John McEnroe

"Please Play On"

A Biography

John McEnroe

"Please Play On"

By

James Harbridge

Published By

CENTRAL PUBLISHING LTD.
West Yorkshire

ISBN 1 903970 00 8

Printed and bound in Great Britain

Photographs courtesy of
Professional Sport
Sports Photography & Picture Library
Hertford, Herts.
www.prosport.co.uk

Cover design by Gary Griffiths.

Publisher

Central Publishing Limited
Royd Street Offices
Milnsbridge
Huddersfield
West Yorkshire
HD3 4QY

www.centralpublishing.co.uk

Foreword by John McEnroe

In this detailed book, James Harbridge has catalogued my career in Great Britain ... from the first ball struck at Roehampton in 1977 right through to my four days at the splendid Royal Albert Hall, twenty years later.*

I hope you enjoy the following pages – and that the years roll back as you read!

Certainly in the main the fans over here have been really positive towards me. This book is especially for those people who tried to understand what I was all about.

Yours in sport

John McEnroe

*Bonus coverage of 1998 – February 2001 included.

Acknowledgments

The author and publishers wish to give thanks to the following in respect of those individuals/entities who have kindly given permission for use of copyright materials:

1   Associated Newspapers Ltd./Mail On Sunday for quotes from articles by Malcolm Folley in 1992 and 1996.

2   John Barrett/International Tennis Federation for quotes from passages by Peter Bodo, Lance Tingay and John Barrett in the annual World Of Tennis (1979, 1980 and 1982 editions respectively) (annual currently published by Harper Collins).

3   Alastair McIver of Tennis World (currently published by Market Link Publishing plc) for quotes from articles by (i) Nigel Clarke in December 1978; (ii) Paul Hutchins in August 1983 and (iii) Henry Wancke in March 1984.

4   Guardian Newspapers Limited for quotes from articles by (i) Frank Keating in 1979; (ii) Richard Evans in December 1980 and (iii) David Irvine in February 1987 (The Guardian © 1979, 1980 and 1987).

5   Guardian Newspapers Limited for quotes from articles by (i) Ron Atkin in January 1979 and (ii) Richard Yallop in October 1992 (The Observer © 1979 and 1992).

6   Alastair McIver of Tennis World for quotes from articles in UK 'Tennis' magazine and Top Tennis by (i) Sam Lippe in August 1977; (ii) Jean Rafferty in March 1979; (iii) Vicky Gilbert (Letters' page) in 1981; (iv) Catherine Bell in 1981; (v) April Tod in June 1984 and (vi) Charles Arthur in 1984.

7   Ace Tennis Magazine for a quote from an article by Linda Pentz in November 1997.

8   Hugo Drayton/Telegraph Group Limited for a quote from an article in The Daily Telegraph by Robert Philip in June 1997.

9   Roger Hughes of Radio Times/BBC Worldwide Limited for a quote from articles in Radio Times by (i) Paul Theroux in June 1979; (ii) Bud Collins in June 1979 and (iii) Henry Fenwick in June 1985.

10   Hugo Drayton/Telegraph Group Limited for quotes from articles by (i) Ian Brodie in Sunday Telegraph Magazine in June 1979 and (ii) Ron Atkin in The Sunday Telegraph in early 1997.

11   Simon Greenberg of The Evening Standard/Associated Newspapers Limited for a quote from an article by John Oakley in The Evening News in June 1980.

12   Mirror Group/MGN Limited for three quotes from the Sunday People of 12 June 1983.

13   Random House for a quote from the book Sportsmen Under Stress by Angela Patmore (published by Hutchinson).

14   Henry Wancke of Abbott Media Services for quotes from articles in Tennis Today by (i) Linda Marie Singer in November 1980 and (ii) Dennis Cunningham in January 1981.

15   WOMAN magazine/IPC Magazines Limited for quotes in WOMAN magazine by (i) Adam Edwards (23 June 1979 issue) and (ii) Donald McLachlan (25 June 1982 issue).

16   Woman's Own/IPC Magaziines Limited for a quote from an article by Simon Kinnersley in June 1989.

17   Woman's Realm/IPC Magazines Limited for a quote from an article published in June 1982.

18   Douglas Keay for a quote from his article which appeared in the 30 June 1979 issue of Woman's Own.

19   The Washington Post for a quote from an article by Dave Kindred, © 1982, The Washington Post. Reprinted with permission.

20   Bill Simons of Inside Tennis magazine for four quotes from an article by Jay Axelbank (which was reprinted in the May 1988 issue of UK Tennis magazine).

21   Stephen Weiss of Racquet magazine for three quotes from an article by Matthew Tolan in the Fall 1994 issue.

22   Express Newspapers Limited for quotes from articles in The Daily Express by (i) Ian Barnes in November 1978 and (ii) Jean Rook in June 1979.

23   Express Newspapers Limited for a quote from an article by Bryan Cooney in June 1983, and for an article by Alasdair Buchan dated 15 June 1984 (quoted in full).

24   Express Newspapers Limited for a quote from an article in The Express On Sunday by Clive Hirschhorn (dated 27 June 1982).

25   MGN Limited for quotes from articles in The Mirror by (i) Anthea Disney and Rita Grosvenor (June 1979); (ii) Noreen Taylor (June 1982); (iii) Hugh Jamieson (March 1991), and for a quoted passage from The Mirror editorial of 2 July 1979.

26   News International Newspapers Limited for two quotes from articles by Rex Bellamy in The Times on 4 July and 9 July 1984 © Times Newspapers Limited, 1984.

27   News International Newspapers Limited for quotes from articles in The News Of The World by (i) Fiona MacDonald Hull (17 June 1979); (ii) Fred

Burcombe (19 June 1983, 26 June 1983 and 3 July 1983), © News International Newspapers, 1979 and 1983.

28   News International Newspapers Limited for quotes from articles in The Sun by (i) Chris Martin (June 1989); (ii) John Kay (22 June 1981); (iii) Sun editorial (9 July 1984); (iv) Hugh Jamieson (23 June 1984, 25 June 1984, 30 June 1984, 2 July 1984, 10 July 1984, March 1985 and 24 June 1985); (v) Peter White (22 June 1992) and (vi) Steven Howard (June 1997), © News International Newspapers, 1981, 1984, 1985, 1989, 1992 and 1997.

29   Associated Newspapers Limited/Daily Mail for quotes from articles by (i) Shaun Usher (8 March 1979); (ii) Laurie Pignon (25 June 1979); (iii) Tony Burton (7 June 1980); (iv) Sue Mott (8 September 1981) and (v) Malcolm Folley (14 December 1984).

30   Chris Gorringe, Chief Executive of The All England Lawn Tennis and Crocquet Club, Wimbledon, for kind licence to quote within this book from various transcripts of John McEnroe press conferences during The Championships.

31   British Broadcasting Corporation (BBC) for quotes from the following programmes:

-   Clash Of The Titans (17 June 1996)
-   Chalk Flew Up! (10 June 1996)
-   Coverage of Masters Tennis Final, from New York (January 1985)
-   Coverage of Stella Artois Championships (17 June 1984)
-   Coverage of Wimbledon (3 July 1985)
-   Coverage of Wimbledon (26 June 1990)
-   Wogan (19 June 1991)
-   Coverage of Wimbledon (4 July 1992)
-   On Side (1 December 1997)
-   Clive Anderson Show (4 December 1997)

32   Newsweek for a quote from an article by Pete Axthelm (January 1979).

33   Der Spiegel for two quotes from an article by Helmut Sorge and Teja Fiedler in 1985.

34   Excerpt from "Portrait In Motion" by Arthur Ashe and Frank Deford, copyright © 1975 Stanley Paul, reprinted by permission of Houghton Mifflin/Sterling Lord.

35   Tennis USA for three quotes from an article by Murray Janoff in 1977.
36   World Tennis, for quotes from articles by (i) Vicki Berner (June 1977); (ii) Mike Lupica (1978) and (iii) Neil Amdur (1984).

37   Excerpt from "Sports Star: John McEnroe" copyright © 1979 by Sue Burchard, reprinted by permission of Harcourt Brace & Company.

38   US Tennis magazine, for quotes from articles by (i) Robert Cubbedge

(July 1978); (ii) instruction section (January 1979) and (iii) Tracy Leonard (1982) and Peter Bodo (1981).

39   New York Post for a quote from an article in December 1984.

INTRODUCTION

Some of you might ask, "Why write about John McEnroe when he last played in a singles match on Centre Court in 1992?"

In answer, I should first point out that if the New Yorker received a wild card into the men's singles at the All England Club, he would still be the major attraction. It may be a particularly overused cliché, but it is true: He Has Personality.

Secondly, it is now over twenty years since John's Wimbledon debut. We may never again see such an artist with a racquet, so his talent-laden career deserves to be remembered and cherished.

And thirdly, lest we forget … despite possessing a legion of admirers, both young and old, John McEnroe was, at one time, probably the most vilified sportsman ever. No matter which country's press one cares to examine, McEnroe was often described as "belligerent", "controversial" and "temperamental".

Unfortunately, it is all too easy to passively accept the media's interpretation of events. But sensational reporting often reveals a failure to grasp the relevant issues. So often the press are fast off the mark to chastise, but quite reluctant to attempt an understanding of, and explanation for, people's actions.

Look at a handful of incidents, in England alone, where McEnroe's side of the story was completely ignored.

Benson and Hedges Final, 1978. Three minutes' demonstrative McEnroe shouting is required before the linesman admits a shot had hit his, the linesman's, nose! "I suspect the linesman just wanted to teach John a lesson," one journalist told me.

Stella Artois Third Round, 1979. McEnroe is unfairly docked a penalty game after the Umpire wrongly implements the Code of Conduct.

Wimbledon first Round, 1981. Umpire Edward James censures John for obscenity after mishearing his "pits of the world" comment.

Stella Artois Final, 1984. Umpire overrules his lineswoman, deeming a McEnroe shot "out." But Grand Prix Rules stipulated that the overrule should be made 'promptly' and John had, in fact, sat down in his chair having changed ends when the Umpire made his decision …

So if we decide to peer behind the downright stupid labels that newspapers have given McEnroe, what do we actually see? Are the insults justified?

There are many popular misconceptions. The first is that John is a tormentor, proud of his temper and one who actually enjoys exposing people to angry outbursts.

Yet he has always been contrite. As we shall see, time and time again John showed real remorse. "My behaviour is unnecessary. No one is to blame but myself ..." "I made a mistake and I feel bad about it. I said something obscene and I can't justify that ..." "I do try to have manners," were typical McEnroe lines.

And when he said, "Everybody regrets things they say. It is nothing personal. Linesmen have a thankless job, everyone is human," he was sincere. Put simply, John McEnroe is an honourable man. "Oh yes, who says so?" I hear you ask. Just about everyone who has met him away from the strained atmosphere of the tennis world, that's who. "He's charming," says John Ballantine, a former scribe for the quality paper 'The Sunday Times'; "as nice as pie" affirms the player's one-time Malibu neighbour, Marina Gonzalez; "delightful" is the opinion of Stanford University tennis coach, Dick Gould. And so on.

But my favourite testimony to his amiable, modest character comes from his ex-schoolmate, Tory Kiam: "He would win so easily in school that no-one really understood how good he was. But he'd never beat anyone love and love, even when he could have. He'd let a set go to 2-2 for example, so as not the humiliate the other guy."

Kiam adds that when John was sixteen and beat Charlie Pasarell and Bob Lutz in a tournament before losing to Ilie Nastase, he didn't mention it at school the following Monday morning – his friends only learned about it from the newspapers.

How many other teenagers would have been able to keep quiet and not boast? Most, I'm sure, would have been dying to impress their classmates with the news.

Also, if John really was as arrogant as he's often been portrayed to be, why did he partner Peter Fleming in the Wimbledon doubles when Peter was ranked below 600 in the singles ratings? Why, after their loss of form in 1980 and Fleming's contention that he should take the blame for his 'crap' play, did John say it was as much his fault and that they were a team? Arrogant? I do not think so ...

John McEnroe said wistfully in 1980: "I want the English public to see I am not just the big bully boy they all believe I am."

That comment coincided with a concentrated McEnroe effort to knuckle down and behave. It indicates, I think, how this self-effacing man yearned to have a crowd behind him.

In 1988, he told an interviewer, Jay Axelbank of US magazine 'Inside Tennis', how happy he had been a year earlier in Rome: "When I was at the Italian Open, it was the best crowd I ever played before. Feeling good about the crowd and having people come up to me and say, 'John, you are one of the best whoever played the game', those are the best sensations a tennis player can have."

Clearly John can never be remembered just for his tennis ability. But at the same time it is worth remembering that we cannot fault his altruism. That doyen of tennis writers, the late C.M. 'Jimmy' Jones, described John's charity activities as 'immense'. And many readers will be aware of his intelligent 1980 decision to snub an invitation to face Bjorn Borg in the black South African state of Bophuthatswana for a guaranteed $800,000 and to play free for the World Hunger Project instead. He was concerned that he was being asked to publicise a 'supposedly black state' which seemingly existed for the benefit of the South African government.

Really, no-one can accuse John of surveying the world through selfish eyes. For instance, he has said, "I have noticed that I respect parents a lot, being one myself. I respect a mother who raises three or four kids by herself. I see how tough it is with one or two."

His sense of perspective is rich and mature. Talking to Jay Axelbank he continued: "I feel strongly that teachers, policemen and firemen are badly underpaid people. They do lifesaving jobs. The fact that a tennis player can make a million dollars a year doesn't make sense to me."

What other misconceptions are there? That John is excessively bitter about the media. But what have they done to him?

Apart from those irritating adjectives, they consistently failed to try and understand him. However well behaved, he was still 'Superbrat' to many reporters. Indifferent to his outstanding tennis, which probably reached its peak in the '84 Wimbledon Final, when 1938 Grand Slam winner Don Budge called John's play that of a 'genius at work', they looked only for poor behaviour. So every word, every gesture, every dropped racquet was scrutinised, then sensationalised.

And if there were no tantrums, they goaded him with inaccurate stories. And they employed tactless questions at press conferences – "Have you any previous convictions?" ... "Have you and Stacy split up?" ... "Why haven't you got a sense of humour?"

John, to give him credit, remained very helpful at these player-press meetings, always giving good copy. But if he was hostile occasionally, could you blame him after the way his name had been dragged through the dirt?

Despite his fading resentment, John is a well-balanced, doting father. His wife, Patty Smyth, who gave birth in December 1995 to McEnroe's second daughter, Anna, told Malcolm Folley of 'The Mail on Sunday' "It's wonderful having a baby in the house. We might have more ..."

Indeed, John has always been close to his family. When his maternal grandfather passed away on the eve of Wimbledon '84, his selflessness shone though. "That was for you Mum!" he said on TV, once he'd banked the title.

What of his on-court behaviour? "I was brought up to be serious," says McEnroe and you can tell. His spellbinding early ball tactics demanded total dedication and aggression, entire absorption in every point. With the adrenalin flowing, it could hardly come as a surprise that he was a different man once inside a tennis arena.

Mary Carillo, John's one-time mixed doubles partner, has spoken of his desire for perfection. "He has a real sense of beauty about the game. To him everything should be just so. No noise from the fans at the wrong time. Excellent officiating. If something happens that wrecks it for him he gets upset. He believes it's phoney not to show how you feel." She adds: "He has always been a tough guy to put down, the kind who didn't want to get beat at anything. When we were just kids, maybe he was ten and I was twelve, I was playing a game and he was fighting a war."

Sir Thomas Browne (1605-1682) put into words how John McEnroe must feel on a tennis court. He wrote: "There is another man within me, that's angry with me, rebukes me, commands and dastards me."

But John has been a paragon of honest endeavour, one who fights on to the bitter end – a British type of hero in many respects. Yet our mentality dictates that it is wrong to show how you feel, to wear your heart on your sleeve. George Mikes got it right: "In England it is bad manners to be clever, to assert something confidently. It may be your personal view that two and two makes four, but you must not state it in a self-assured way, because this is a democratic country and others may be of a different opinion."

McEnroe has often felt helpless in the face of criticism, commenting, "People are going to say what they want to say, write what they want to write."

But I have always had time for John. He has never disappointed me. He played tennis with passion, with ambition. It's the way we

iv

should daily live our lives. During his career one empathised with the desolation he felt in defeat, but equally one experienced vicarious pleasure from the exhilaration he displayed in victory.

Sure, he got angry. If he had one failing it was that sometimes he cared too much and tried too hard. On court he would immerse himself in the desire for success. On those occasions his unswerving determination and sheer hunger mesmerised me. It gave myself and many others the hope that through conviction and belief, personal fulfilment could be attained. And giving such inspiration is McEnroe's legacy.

So hopefully John Patrick McEnroe's true personality will become apparent in the pages that follow. In the final analysis I hope we realise how privileged we were to see such an abundance of tennis riches in one man.

A BRIEF CHRONOLOGY

1. John Patrick McEnroe Jr. was born on 16 February 1959, in Wiesbaden, West Germany, where his father John Senior was serving in the US Air Force and his mother Kay was a nurse.

2. When John was nine months old his parents moved to Newburgh, New York. A few years later Flushing, Queens, a borough of New York City, became their home. Mr. McEnroe had now left the Air Force; he worked as an office manager and attended law school at night. Kay gave birth to a second son, Mark, on 2 February 1962 and they finally settled in the New York suburb of Douglaston. Patrick completed the family, on July 1 1966.

3. Mr. McEnroe went on to become a prominent lawyer at the prestigious Manhattan law firm named Paul, Weiss, Rifkind Wharton & Garrison. In other words, he attained his American Dream. Simultaneously, John was quietly moving towards fulfilling his. At eighteen months came the first signs of athletic prowess – he could time the hitting of a ball with a plastic bat. Soon John was slugging the sphere so hard that a woman in New York's Central Park asked his father, "Is that a little boy or a talented midget?"

4. John's education began at the Buckley Country Day School in Roslyn, Long Island. He earned a reputation for being a conscientious student who achieved good grades. Whilst there, around the age of eight, his father took him to the Douglaston Club. "He had never played tennis. We started group lessons together. He was good for a beginner and I was pretty good, too," John told Sam Lippe of 'Tennis' in August 1977.

5. But young John had no idea where tennis was going to lead him. He told Lippe, "I liked football, basketball and baseball, like most kids. I couldn't see myself putting a lot of time into tennis."

6. Yet two weeks after using a racquet for the first time (a cast-off from a family friend, Frank Prior), John won a tournament for under 12s. It was that exceptional debut performance which

eventually prompted his Douglaston Club coaches, Don Dwyer and George Seewagen Snr., to recommend the Port Washington Tennis Academy to the youngster's family.

7.   The head coach at Port Washington was legendary Australian Harry Hopman, who was assisted by former Mexican Davis Cup player, Tony Palafox. Before his death in 1985, Hopman told me: "The first night I was on the courts in the year I turned a professional coach, 1970, John, then aged 11, was one of the pupils, among older boys and all playing well. I was on the court coaching for six hours on a Friday evening from 5.00 p.m. to 11.00 p.m. It had been a long day and I was tired, but I recall easily I was not too tired to reply to the query, "What do you think of the little left-hander you had on your court?" with enthusiasm about his racket work, stroke-making in general and good potential if he had an opportunity to enjoy good practice often."

8.   When he was 13 years old John joined Trinity School on Manhattan's Upper West Side. It is a private school of excellent academic standards, found in 1709. Dr. Robin Lester, initially a history teacher at Trinity, then the headmaster towards the end of McEnroe's five-year stay, will never forget the impact of the star-to-be.
Speaking by phone from Chicago on McEnroe's 35th birthday, Dr. Lester explained to me:
"He was remarkably well-balanced, but also a shy boy. I've heard it said in the media that he was a troublemaker at school, that he wore a denim jacket instead of a blazer. But he was never out of dress code. I don't remember a single instance of him being inappropriately dressed.
"This was not an angry young man as the English would put it. This was a wonderful man from a tight-knit, model Catholic family going to an Anglican school and there was never any tension because of that.
"He was a very fine student. Keep in mind the fact that he was taking college-level physics and Latin in his last two years at Trinity.
"I taught him history for a full year and it wasn't one of his favourite subjects. He always sat at the back of the class and had a habit of rubbing his forelock over his forehead as he took notes.
"But he was very witty. When there was a discussion, John would constantly deflate any pretentiousness that the teacher – me! – put into the proceedings. I never took umbrage. He was never making fun of people, just the situations."

Improbably, McEnroe's favourite Trinity teacher was his Latin master, an Englishman named Frank Smith. He, too, has fond memories of the tennis genius. Over a pub lunch in Kenilworth, Warwickshire, this quirky, elderly man said: "I taught him for five years. He was a good Latinist and we got on well with each other after a battle of wits. To begin with, it was a question of who was going to tame whom. Eventually, he submitted to me and agreed to learn something! "I'll do what you tell me," he said.

"He had a good sense of humour and we clicked. Also, the fact he was never late brought us together. He was a good worker with an exceptional character who would say: 'I'm no genius, I know that, but I'll do as well as I can.'

"His father was paying private school fees and John told me: 'You can't understand the pressures I have when I get home.'" (Kay McEnroe has confirmed the substance of a 'Sunday Times' report by Danae Brook in which the journalist claimed that if John got 96 in an exam, his mother wanted to know what happened to the other four marks.)

However, McEnroe maintained a B minus average at Trinity, even though he found it hard to study. "When I start thinking I might play pro tennis in a couple of years, the day-to-day grind of school loses its importance," John disclosed to Sam Lippe in 'Tennis'.

But McEnroe didn't confine his sporting skills to the tennis court. He was the football quarterback, captain of the basketball team, the baseball pitcher and a skilful left-winger on the soccer field. In fact, Terence Bruner-Smith, the school's alumni secretary, confides: "We always considered John McEnroe as much a soccer player as a tennis player." And Dr. Lester remembers that John's corner kicks "were ferocious things – with the same lefty curve as his serve into the ad court."

Which brings us to John's school tennis record. In all, he accumulated a 37-1 win/loss ratio over four seasons. Selfless McEnroe said that winning the Ivy League (private school) Championship "was almost like winning the US Open. His friend Alex Seaver commented to Sam Lippe: "John's so modest that the people at Trinity don't realise how good he is."

McEnroe's parents never begged permission to pull John out of school for a tennis tournament. When he narrowly lost to Ilie Nastase at Virginia Beach, it had been a weekend match which Dr. Lester only found out about via his newspaper. "He was very modest," Dr. Lester says of John. "It goes with his timidity, shyness and self-effacement."

But despite his low profile McEnroe was well-known throughout Trinity. Says Bruner Smith, "The little fellows lower down in the school thought he was "It" with a capital I. He had a great fan club."

Yet the last word on John's school routine should go to his mother, who instilled such drive in her first-born. Kay informed Murray Janoff of 'Tennis USA': "He had long schooldays in high school. He'd take a 7.20 a.m. train to Manhattan every day. School started at 8.20 a.m. and let out was at 4.10 p.m. Then he'd play a sport and get home about 7.15, have some dinner and study. He never left the house Sunday through [to] Thursday nights."

What of John's tennis away from Trinity? In July 1975 Harry Hopman left New York for Florida. Shortly afterwards, Palafox would also move, but only as far as the Cove Racquet Club in Glen Cove on Long Island. In 1976 McEnroe joined up again with the Mexican and by the summer of '76 "the strokes were all there," according to Palafox. The coach also observed McEnroe's great drive, his anger when things didn't go right and his intense concentration.

John's efforts saw him win the national clay court under 16's in '75, the same title in the 18's category in '76, together with the Orange Bowl and a plethora of junior national doubles titles as well. And in 1977 he seized glory and his life changed forever ...

John McEnroe – Please Play On

1977

In the following yearly results, unless otherwise stated, the opponent listed is the last player John McEnroe faced in the singles of each tournament. Thus, where McEnroe has won the singles, the name listed is that of the runner-up. In all other cases, the name listed refers to the player who defeated McEnroe in the event.

The scores of all the singles and doubles matches played in the British Isles involving John McEnroe can be found at the back of this book, in the Appendix.

Ocean City	1st Round	Nastase	75 64
Virginia Beach	Semi-Final	Nastase	75 46 63
Downeast Classic	Semi-Final	Fleming	76 76
French Open	2nd Round	Dent	46 62 46 63 63
Wimbledon	Semi-Final	Connors	63 63 46 64
Newport, USA	2nd Round	A. Amritraj	63 16 63
Cincinnati	Quarter-final	Fagel	61 62
Washington	1st Round	Solomon	76 75
South Orange	Semi-Final	Vilas	62 26 60
US Clay Courts	Semi-Final	Dent	64 76
Toronto	3rd Round	Alexander	75 67 62
US Pro Champs	2nd Round	Connors	57 62 75
US Open	4th Round	Orantes	62 63
Los Angeles	2nd Round	Teltscher	64 67 75
San Francisco	Quarter-final	Walts	63 67 63

John was still at school at the beginning of the year.

But he won the junior Banana Bowl Championships in April '77, beating Ivan Lendl 6-2, 7-6.

In May, Trinity School decided that playing the French Open and Wimbledon should be John's "Senior Year Project".

"It's an attempt to deal with students who have already been taken on by universities," explains Dr. Robin Lester.

As a result, McEnroe had to miss his Graduation Day and it upset him.

"We were sad, too," says Lester.

But John didn't forget his school. He has gone back to raise funds for the under-privileged youth of New York and Dr. Lester comments, "After a formal press conference, he did something wonderful. He held a mock press conference with children from Trinity. They asked embarrassing questions about his behaviour and unerringly his response was, 'Don't do as I do, do as I say.'

"I think his finest moment was with children. I've seen him with my own and he's gentle, a little shy. Children instinctively trust the man."

At the French Open, John was a little too honest for experienced pro Phil Dent. The youngster had always called line decisions in his opponent's favour because he didn't want to be accused of cheating. When this philanthropy benefited Dent, the Australian told John, "Listen, sonny. This is the pros here. We don't play that way. We play the calls."

The 18-year old took the message to heart after losing to Dent in a second round five setter.

He may have lost a little innocence, too, but he won the junior title in Paris (beating Australian Ray Kelly) and the senior mixed doubles title with Mary Carillo, who also hailed from Douglaston, New York.

The two had practised together at the Douglaston Club, but had never teamed up before doing so at Roland Garros. They took the title by overcoming Ivan Molina (Columbia) and Florenta Mihai (Rumania) 7-6, 6-3.

Carillo, 23 months older than John, said at the time, "People have to understand he's only 18. His problem is he wants every point."

And that uncompromising attitude was then transported to London SW19. Amateur John's awesome run to the Wimbledon semi-finals surprised even Harry Hopman.

"Very, very few players find their best form so early at Wimbledon," the Australian declared in 1985.

But John did. Yet he remained an amateur and passed up $40,000 in prize money that summer in order to take up his scholarship at Stanford University in the autumn.

Amazingly, a fourth round US Open showing didn't tempt him to change his mind, nor did his semi-final doubles appearances at Los

Angeles and San Francisco with new partner, Peter Fleming. After a month on campus he told Murray Janoff of 'Tennis USA', "The area, the people and the weather are just great. I'm glad I made the decision to go to college. But then, I didn't want to go when I was 28."

⚚⚚

At the end of 1975 John had been placed not first, but second, in the United States under 16 rankings – behind Brian Gottfried's younger brother, Larry.

Gottfried was No.1 twelve months later in the under 18s, but by the close of '77 John had left him totally and utterly behind. Indeed, in the BP/ITF Yearbook, McEnroe was hailed as one of the "Players of the Year", along with Borg, Connors and Vilas.

Harry Hopman had always maintained that John had greater potential than Gottfried – and once again he'd been proven right.

Wimbledon Qualifying Event

Wednesday, June 15, 1977

Shortly before John McEnroe Junior left New York to embark on his Senior Project, he had one last conversation with Latin teacher, Frank Smith.

"You're going to London, you'd better behave yourself," the Englishman gently chided him.

"Why should I?" grinned John, a lover of argument for argument's sake. Doubtless with a postcard image of Buckingham Palace in mind, he added, "I can cope with those guardsmen."

"That's what you think," responded Smith. "They might beat you up!"

"That'd be the day," laughed John, blissfully unaware of all his adventures in the British Isles that lay ahead.

⚚⚚

Despite his achievements in Paris, McEnroe's goal on this, his first trip to England, was the junior title. The United States Tennis

3

Association entered him for the qualifying event almost as an afterthought.

The teenager was staying in £12 per week accommodation in Roehampton, near the Bank of England Sports Ground in Priory Lane where he was due to play Christophe Roger-Vasselin, a 19-year old of dual nationality (England and France).

It was not an auspicious location from which to make a bid for stardom. The sixteen courts lack the quality of their All England Club counterparts. There are few spectators, although admission is free, and jets from Heathrow Airport frequently fly overhead. Furthermore, in 1977, the lack of ball-boys or ball-girls meant there was no pampering of over-sized egos.

But the sobering conditions did not distress young John. On a day plagued by drizzle and a temperature which refused to rise above 12 degrees centigrade, he crushed Roger-Vasselin 6-4, 6-3 for his first success on English grass.

Fifteen years later, McEnroe's London-born opponent could still recall why John had won their encounter. He told me, "McEnroe was a very difficult player to play against. One never knew what he was going to do and all his strokes were very difficult to read, especially his serve. He had a great eye to see the ball very early. He had a great touch and a big variety of shots to choose from. He was also very fast and he came to the net very fast behind his serve and covered the court very well. His desire to win was tremendous."

And what of Roehampton? If John had read the June 1977 edition of the American publication 'World Tennis', he would have seen an article by perennial Wimbledon qualifying competitor Vicki Berner. She wrote " … more often than not it's just one player against another with a chair umpire keeping a close watch. Tempers are short, balls are blasted over the fences, and rackets are launched like rockets with alarming regularity. Choking is the order of the day. Few qualifiers escape the paralysis that seems to strike on every key point."

So could 18-year old McEnroe stand the pace?

Thursday, June 16, 1977
Beat Uli Marten 6-8, 6-4, 6-4

This was McEnroe's first tough day on English soil.
By his own admission, grass was Marten's favourite surface and

the six foot three inch 21 year-old from Schweinfurth, Germany soon led by a set and a break.

John was troubled by a very bumpy court and irked by some of the umpire's line decisions. Marten says that McEnroe swore at the umpire, but when the official left the court and walked across the cricket field to the referee's office, it was not in order to default the young American.

Instead, the umpire returned with four linesmen which suggests he felt that McEnroe's complaints were justified to some degree.

In the end, Marten lost a close match and was impressed by John's serve and touch.

Friday, June 17, 1977
Beat Gilles Moretton 6-2, 6-4, 6-4 (best of five sets)

John McEnroe cruised past the 19-year old from Lyon and thus qualified for the Wimbledon Championships at his first attempt.

Seventeen years later Moretton, a tournament director, would call the New Yorker "a genius" who "had the quickest eye ever in tennis."

It is also worth noting that Gilles could recall no histrionics from John in what was a crucial match for both teenagers.

❧❧❧

Somewhat surprisingly, McEnroe's attempts to qualify in the men's doubles were not successful. His partner was Gene Scott, a 39-year old New York lawyer who had played at Wimbledon since 1958. Gene had been a member of the United States Davis Cup team between 1963 and 1965, and had won the 1963 Wimbledon Plate. He'd also been a TV commentator for the 1973 Billie Jean King/Bobby Riggs 'Battle of the Sexes' clash.

As regards McEnroe in 1977, Gene recalls, "I was signed unofficially by his parents to look after him. I had played doubles with him when he was 15 at the Eastern Hardcourts – I was 36, 37, and we won the tournament. Everyone thought it was because of my wisdom and experience. But I knew it was because John had an eye for the doubles game that no-one of 30, 50 or 80 would ever have.

"He had a unique aptitude for the game and doubles in particular.

5

"In the 70's I just took my holidays at Wimbledon time and hoped my ranking was good enough to get in. That year was the first I didn't get direct entry and I assumed John and I would coast through the qualifying, but as it was…"

As it was, Gene and John ousted Frank Crawford (New Jersey) and Bill Lofgren (Illinois) 7-5, 2-6, 6-1, before Scott Carnahan, playing on turf for the first time, and Briton Michael Wayman beat them 4-6, 9-8, 6-3.

At the time, Carnahan was in the Guinness Book of Records. In September 1976, at Los Angeles, he had hit the fastest serve timed with contemporary equipment; his cannon-ball delivery had clocked up 137 miles per hour.

Nevertheless, Gene and John "underestimated" their opposition, according to Wayman himself.

The Briton, who has coached in California, adds, "At the beginning [Gene] Scott played the steadier tennis. John made more unforced errors, but set the points up better; i.e. changed service direction better, mixed up returns, poached more. He exhibited qualities to be seen later – quick pick-up returns followed by low volleys and good change of direction on his volleys.

"John's temperament was extremely competitive. He became argumentative in the tie-break after he passed me down the line – his shot was [called] wide. Carnahan hit a couple of winners off John's serve during the tie-break and I managed to make a reasonable return to win the tie-break.

"[In the third set] McEnroe missed a crucial smash for us to break and serve for the match. He argued quite a bit. He tried to dominate the match, but was taken out of it by us concentrating on Gene Scott who couldn't hurt us as much.

"Gene Scott was a calming influence during the match, but John was definitely top class at that stage."

Thinking of his own job, Wayman says point blank, "I don't think you can teach a student to play like McEnroe.

"The truth is he is a player unto himself. Technically, you can point out his movement to volleys, shortness of swing on volleys, use of balance, etc. – but I've always found it amusing to see juniors and adults attempt to emulate McEnroe's serve without understanding how it works. McEnroe's control and feel for the ball is not teachable."

Gene, for his part, is concerned to put the record straight about

6

John's behaviour in 1977.

"He appeared to listen. He was not that bad. He just seemed a very talented, somewhat out-of-control teenager.

"Off court he was shy to the point of being amusing. And he was definitely alert to his behaviour. In '77 he used to ask endearingly at the end of a day's play, 'How did I do? Was I any better?' And I would answer, 'Frankly, no,' or 'Frankly, yes,' because he didn't misbehave every day."

Wimbledon

Monday, June 20, 1977

So John, just out of school and youthfully exuberant, had arrived. The draw for the 1977 Wimbledon meeting was duly made, with the result that the burly Eygptian left-hander Ismail El Shafei became his first round opponent.

29-year old Ismail's best days were most definitely behind him, though he could not have been considered a soft touch, having enjoyed some success on the All England Club's lawns. He had been the vanquished finalist in the 1963 Junior Invitation event, a year later he won it and at the 1974 Senior Championships he only succumbed at the quarter-final stage, thrashing Bjorn Borg along the way.

But McEnroe was quite fearless. On a dank, chilly evening, by the time the match was called for darkness, he had convinced himself that El Shafei was distinctly beatable.

Overnight score: McEnroe led El Shafei 6-0, 5-5

* In June 1992, McEnroe would tell Malcolm Folley of the 'Mail on Sunday': "I didn't even know that my first-ever opponent, El Shafei, was a leftie. We didn't have coaches like the kids today. [24-year old fellow player] Jim [Delaney] befriended me and he told me to jump on El Shafei from the off as he was a slow-starter."

Tuesday, June 21, 1977

Since the first Tuesday of the Championships is by tradition Ladies' Day, a women's match was played on John's court –

Number Eight – before he resumed with El Shafei.

Spectators first saw the South African player Brigitte Cuypers beat Regina Marsikova – an 18-year old from Prague for whom John had once ball-boyed at the Junior US Open event – 6-0, 6-4. Then McEnroe notched up his first main draw Wimbledon win, 6-0, 7-5, 6-4.

Afterwards, the teenager from New York returned to a hotel room at the Cunard International, near Queen's Club, where he was practising. The only problem was that the room was not his own – he was sharing it with two Californian juniors, Eliot Teltscher and Robert Van't Hof, to defray expenses. But at least John was feeling a whole lot better than El Shafei. The Egyptian still sounded bewildered when he discussed the contest with me years later.

"McEnroe was just out of qualifying, just a rookie. I knew nothing about him at all. No-one knew his name. But he played a good match. I was surprised he could handle himself so well. He had flair and was able to play with a lot of deception. He definitely had the game for grass."

That last comment goes without saying!

Wednesday, June 22, 1977
Beat Colin Dowdeswell 9-7, 6-3, 6-1

"The main reason he was such a good player was that he had a wicked serve, probably the best serve in the game. It was very difficult to judge his ball toss as to where he was going to hit the ball, and particularly on the left-hand court he took you so wide, making the return very difficult, as he was on the net so quickly and then often had the open court to volley into. He was just an all-round great player with no weaknesses which made him very difficult to play against." (Colin Dowdeswell)

Thursday, June 23, 1977

On undistinguished Court Six, John dismissed Karl Meiler 6-2, 6-2, 5-7, 6-3 in a battle that highlighted both his considerable promise and keen competitive spirit.

His perfectionist tendencies were already well developed at this tender age, a fact that was typified by his disgust after executing poor shots.

Centre Service linesman Albert Taylor, from Bolton, recalls a small incident that might have ruffled the 18-year old. Mr. Taylor called a McEnroe serve out, except it swung in late and so he quickly reversed the call. The umpire, Bill McDonald from Perth, asked McEnroe to play a let and John accepted this decision without a flicker of dissent.

Play began in the early evening at 5.11 p.m., and ended in South London sunset 1 hour and 54 minutes later at 7.05 p.m. Meiler never managed to match the tenacity and heart of his unknown adversary, but McEnroe was well satisfied and prior to his fourth round confrontation with fellow American Sandy Mayer, a Wimbledon semi-finalist in 1973, the junior was heard to say, "There's no way this guy can beat me, no way." Already the crowds were beginning to take notice of him – not merely for his sheer tennis ability, but due to his burgeoning confidence as well.

Friday, June 24, 1977

With Mary Carillo, beat Bobby Wilson and Jackie Fayter, 5-7, 9-8, 7-5.

Wilson, 23 years John's elder, recalls, "He was an extremely good player generating terrific pace in a similar manner to Rod Laver and Tony Roche.

"However, his antics on court left much to be desired. In fact they were so extreme that I lost concentration when leading 5-1 in the second set which led to our loss of the match. At one stage he said quite loudly, 'I give up' and I walked up to the umpire and requested the match as McEnroe had said he had given up. Unfortunately, the umpire didn't agree and the match continued."

Saturday, June 25, 1977

25-year old Sandy Mayer, a political science graduate from Stanford University, had stunned Wimbledon in 1973 when he overwhelmed the favourite, Nastase, en route to the semi-finals.

But today Sandy was himself stunned, 7-5, 4-6, 6-3, 6-1, by John McEnroe on Court No.6.

John joked, "I hope they keep me back here all the time," referring to the fact that all his wins had been on outside courts.

Becoming more serious, the 18-year old added, "I never even

dreamed I could get into the tournament, let alone have a shot at the title. The best I hoped to do was qualify."

Monday, June 27, 1977
With Mary Carillo, beat John Lloyd and Monica Simmen 6-4, 6-3.

"It's nice to think back and remember a very nice time of my life – my tennis life!

"I am now married and have two beautiful children. I remember the match very well, I was very nervous! To play on a big court [Court 14] at Wimbledon with John Lloyd, that's a big thing!

"John McEnroe was a great player and I was a little scared to play against him … and his serve! He was young, me too, and when you play a match you, know you, want to win and you'll do everything necessary – so I thought he would not take into consideration a woman in front of him.

"But I was very surprised to play a real gentleman. This is obviously a big compliment to him. Unfortunately I had no more contact with John, but playing against him was a positive experience and very memorable." (Monica Simmen)

Tuesday, June 28, 1977

John McEnroe, oozing with confidence, eliminated the experienced Phil Dent in a tortuous battle on Wimbledon's Court No.1.

The young left-hander's win was made all the more creditable considering it was his first ever match on a true show court. Also, never before had he been allowed to reside in the dressing room annexed by the established stars. Earlier in the tournament the teenager had had to make do in the confined space of the No.2 dressing areas.

McEnroe's aggressive display forced him to scratch from the Junior event, his priority a month earlier, but inevitably that was no disappointment. "I came here expecting to be lucky to win two games a set and I can't say, even now, that I feel like one of the guys on the international circuit. I shall have to talk to my parents about whether to make tennis a full-time business," he said, obviously relishing the prospect of a semi-final with Jimmy Connors in the intimate theatre of Centre Court.

John's opponent, the thirteenth-seeded Phil Dent from Sydney, Australia, was hampered by a nagging thigh injury, but still struggled manfully, producing some great passing shots to frustrate the 18-year old when the junior stood on the brink of victory.

But after three hours and nine minutes of courageous endeavour McEnroe finally hammered a service winner on his fifth match point. He leapt into the air, the most successful qualifier in the history of The Championships and the youngest semi-finalist ever.

Later, he revealed how anxiety had gripped him in the final stages.

"For the first time I started to feel nervous and I kept telling myself to keep my head. I don't let Wimbledon or the opposition intimidate me. That's the way to lose matches." But he also joked, "If I beat Connors, I might drop dead right on Centre Court!"

McEnroe began in scintillating style, breaking Dent in the seventh game with a sweetly struck backhand return. Always playing competently and often splendidly, he snatched the set 6-3. The deficit was by no means insurmountable for Dent, but prospects looked a little bleak for him when he came to grief again on serve in the first game of the second set, delivering three double faults. However, the Australian stormed back, harrying John and he levelled at 3-3.

A prolonged spell of American pressure saw the momentum shift back to the teenager and when he reached set point at 7-6 in the tiebreak he appeared to be sustaining concentration. Then suddenly his explosive temper simmered over. McEnroe hit a deep second serve and the return from Dent landed beyond the baseline.

"Fault," said the umpire.

"What?" retorted McEnroe, incredulous.

"The serve was out," the umpire replied firmly.

Muttering about the "stupid linesman", McEnroe conceded his next service point and then the set, when Dent served successfully to make the points score 9-7. John flung his racket down and kicked it towards the net.

For a while he looked as if he'd pay dearly for his outburst and there was an air of desperation in his play. Fatigue exacerbated the situation and his 27 year old opponent wasted no time in securing the third set by a 6-4 scoreline.

After that setback McEnroe's will to win returned and with his serve again functioning as a potent weapon, he forced the issue to a final set.

Fighting well in the crises, Dent saved three break points in the opening game, but he couldn't weather the storm six games later when John broke for a vital 4-3 lead.

Dent was unable to claw back and John completed the job in fine style. The match was his: 6-4, 8-9, 4-6, 6-3, 6-4. When asked for his thoughts on the absorbing plot, the boy replied simply, "I'm just happy to be playing well."

* After this rousing quarterfinal, according to S.H. Burchard, author of 'John McEnroe – Sports Star', an "official in a blue blazer not at the match came up to John and asked, "Did you win today, McEnroe?" "Yeah, the unbelievable happened ..." John said."

* McEnroe's headmaster, Dr. Lester, watched the contest on television. It was his pupil's first Wimbledon game to be broadcast in the States. He was "astonished to see John's behaviour. That was the first indication I had ever seen of it. I've never heard a proper explanation," he adds. "But John has hinted that when he started out promoters favoured the surly McEnroe to the prep school boy."

* John told Chris Martin of 'The Sun' in June '89: "I will never forget the very first time I made headlines at Wimbledon. I was playing Phil Dent in the quarter-finals and lost the second set on a tie-break. I was so mad with myself I threw my racket down.

"The crowd booed me. I couldn't believe it.

"I remember thinking I was the one who should be unhappy, not them. So I kicked my racket and they booed even louder.

"Suddenly I was the new Attila the Hun."

Wednesday, June 29, 1977
With Mary Carillo, beat Bob Carmichael and Ilana Kloss[1], 6-2, 5-7, 6-2

John and Mary triumphed in an evening clash on Court No.1. And on the eve of the singles semi-final, interest in the New Yorker was gathering apace. When the player was asked about fan worship, he replied quietly, "I can do without that."

---

[1] As he had for Regina Marsikova, so too, had John ball-boyed for Ilana Kloss during the US Open Junior Event one year.

After the win, John and friends went out to dinner at a cheap pizzeria that he had frequented throughout the tournament. Suddenly the enormity of his achievements seemed to seize him.

"You know," he said, "if I beat Connors tomorrow and Borg breaks his leg or something, I win Wimbledon."

In 'World Tennis' Mike Lupica wrote, "That was it. He went back to his pizza."

Thursday, June 30, 1977

A few hours before McEnroe's semi-final sunshine battle with number one seed Jimmy Connors on the worn carpet of Wimbledon's Centre Court, speculation was rife that the 18-year old might never appear at The Championships again. The rumours were based on comments allegedly made by John's father after he and Tony Palafox had flown 3000 miles from New York to witness the match. Mr. McEnroe said, "John tells me that if he wins Wimbledon he will turn pro. But I want him to go to university and study Law. Wimbledon is only one tournament. He can't play tennis forever and I feel he would be better off with a good, solid education behind him."

His son also had thoughts on the dilemma, recognising the difficulties in choosing between going to Stanford University and becoming a pro.

"It's sure gonna be a hard decision to make. I love tennis and I realise the sort of money I can earn in a short space of time. Tennis, however, doesn't last forever and I can understand my parents wanting me to look beyond the game. We'll just have to sit right down and talk it over when Wimbledon is over."

And so the stage was set for the biggest match of McEnroe's short career thus far.

᪥

Jimmy Connors was well versed with the role of precocious youngster as they stepped onto Centre Court at two o'clock. Earlier in the tournament the left-hander from Illinois had insensitively snubbed the centenary ceremony of past champions, and, along with

Ilie Nastase, he was known as the game's bad boy. The crowds, on the other hand, saw John as the heroic underdog, and for two hours and thirty-six minutes he gave the older Connors many anxious moments.

Right from the outset McEnroe meant business. Despite a double fault in the initial game, his first of eight, he fired in two winners. When Connors first served, the Douglaston junior reached deuce with a great backhand pass.

It was the seventh game before John's understandable nerves were uncovered – twice he double-faulted and a forehand down the line gave Connors the break. McEnroe fell further behind at 3-5 and his fourth double fault enabled Connors to win the first set 6-3 in thirty minutes.

The second set followed a similar pattern, the break coming in the sixth game after McEnroe had fended off four break points.

But in the third the 18-year old cleverly changed tactics, electing to slowball Connors. The move brought immediate dividends as Jimmy's suspect forehand betrayed him. But at 4-4, 30-0 when a pigeon distracted the server, McEnroe, it looked to be the challenger's end. The bird flew across his line of vision and he netted a forehand. Fortunately the portent was false. John held serve and by courtesy of two successive stinging backhands he grabbed the set.

Only now did the contest sparkle, but John was overawed by the prospect of a fifth set and indifferent serving proved his downfall. Connors broke straight away at the start of the fourth, was pulled back, then finally got ahead 4-3. McEnroe became increasingly ragged and surrendered speedily.

"I wish I could have won. Jimmy was always hitting winners off my serve. I thought I had a chance when I won the third set but he just played the big points better than I could," confessed McEnroe.

"If I were him and had a first year like that I'd be proud of myself," opined the victor.

It had been a fortnight of miracles for McEnroe, from the anonymity of Roehampton to the semi-finals of the greatest tournament in the world.

He had played nine matches to reach it. No one before had ever done that – not even Bill Tilden in the days of the challenge round, who played eight in 1920.

No wonder the late Arthur Ashe asserted, "He's good – you'd better believe it."

⥊⥻

With Mary Carillo, lost to Dennis Ralston and Martina Navratilova 6-8, 6-3, 10-8.

John returned to Centre Court to partner Mary in this tense mixed doubles quarter-final against vastly more experienced opponents.

John Feinstein has written in his book 'Hard Courts' about an incident at 8-8 in the third set when Ralston, a Wimbledon singles runner-up in '66, hit Carillo with a shot. McEnroe has always thought it was an intentional strike, and his love of tennis has led him to plead, "That's not the way you play the game. You don't go around trying to hit the girl."

Ralston has told me, "I have never tried to hit anyone." On a less contentious note, he adds, "McEnroe and Carillo played well and it was a close match. I didn't notice any weakness in his game. He was very good."

* In the December 1977 issue of 'Tennis USA' John McEnroe Senior told Murray Janoff, "I've read how people say I want Johnny to be a lawyer like me. I don't know where they came from. I don't remember any discussions with him about being a lawyer. My wife and I believe in education. We have always encouraged school. I'd support his desires if he wants to study Law, but I never influenced him."

* Eight years after John's Wimbledon debut, All England Club Chairman Sir Brian Burnett divulged this information to me, "I happened to run into him [McEnroe] in the Secretary's Office, where he was appealing against a fine imposed on him for bad behaviour on court. I think it was for racket abuse and slashing the canvas backstop during a mixed doubles match. After hearing what he had to say, including a promise that he wouldn't ever do it again, I decided to let him off.

"However, before doing so, I spoke to him like a 'Dutch Uncle' and said I thought he would be a better player if he learned to control himself. He seemed to accept this and again promised to behave in the future."

" ... and again promised to behave in the future..." The point surely is that throughout his career John endeavoured to project himself in a better light: *"Maybe I need to get defaulted. Maybe that would straighten my head out,"* but all to no avail: *"The crowds weren't*

annoying me today – I don't know why I told them to shut up."

* *During the BBC TV 'Clash of the Titans' series, broadcast in June 1996, Gene Scott said, "I would go to all his [John's] press conferences [during Wimbledon '77] and hold his hand and try to generally lend a parental arm... There was the sense of a time-bomb just starting to tick then."*

* *Over the years, Mary Carillo has spoken about her visit with McEnroe to Speakers' Corner in Hyde Park. "John picked a fight with one of the speakers," she says playfully. Apparently they also went together by tube to the Wimbledon ball – after John had borrowed a jacket.*

1978

US Pro Indoors	Quarter-final	Gottfried	61 63
Ocean City	1st Round	Taroczy	36 76 63
Washington	Quarter-final	Orantes	46 64 63
Smythe Grand Prix	Semi-Final	Mitton	16 64 64
Las Vegas	2nd Round	Newcombe	16 62 63
Rawlings International	Runner-Up	Roche	86 97
Wimbledon	1st Round	Van Dillen	75 16 89 64 63
Forest Hills	Semi-Final	Nastase	63 76
Washington	3rd Round	Orantes	67 61 75
South Orange	Semi-Final	Clerc	62 46 63
US Clay Courts	Quarter-final	Connors	36 61 61
Toronto	Quarter-final	Dibbs	61 62
US Pro Championships	Quarter-final	Solomon	62 62
US Open	Semi-Final	Connors	62 62 75
United T'gies Classic	WON	Kriek	62 64
San Francisco	WON	Stockton	26 76 62
Hawaii	Semi-Final	Scanlon	62 36 63
Swiss Indoors	Runner-Up	Vilas	63 57 75 64
Cologne	Semi-Final	Fibak	57 61 61
Stockholm	WON	Tim Gullikson	62 62
Benson & Hedges	WON	Tim Gullikson	67 64 76 62
Bologna	Semi-Final	Fleming	64 61
DAVIS CUP			
V Chile:	With Brian Gottfried bt Prajoux/Fillol		36 63 86 63
V Great Britain	Bt J. Lloyd bt Mottram		61 62 62 62 62 61

1978 was a year of two halves for John. Now expected to make the final stages of tournaments due to his sensational Wimbledon debut the previous June, he stuttered in the first six months, until, brushing aside Sherwood Stewart, Jaime Fillol, Peter Fleming, Colin Dowdeswell and Butch Walts, he achieved a semi-final showing in the US Open.

McEnroe's proudest moment in the first half of the year had been his win over John Sadri which landed him the NCAA's (National Collegiate Athletic Association) title as a freshman.

In the autumn John triumphed in four Grand Prix events – the United Technologies Classic, the Transamerica Open, the Stockholm Open and the Benson and Hedges Championships. His title in Sweden included a one hour fourteen minutes' rout of three-times Wimbledon Champion, Bjorn Borg, in which he only dropped seven points on serve.

Furthermore, he was a runner-up at Basle and reached three semi-finals – in Hawaii, Cologne and Bologna respectively – thus qualifying for the '78 Masters Tournament, which was played in January 1979.

The United States Davis Cup selectors couldn't let such remarkable exploits go by unrewarded. Santiago, Chile saw McEnroe's debut in the competition – he and Brian Gottfried beat Jaime Fillol and Belus Prajoux 3-6, 6-3, 8-6, 6-3, as the US captured the American Zone Final.

But it was in the Final Proper, held at Palm Springs, where John really proved himself. Great Britain was slaughtered 4-1, with the 19-year old destroying first John Lloyd, 6-1, 6-2, 6-2, then Buster Mottram, 6-2, 6-2, 6-1.

Peter Bodo wrote in the BP/ITF 'World of Tennis' book, "[McEnroe's] tennis was simply superb – a sagacious mixture of spin and pace that dissected Lloyd's game with surgical precision. 'I've never been made to look like an idiot on the court before,' Lloyd commented afterwards. 'Not by Borg, not by Connors, not by anyone until I played McEnroe today.' "

Rawlings International

Monday, June 19, 1978

After all the press speculation as to whether John would join the circuit full time or go to Northern California's Stanford University, he chose the latter opportunity.

Dick Gould, tennis coach during McEnroe's one year stay, remembers, "The first time I saw John play was on television when he was at Wimbledon [in 1977]. I was impressed most of all with his quickness, both with his hands and his feet.

"He was very well liked here at Stanford. He was just a normal student as far as the rest were concerned. There are many special people here in areas in addition to athletics and John was treated just like anyone else. To my knowledge, he didn't receive any special adulation or privileges. John was also one of the greatest team players I have ever seen. He was very quick to congratulate a team member after a win and just as quick to console a losing member. There were only two occasions when I saw John become upset with an umpire or linesman. One was in a match against Eddie Edwards here at Stanford towards the end of the season when we played Pepperdine, and the other was in the NCAA Championships when he had unbelievable pressure on him. Certainly in his day-to-day relationships with his teammates and other people on campus he was not 'self-righteous, self-absorbed, aggressive, overbearing and rude.'[2]

"John has been very quick to help Stanford. He has come back to play at fund-raising exhibitions and has supported this school financially as well. In spite of his short-comings under pressure on the professional tour, I remember him here at Stanford as being delightful, quick of wit and with a little bit of the 'devil' in him. He was truly a fun person to be around. It is too bad the people only see one side of him in a match and thus judge his entire personality on this basis."

Gradually during his twelve months' college McEnroe realised his career lay in tennis. In February 1978 he discussed with his parents the possibility of leaving Stanford. They, too, were beginning to understand their son's compelling potential.

Having won the prestigious NCAA Championships – team and individual singles – John left university in June and turned professional.

The Rawlings International at Queen's Club represented his first event as a pro and it was none other than his doubles partner Peter Fleming whom John beat, 4-6, 7-5, 6-3, in the opening round.

Six foot five inch Fleming was born on January 21st, 1955 at

---

[2] Michael Mewshaw, author of 'Short Circuit', a 1982 book about the men's tennis circuit, used these words when he described John to me.

Summit, New Jersey. Given his height, people were always telling him to play basketball, but his father escorted him to the nearby tennis club and Peter was soon playing the game constantly.

Fleming was 16 years old when he met John, four years his junior, at the Port Washington Tennis Academy.

They first played doubles together in the autumn of 1977, reaching the semi-final at Los Angeles and San Francisco. For believers in biorhythms, their match on this day was a foregone conclusion. McEnroe was near his peak in physical, emotional and intellectual terms, whereas Fleming was at his lowest point physically.

Tuesday, June 20, 1978

"Wimbledon 1977 changed my whole life."

John put his fearsome serve and volley game into top gear as he outclassed Ismail El Shafei 6-3, 6-4. McEnroe was unusually cheery afterwards: "I turned professional two weeks ago so this is my first tournament pay day. It's a nice feeling."

Had his Wimbledon experience been the main reason why he turned pro? Yes, definitely, according to McEnroe himself. He suddenly realised that he could compete with the "really good guys."

"My confidence and outlook changed dramatically."

Someone then asked what his immediate goals were.

"I keep working at the basis of my game, aiming at consistency. Oh, I know that if I get lucky I can have a good result against anybody. What I want to do now," he added ominously, "is play the same high level game day in and day out."

Judging by this performance, El Shafei, not to mention many other players, were surely hoping McEnroe wouldn't attain his objective.

Wednesday, June 21, 1978
Beat Gene Mayer 7-5, 6-0

It could have been on this day that John lunched at Queen's Club and said diffidently, "I may never make the semi-finals [of Wimbledon] again."

Certainly McEnroe uttered those words at Queen's Club within earshot of World Tennis' Mike Lupica "one afternoon before the 1978 Wimbledon."

As regards Gene Mayer, he too had been coached by Dick Gould at Stanford University. But Gene and John were not at Stanford at the same time. It was not until the early '80's that they played a hilarious exhibition match against each other to raise funds for Stanford's scholarship system.

Thursday, June 22, 1978

"I'll play my quarterfinal on Friday and if I'm still in, my semi on Saturday and my final on Sunday." *(Rain postponed his match.)*

Friday, June 23, 1978

John, named as the eleventh seed for Wimbledon, soon found himself involved in a tough, uncompromising battle with Tom Gullikson of the United States. He had to try to cope with violent winds, depressing drizzle and raging thunderstorms on a day that proved frustrating for both players and officials alike.

At just past 5.00 p.m. the organisers abandoned play for the day, with the intention of re-starting the following morning at 10.30 a.m. Although John had conceded the opening set he'd resuscitated his challenge and was a break up in the third at the close.

After 20 minutes of the Gullikson affair, the score stood at 4-4 with no service breaks along the way. Then down came the rain and play was suspended for one and a half hours. When they returned Gullikson forged ahead 5-4, displaying a readier awareness of what was practicable and what was not, as McEnroe twice slipped chasing shots. Sure enough, in the next game the youngster blew a simple volley to present Gullikson with two break points. A similar error gave Tom the set.

At 1-1 in the second set the match was again halted – only 17 minutes play had been allowed – and this time the break was a mentally taxing two hours, two minutes.

Maybe the wait disturbed Gullikson, maybe it was simply that John played superlatively well, but on the resumption Tom lost the second set 6-2 in ignominious style. The third interruption came just 28 minutes after the previous one; the final set score stood at 1-0, Gullikson. The delay was a comparatively mere 33 minutes and when they returned McEnroe broke serve to lead 3-2.

Prospects for the 19-year old looked good, but this playing spell, spanning 21 minutes, was swiftly curtailed by further thunder and lightning.

Overnight score: McEnroe led Gullikson 4-6, 6-2, 3-2.

Saturday, June 24, 1978
Beat Tom Gullikson 4-6, 6-2, 6-4
Beat Colin Dibley 6-3, 8-9, 6-2

The fact that John was a service break up overnight meant he needed just fifteen minutes in the morning to complete a 4-6, 6-2, 6-4 victory. The protracted duel ended almost twenty-fours hours after the first ball was struck. Playing time however, was only about one hour and forty-five minutes. The 3-2 lead that McEnroe possessed quickly became 4-2 and from there he never looked like losing the initiative. He won his last two service games to love.

What of his encounter against a former Customs Immigration Officer, Colin Dibley of Australia? Well, one member of the press described it as "a dull, one-sided match," but John must have been pleased to beat a man who had reached Wimbledon's last eight in 1971 and 1972.

Sunday, June 25, 1978
Lost to Tony Roche 8-6, 9-7

It was no disgrace for 19-year old John to fall to Roche, who in his prime had been ranked No.2 in the world behind Rod Laver.

The Australian victor praised John's mature game as he appreciated he had been severely tested. John had led 2-1 in the second set with a service break and later saved five match points before Roche struck a backhand service return winner to collect the title and cheque for £9,770.

On the positive side, the 'Daily Telegraph' voted the fight "as good a final as Queen's has seen." On the negative side, John would be labelled "a self-cursing, line-questioning, fidgeting neurotic" in 'Tennis Today's' report on the tournament.

Wimbledon

Thursday, June 27, 1978

"It was a strange feeling. As I walked out the umpire asked me if I'd ever played 'Flash' before. It wasn't so long ago that I was the wonder boy coming through. This year I wasn't even seeded for the qualifying tournaments." (Erik van Dillen)

Young John crashed unexpectedly in the first round by the score of 7-5, 1-6, 8-9, 6-4, 6-3 to a determined man ranked 120 rungs below him on the ladder of world tennis. In an invigorating late afternoon contest on difficult Court No.7 McEnroe was near enough to sight victory before the quick-witted van Dillen snatched it from him.

The 19-year old appeared to have established a firm grip after easily taking the second set, and when he won the third on a tiebreak, he looked unlikely to slide down the slopes to destruction. They moved to 4-4 and Charlie Pasarell, van Dillen's former Davis Cup partner, suddenly shouted to him, "Hit the ball, hit your returns."

The six-foot tall Californian responded by attacking, then crowding his opponent. Later he said, "I just blasted straight winners. I had never done anything like that." The underdog broke McEnroe's serve for a 5-4 lead, only to find his rumbustious play faltering. Regaining composure quickly, van Dillen managed to hang on for a fifth set.

At 2-2 the teenager could not prevent an inspired attack that left him 0-30 down on serve. Although he salvaged the next point, the little-known American progressed to 40-15 and a hard backhand induced a McEnroe error.

Later, again serving, this time to save the match, the eleventh seed saw van Dillen sweep to match point. Twice John hit smashes, but both were returned and finally he was stranded. After the handshake the weary loser retired to his seat and hid beneath a towel. In marked contrast, Erik's racquet went flying as he jumped the net, and then embraced his wife Lailee, who had watched courtside.

At Queen's Club earlier that month John had won £4,000 for his endeavours – his three hours eight minutes' Wimbledon effort brought him a mere £250.00. At least he could take heart from van Dillen's comment, "That kid will be back. You get a lot of shooting stars who burn themselves out, but not McEnroe. He's got too much class for that."

John, close to tears, was furious with his inability to close out the match and remarked bitterly, "You just don't expect to find guys playing out of their skins in the first round of Wimbledon. Yes, I'm taking it pretty hard. I expect more of myself. I always want to do well."

* John's press conference lasted a tense five minutes in which he fidgeted continually with the silver buckle on his watchband. Asked if a first round loss was particularly upsetting after his fine show in 1977, the youngster deadpanned: "No-one likes to lose in the first round."

July 1978

In US 'Tennis' magazine, Tony Palafox informed Robert Cubbedge that John's eleven-year old brother Patrick "has tremendous potential."

But Mr. McEnroe declared, "We're not trying to make a tennis player out of him ... obviously he's got something to shoot at with John as his brother. I'm sure some people will say that's good, some will say it's bad. I don't know what the answer is. But we're not pushing him – or comparing them together."

It was further revealed that John often gave Patrick "pointers" with his game. However, "if he tells me something and I do it wrong again, he gets mad and starts yelling at me," commented the younger brother.

John admitted it was true: "Whenever I tell anyone anything, I want them to do it right away. With Pat, I want him to do it faster. He's my brother."

Apparently Patrick didn't yell back, though John joked, "Give him a few years ... What the heck, he's a McEnroe."

Monday, July 3, 1978
With Stacy Margolin, led Tony Lloyd and Ros Lewis 3-0

John was competing in the mixed doubles with his girlfriend, 18-year old Stacy Margolin from Beverly Hills, California. They had met whilst playing the same junior competitions.

Blonde Stacy had graduated from Beverly Hills High School in June 1977 as a 'straight A' student. Coached by Robert Lansdorp and her brother Mike, she was a left-hander with a topspin forehand and double-handed backhand. She was not yet a professional because she was majoring in Psychology at the University of Southern California.

As for the match itself, opponent Ros Lewis recalls, "It was a great thrill to play McEnroe. The Wimbledon of '78 was extremely wet and I remember beginning the match on Court 13 (it was a show court in those days) and we had to come off for rain before we began the match.

"Because Tony Lloyd was the third brother there were many spectators and of course McEnroe's reputation was already beginning to spread.

"We resumed the match late (7.45 p.m.) that evening and the light was bad and it was cold. The umpire asked McEnroe to take off his tracksuit, which provoked a protest. The umpire relented.

"I must say I was very surprised that he [John] took the match so seriously. He glared at the linesmen several times and queried a number of calls. No major tantrums, though.

"It was obvious to me that he and Stacy would win but there was no let up on his part – he just got on with the job, a true professional already."

Only the inclement weather could stop him that evening.

Tuesday, July 4, 1978
With Stacy Margolin, beat Tony Lloyd and Ros Lewis 6-2, 6-2

Ros was very pleased because she managed to return McEnroe's serve: "It wasn't the most powerful one I'd faced." But Tony Lloyd believes John "did not play full out – he was very nice to my partner by not hitting the ball too hard."

Ros agrees to some extent: "He didn't exploit me as the weakness at all, which made me feel he was a gentleman."

And Lloyd, who was anxious about possible intimidation, now admits, "McEnroe was very laid back. He seemed to enjoy playing, smiling and joking with Stacy. Certainly for me, McEnroe was the best player on grass courts. Sometimes I think he was unplayable on fast surfaces."

Wednesday, July 5, 1978

On Court No.6, John and Stacy led Chris Kachel (Australia) and Ilana Kloss (South Africa) 9-8, 5-7, 2-0. They played late in the evening.

Thursday, July 6, 1978
With Stacy Margolin, lost to Chris Kachel and Ilana Kloss, 8-9,7-5, 9-7.

"The game plan was to keep McEnroe out of the match as much as possible – this obviously worked as the lines of communication with his partner broke down.

"McEnroe had the best serve in the world at his peak – it was just so difficult to anticipate. He was a champion player who unfortunately would self-destruct when things were not going his way. I can recall him smashing a ball or two into the nearby road after this match." (Chris Kachel)

Saturday, July 8, 1978
With Peter Fleming, lost to Frew McMillan and Bob Hewitt 6-1, 6-4, 6-2.

David Irvine reported in 'The Guardian' that the unseeded pair of John and Peter had been "comprehensively out-manoeuvred" in this men's doubles final.

Frew McMillan adds, "We won pretty handily. McEnroe was very restrained in his tennis and temperament, showing I think his great respect for Wimbledon in this his first Wimbledon final. Additionally, I do remember saying that I thought the Fleming-McEnroe partnership was unlikely to be a great one!

"McEnroe's genius, to my eyes, was obviously still very tightly wrapped in its bud."

Benson & Hedges Championships

Wednesday, November 15, 1978
Beat David Lloyd 6-4, 6-2

"I do remember playing McEnroe as we reached the Davis Cup Final that year and I was playing fairly well. I enjoyed the match against John and my main memory is the fact that he served so very well. His left-handed serve was impossible to pick. He seemed to hit it so easily and yet it went so very fast. His backhand was, for a left-handed player, superb. He did so much with it and I would say it was possibly his strongest return of serve. In my opinion, he is probably the most talented player of all time.

"Bjorn Borg, for instance, was easier to play against, as he was more predictable. He couldn't do the unusual, whereas John, at any given time, could hit a topspin lob or a drop volley without showing his intention." (David Lloyd)

Thursday November 16, 1978
Beat Tom Okker 6-2, 6-3

"I was on my way down – John was playing a lot better than me. I had a lot of respect for his game. I couldn't read his serve – he hit it very wide to my backhand.

"I preferred the way McEnroe played – with a lot of feel and imagination – to the way Borg played.

"John was pretty quiet off the court, very kind." (Tom Okker)

Friday, November 17, 1978

Experienced Italian Corrado Barazutti fared little better than Okker in the quarterfinals, as John's bold show of aggression sapped his confidence right from the outset.

A flurry of American brilliance coupled with Corrado's lack of adventure gave John the first set 6-0, with the loss of just seven points.

Barazutti was still stumbling around at 0-4 in the second, but then the thought of a bitter defeat acted as a powerful spur. At last his virtually untapped energy poured forth and a string of five games bemused McEnroe. The assault only staved off defeat briefly, though. Responding with admirable determination, McEnroe took the crucial tiebreak by seven points to three.

Afterwards the American felt groggy and was ordered back to his hotel bed by a doctor to catch some sleep. Rumours were that John had tonsilitis and a 100 degree temperature, but he said he hoped to be fit for his semi-final clash with Dick Stockton.

Saturday, November 18, 1978
Beat Dick Stockton 6-4, 6-3

"He's a lot better at age 20[3] than most players even dream of being in their life. He's already a better player than Borg in some respects because he has shots which Bjorn doesn't have, and I think he can win Wimbledon next year. He's capable of it." (Dick Stockton)

Sunday, November 19, 1978

Since his last visit to England John's consistency of performance and match toughness had risen sharply. From South Orange to San Francisco, Boston to Basle, the imperfections in the youngster's game had gradually subsided as he compiled a 49-10 win:loss ratio. The icing on the cake had been the clinically efficient 6-3, 6-4 Stockholm subjugation of Bjorn Borg.

"There was little I could do," said the Wimbledon Champion, bewilderment registering on his normally impassive face. "John simply played too well for me."

A week later, under the warm lights of the Wembley Arena, McEnroe was aware that another Grand Prix victory, his fourth of the year, would almost certainly assure his entry into the Colgate Masters event in January.

Pitted against the late Tim Gullikson, the player he had so easily defeated on a fast court in the Stockholm final, the 19-year old figured to pummel his opponent, but the anticipated one-sided affair never materialised. The capacity crowd saw a titanic struggle as two combative young men embarked on a dour adventure that required them to dig deep into their resources of courage and strength.

The intensity of their desire was first epitomised by an absorbingly close opening set. At 6-6 a gripping tie-break sequence prevailed. McEnroe assumed the initiative, but at 5-1 he suddenly became frail. Gullikson responded immediately and at 6-5 held a set point.

---

[3] McEnroe was, in fact, only 19 years old.

McEnroe served. Gullikson's backhand return drifted tentatively into the tramline, but remarkably, perhaps in the absence of a call, or perhaps due to a bizarre moment of absent-mindedness, umpire Roy Cope-Lewis awarded the set to Gullikson. The absurdity of this decision was made all the more acute because the ball had actually skimmed the net-cord judge's nose!

There followed, not unnaturally, three minutes' passionate debate as John, never one to tolerate errors, protested vehemently about what seemed an obvious mistake. His ire roused and wrath kindled, the American breathed fire and fury in an emotionally charged plea. When the umpire remained stubborn, McEnroe declared with a resigned glare, "That's it then, man. I'm not playing any more."

Referee Mike Gibson was then summoned to restore order. Sheepishly, both linesman and net-cord official now chose to enlighten the umpire and he sharply reversed his decision. Yet if it hadn't been for McEnroe's lengthy debate, which swung the crowd against him, one doubts if justice would have been seen to be done.

Freelance writer Jean Rafferty told me, "I suspect the linesman just wanted to teach McEnroe a lesson. He sat there and said nothing while the crowd slow handclapped and booed McEnroe. I've never seen a player face so much collective HATE."

The rattled New Yorker lost the tie-break 9-7. However, far from being disheartened, he displayed the value of composure in the second set, winning twelve of the last thirteen points to dig in at 6-4. Persistent attempts to break down Gullikson's defences rewarded John in the third and after another tie-break he at last led.

The teenager now forgot the earlier fracas and as he continued to step up his challenge, so his opponent's competitive fires faded. Fatigue affected Tim to such an extent that he finally surrendered with two double-faults.

McEnroe thus became the youngest winner of the Benson and Hedges trophy and later, teaming up with Peter Fleming, he exacted revenge on the couple that beat them in the Wimbledon Final, Bob Hewitt and Frew McMillan.

It was John's first major triumph in England and his anger during the final made him an unpopular champion. The £18,200 cheque came with new enemies that November night.

 * *John rewarded himself with a trip to Wolfe's Restaurant at 34 Park Lane. According to a staff member there, "All the players used to come to us, but since they now rent houses around Wimbledon and*

no longer stay in the Park Lane hotels, they have stopped coming."

Another of John's favourite eateries on his early visits to England was Alexander's in the King's Road, but proprietor Jose Neves confided in 1988, "John McEnroe has not been here since 1982."

* *Wembley '78 was the first time Jean Rafferty met John McEnroe. She says, "When he spoke at his press conferences he was amusing, intelligent, with an unexpectedly quiet and sensitive side to him. He talked about wanting to see art while he was in Europe. It seemed to me that he was basically a very decent 'normal' person."*

In a Benson & Hedges conference McEnroe had said, "You find interests by travelling. Like art. I never thought about art at all before. But you see so many beautiful buildings and things. The fact that I even look twice is amazing. I'll probably learn a lot about that later."

Thursday, November 21, 1978

Ever wondered where that cruel 'Superbrat' tag came from?

On this day, an article in 'The Daily Express' by Ian Barnes began, "Tennis pros who nicknamed John McEnroe 'The Brat' only a year ago are looking over their shoulders at the upstart emerging as the next superstar."

The headline read "Super Brat Has Them Worried."

Says Barnes, "It came up in general conversation that he was being called the Brat in the locker room, especially by the older players. My sub-editor made it two words, 'Super Brat'. But the following summer the tabloids made it one word."

Yet thinking of the 'Superbrat' label in 1984, John Ballantine of 'The Sunday Times' would opine, "John was treated disgracefully on his early visits to Wimbledon."

December 1978

In 'Tennis World', Mary Carillo says of John: "He has no subtlety; he doesn't go out of his way to impress people. He doesn't care what they think. Tennis is a simple game to him, when things go wrong he gets mad."

1979

Masters[4]	WON	Ashe	67 63 75
US Pro Indoors	Quarter-final	Tanner	76 62
Richmond	Semi-Final	Borg	46 76 63
Boca Raton	Third Place	Vilas	64 62
Palm Springs	2nd Round	Teltscher	67 75 76
New Orleans	WON	Tanner	64 62
Milan	WON	Alexander	64 63
Rotterdam	Runner-Up	Borg	64 62
San Jose	WON	Fleming	76 76
Las Vegas	Semi-Final	Connors	75 64
WCT Finals	WON	Borg	75 46 62 76
Gunze International		Dupre	John led 76 32 retired
Stella Artois	WON	Pecci	67 61 61
Wimbledon	4th Round	Tim Gullikson	64 62 64
Forest Hills	Round Robin	Lost Pecci Beat Alexander Beat Vijay Amritraj	36 75 76 63 60 62 16 61
South Orange	WON	J. Lloyd	67 64 60
US Clay Courts	Semi-Final	Vilas	64 75
Toronto	Runner-Up	Borg	63 63
US Open	WON	Gerulaitis	75 63 63
Los Angeles	Runner-Up	Fleming	64 64
San Francisco	WON	Fleming	46 75 62
Stockholm	WON	G. Mayer	67 63 63
Benson & Hedges	WON	Solomon	63 64 75
Bologna	Semi-Final	Walts	64 67 63

---

[4] Part of the 1978 Tennis Year.

Davis Cup:

V Columbia beat Betancur 6-2 6-1 6-1; beat Molina 6-4 6-3 6-2;
with Fleming, beat Molina/Agueldo 6-4 6-0 6-4
    V Argentina beat Vilas 6-2 6-3 6-2; beat Clerc 6-2 6-3
    V Australia beat Alexander 9-7 6-2 9-7; beat Edmondson 6-3 6-4
    V Italy beat A. Panatta 6-2 6-3 6-4; beat Zugarelli 6-4 6-3 6-1

In 1979 John McEnroe established himself as the world's No.2 –
with only Bjorn Borg ahead of him.

He celebrated the beginning of the year by capturing the '78
Masters and in May the WCT Finals in Dallas fell to the dexterity of
his racquet. At the latter tournament McEnroe shocked both Jimmy
Connors and Borg, the first time a player had beaten those supposed
immortals back-to-back since Arthur Ashe at Wimbledon '75.

By June, when he blitzed through the field at Queen's Club,
John's unique serve was a familiar sight to English audiences. As he
had told US 'Tennis' magazine six months earlier " …maybe it looks
a little weird, but it helps me to get my rhythm going and also helps
me to hit the ball out in front, with my body fully extended. In that
way I can get a lot more power on my serve and still keep it in."

Not that the English press was interested in technical discussion
regarding John's game. Despite being the victim in a dispute during
his Stella Artois win over Vijay Amritraj, the media attacked him
mercilessly from that point onwards. Respected journalist Lance
Tingay wrote in the BP/ITF 'World of Tennis' book, "I doubt if ever
in the history of the game a player was meted out such rough
treatment as was given to McEnroe immediately prior to the
Wimbledon Championships."

An injured left thigh contributed heavily to McEnroe's loss at the
All England Club to the late Tim Gullikson, but he bounced back two
months later to capture his first Grand Slam title, the US Open, by
virtue of immense skill allied to a courageous sprit. Singles was not
John's only success – in harness with Peter Fleming he finished
victorious at Wimbledon and Flushing Meadow and they won many
other doubles titles.

The 20-year old New Yorker beat arch-rival Borg twice (New
Orleans and Dallas), but lost three times to the Monte Carlo resident
(Richmond, Rotterdam and Toronto). But the Swede feared

McEnroe, openly admitting, "If you play John you have to be at the top of your game to beat him."

No-one could defeat McEnroe in the Davis Cup. After the United States' 5-0 whitewash of Italy in the final, John had yet to lose in the competition.

Braniff Airways World Doubles

Wednesday, January 3, 1979
With Peter Fleming, beat Paulo Bertolucci and Adriano Panatta 6-1, 6-1

A small but enthusiastic crowd at Olympia in London saw the Americans take less than 40 minutes to demolish their Italian opposition.

McEnroe and Fleming dropped just 11 points in each set whilst poor Bertolucci lost his serve on every occasion.

Thursday, January 4, 1979
With Peter Fleming, beat Ilie Nastase and Sherwood Stewart 7-6, 4-6, 6-3

A whole decade after this match took place, John would confess to Chris Martin in 'The Sun' that the Braniff prize money - $40,000 for the winning pair – had "really opened my eyes. I couldn't believe it. I have always felt there is too much money in tennis."

By 1989 many McEnroe observers had warmed to his honesty. But in 1979 crowds were struggling to comprehend his intense approach. John was aware that he was being misunderstood and as a result he felt a little wary of interviewers. Around this time he would tell Frank Keating of 'The Guardian', "I suppose it will be all the usual dumb stuff , 'Why don't I ever smile?' and 'Why am I rude to officials?' and 'Why can't I be more British?'

"Well, before you get going, let me say I don't smile when I'm concentrating on court – well, do you go around with a grin on your face when you're reading up some really concentrated research? And as for being rude to linesmen, well, I can honestly say I've only ever queried what I genuinely know is a bad call and I just think my eyesight at 20 is better than some old man's of 70, however much he might love tennis."

Friday, January 5, 1979
With Peter Fleming, beat Bob Hewitt and Frew McMillan 6-3, 6-3
Two months earlier, in November 1978, John and Peter had exacted revenge for their Wimbledon final loss by beating this South African pairing both in Cologne and in London.

Today they won again, leaving Frew McMillan to declare, "Their play is full of courage and inspiration – it was like facing IRA bombers."

Saturday, January 6 1979
With Peter Fleming, beat Mark Cox and David Lloyd 6-3, 6-7, 6-3

"I remember talking to Fleming after the match, saying words to the effect that if his partner could just present himself in a better light on the court he would hold the whole world in the palm of his hand." (Mark Cox)

Sunday, January 7, 1979

In an article by Ron Atkin of 'The Observer', John declared defiantly, "OK, I make faces. The faces are me. People pay to watch me play and if they want to boo me, that's fine. Let's put it this way. I'd rather get some attention than no attention. If it's bad, that's life."

Coming off the court having beaten Ilie Nastase and Sherwood Stewart 3-6, 6-2, 6-3, 6-1, Peter and John got rather a lot of attention. They were mobbed by screaming fans and security men had to hustle them to the locker room.

They lost the first set after Peter dropped serve in the eighth game. John was the only one of the four men to hold serve throughout the 1 hour 50 minutes of action.

Pride had been McEnroe's only catalyst because this event was merely part of his build-up for the more important battles of 1979. "This doubles tournament may not have been the best way to prepare for the Masters, but the match play has got me back in the swing of things after two weeks off and I hope it will work out. I feel a lot better now than I did at the beginning of the week."

Monday, January 29, 1979

"I think I've improved a lot. But it doesn't seem to matter. People want to read about my terrible reputation. I'm different on and off the court and I'd like people to know me for what I am – a nice person. There's nothing I can do about the faces I make." (Talking to Pete Axthelm, 'Newsweek')

March 1979

Freelance writer Jean Rafferty profiled John for the new British magazine 'Top Tennis'.

She revealed his belief that he was a "terrible dancer" and introduced us to John's desire for perfection. He said, "I think I can improve everything. There's nothing I feel I can't hit, but I don't have any shot that's great. You can always do something better. Nobody's got anything perfect."

Thursday, March 8, 1979

"All our kids got the same instructions when we sent them off to the courts: 'Play your best. Don't quit. But we want you to be gentlemen.'" (John McEnroe Snr. talking to Shaun Usher, 'Daily Mail')

Saturday, April 7, 1979

At Rotterdam's ABN World Championships, John stormed into the final with a 6-0, 6-3 thrashing of 25-year old Vijay Amritraj.

The Indian was more than impressed by McEnroe's talent. "Right now everybody feels he is the best in the world. He's the toughest to play against and I have played them all. It's like facing a cannon, a machine gun and an air rifle at the same time. There you are trading ground strokes with him and then suddenly you look up and find him at the net. He moves so quickly."

Stella Artois Championships

Tuesday June 12, 1979

After inflicting a straight forward 6-4, 6-4 defeat on veteran Charlie Pasarell in the £70,000 Stella Artois Championships, young star John McEnroe revealed his secret Wimbledon fear.

On May 17 he had sustained a thigh injury against fellow American Pat Dupre at the Gunze World International, Tokyo and it had prevented him from playing either the French Open or a grass court event at Beckenham in Kent. Now, not only was his form so rusty that match practice for Wimbledon was vital, but simultaneously care needed to be exercised so as not to aggravate the suspect left thigh. It was, said the American, a classic catch-22 situation.

McEnroe's affected area was bandaged and although he fell over twice against Pasarell, the match represented no more than one hour and 15 minutes of mild exertion, despite the fact that there was heavy drizzle for the final three games. "The doctor told me to be careful and I wouldn't want to play on really wet grass, but you just have to play a few matches here to know how you are feeling," said McEnroe, dispelling rumours that the tumbles and greasy court had concerned him unduly.

As for his opponent, Charlie Pasarell, fifteen years older and a man with vast grass court experience, he was soon struggling and had to stave off six break points in the seventh game as John began to increase the tempo.

In his very next service game, Pasarell, remembered as the player who stretched Pancho Gonzales to a 112 game marathon at Wimbledon in 1969, was broken when he netted an easy backhand. The error proved costly as the New Yorker ran out the first set 6-4. When Pasarell again conceded serve in the second, it was enough to give McEnroe the match 6-4, 6-4 in a below-par encounter with few noticeable rallies.

Although John lost just nine points in ten service games it wasn't an auspicious start. "I thought Pasarell played well, but while I made some good shots, I didn't really have it all together," was his honest verdict.

Thursday, June 14, 1979

"This is making me sick with myself." (after playing a poor forehand)

Two days can be an interminable amount of time for a tennis tournament and since John's opening match much had happened. Not only had the Stella Artois Championships been plagued by drizzle and subsequently unplayable courts, but an announcement was soon made that the final would be played on the following Monday.

McEnroe was still finding trouble gaining confidence on the slick grass courts and his insecurity grew when he could only practise indoors on wood for his match with Australian John James.

After his 3-6, 6-3, 6-2 win, he admitted it, saying, "I didn't feel anything was right for a while."

During most of the duel one was able to feel an underlying tension, although it receded somewhat after a peculiar incident in the fifth game of the final set. A dying pigeon fluttered onto the court as McEnroe was in his first serve ritual and despite a ball girl's amusing attempt to catch the bird, John flung his racquet down. This was followed by an equally fruitless effort by the groundsman to throw a towel over the young dove, which in the end was carried to safety.

Earlier, McEnroe had pouted his displeasure at BBC cameramen and mocked himself, yelling, "Hit it!" after one particular error. Furthermore, an unavailing run for a ball was met with the sarcastic exclamation, "Good moving."

On several occasions John tumbled on the slippery court and once, thoroughly exasperated, he banged his tousled head on the grass. Fortunately, the left thigh proved no problem and he was also lucky in that his match was one of the few to be played on Centre Court, the rest being staged indoors on wood.

Friday, June 15, 1979

John was still in the news and two journalists of 'The Daily Mirror', Anthea Disney and Rita Grosvenor, told how, "He has little time for girls…"

In their article John was quoted as saying, "You can't say it's fun to just lie on some bed in your room and watch TV between practice and playing, but that's the way I want it.

"You need time alone – to think things out – at least I do. I don't want to socialise much before a match, just lie around and be quiet. When you travel this much, you're in the same place maybe twice a year, so you don't get much chance to make friends. In a way, the more you win the less chance you have to go to parties or whatever. When you are winning a lot, it's tougher on the person, the pressures are just incredible.

"A lot of people want to be around you because you're a tennis player. That's the way it is. I accept that. But when some girl calls up at three in the morning it can be a real pain. I just say to her, 'I'm asleep, call me tomorrow.' Look, I'm having a great time - I'm doing well, I'm making an incredible amount of money, but look at someone like Arthur Ashe who's about seventeen years older than me. I don't think I could stand it for that much longer."

Saturday, June 16, 1979
Beat Vijay Amritraj 7-6, 6-1

Umpire Dick Lumb incensed John by wrongfully penalising him a game, instead of the valid one point.

The clash came when McEnroe exclaimed, "I want more serves," and continued to practise his delivery when Lumb called for the start of play. Lumb reacted by awarding the first point to Amritraj, in line with the Players' Code of Conduct stipulation regarding a Failure to Commence Play.

McEnroe responded, "I'm ready to play," and Lumb suddenly exceeded his powers by next calling "Game to Amritraj." Immediately John yelled to tournament director Clive Bernstein, "Get somebody down here. He's won the match if he's got the game."

The error was rectified and distinguished journalist Lance Tingay wrote in 'The Daily Telegraph': "McEnroe had a kind of moral victory." As for Lumb, he freely admitted afterwards that he had misinterpreted the rules.

But in the match itself John had to really exert himself. He saved one set point at 5-6 with a second serve ace and then he averted another a few seconds later.

After the struggle he said he "might have taken ten more seconds than I should have done."

In addition, "I said a few things to people in the crowd. That's my fault to respond, but when they clap your double-faults …

"A woman shouted at me, 'You're ugly.' I've been called a baby and all sorts of names. They may be true, but it's unnecessary. It's hard enough as it is to go out there with the crowd against me."

Sunday, June 17, 1979

When umpire Roy Cope-Lewis overruled a service call to give Sandy Mayer an ace in the seventh game, McEnroe soon received his second penalty point in as many days. And although referee Jim Moore and Grand Prix supervisor Frank Smith again arrived on the scene, this time the penalty was upheld.

The ace gave Mayer a 5-2 lead in the first set and McEnroe advanced to the chair, asking the official, "What's your name?"

On being told, he said, "I'll make sure you're not on my court again."

John later admitted he wouldn't complain if Cope-Lewis was made umpire for any of his subsequent matches. However, regarding the penalty point, he added, "I don't think that was justified. I did not say anything obscene to the umpire. I just asked his name. Neither do I think I'm always right, there's no doubt about that, but umpires now seem to be a little quick to jump on me."

Later John insisted on complete silence and Mayer sarcastically remarked, "You missed your calling. You should have been an usher."

When, following John's complaints, a tournament official appealed over the loudspeaker for immobility except at the changeover periods, Sandy childishly retorted, "Rigor mortis is required."

Not surprisingly, John's meeting with Roscoe Tanner in the semi-final was, in comparison, a subdued affair. He won handily enough: 6-4, 7-5, blunting Tanner's service ferocity with inspired control off the ground. McEnroe's familiar grievances continued, but it was obvious he was making a great effort to tone down. Anyone moving around or speaking was merely reprimanded with a glare. Mild complaints were made by the New Yorker with regards to noise from the restaurant and a couple of linecalls were half-heartedly queried, but in essence it was a peaceful performance.

So what were his hopes for Wimbledon?

"I'll try to avoid any sort of confrontation, where all you ought to worry about is playing well. The occasion is far too big and important ... I've learned it doesn't do any good to be negative to umpires and linesmen. It only makes them negative to you. I have to protest sometimes, everybody does. Maybe I don't go about it the right way because I never seem to get things changed in my favour, but I'll still do it if I think I'm right. I only say something on court when there is something wrong. My temper is better than it was two years ago and I'm trying to change all the time. When I was a junior it was different. If I asked for quiet whoever was making a noise would turn round and tell me to 'shut up'"

Finally, what was John's reaction to the British press techniques?

"I don't know whether you guys write the headlines, but over here you make it seem as if you have committed a murder or something," he replied quickly.

All in all, it had been a bad weekend.

* *"Don't forget he came onto the stage when only 18," pleaded doubles partner Fleming. "People who have criticised him for his antics don't really know him. Frankly he's very shy – and an amazingly tough competitor."*

* *"I figure people don't know me. They're judging a book by its cover and they don't understand. The trouble is I don't always know what's behind the cover myself. I know I'm shy. I know I always want to win. And that's about it. I may be quite famous now, but I'm still human. I have feelings. Of course I want people to like me. I think there are good things about me ... Sometimes I wish I could just take a year off and go to Hawaii and lie in the sun. Sometimes Stacy and I just want to take off and go somewhere together. But you can't drop any job for six months and disappear, and tennis is my job.*

"I think the only thing that could really hurt me badly now would be if one of my close friends turned his back on me because of what I am and what I've become. I would find that really hard to handle. I'm not complaining about this fame thing but I find it hard to grasp when people call me a celebrity. I feel like a normal kid who plays tennis for a living and is good at his job." (Talking to Fiona Macdonald Hull, 'News of the World')

Monday, June 18, 1979

Arthur Ashe: "You have got to clean up your act for Wimbledon. You can't blame youth or inexperience anymore."
John McEnroe: "I'm going to get my head together this week."

Surprise French Open runner-up Victor Pecci mounted stern resistance in the first set against John, but after that the young American stormed back and the Paraguayan's challenge gradually dissolved as McEnroe blitzed through the South American's increasingly frail defences to come through in a three setter.

The umpire appointed for the match was Roy Cope-Lewis, but McEnroe, as he'd promised, refused to be perturbed.

Indeed, it soon became evident that the New Yorker was making great attempts to keep his emotions on a tight rein. In the second game, which he lost, McEnroe first stared at the line after a Pecci backhand brought up a cloud of chalk and then shrugged his shoulders and continued with the match. In game four, with McEnroe serving at 30-15, his concentration was disturbed when an 'Evening Standard' dispatch rider walked alongside the court. John gave him no more than a sarcastic wave as he waited patiently. Yet the incident clearly distracted the American, who went on to serve three double faults in that game, his fourth in the match.

Looking strangely dormant, McEnroe soon found himself trailing 1-3 and it wasn't until the seventh game that his famed courage was shown. He broke the six foot four inch Pecci before holding serve to 4-4.

That eighth game saw five double faults from John's racquet and when he had finally recouped the leeway he showed mock appreciation by clapping himself. There were no sudden changes in fortune and as proceedings moved towards a tie-break he was continually on the back foot.

The cumbersome first set reached a conclusion after 55 minutes when Pecci took the tie-break 7-2, with McEnroe serving a twelfth double-fault.

But the American changed his shirt at the changeover and with it came a remarkable switch. He produced a counter-offensive of gargantuan proportions. At last he demonstrated the depth of his mental ability and Pecci, wilting visibly, virtually collapsed under the frenzied pressure.

"I sensed he was getting tired. He's had a lot of very tough matches recently and I think my game picked up from the start of the second set whereas his didn't. Other than my serving in the first, I was always playing well and able to make him make the errors," was the winner's explanation for the dramatic transformation in events.

The 25 minute 6-1 second set began with a fierce smash plus two blazing aces from McEnroe, and when he captured the third set by the same margin he pocketed £9,392 for his efforts.

John's behaviour gave no cause for concern. True, he stopped three times to re-tie laces and threw a few stern looks at the line officials, but that was all. Inevitably his stupendous grass court play in the latter stages was of no interest to the media. Why did he see to those shoelaces, one fellow wanted to know?

"I don't do it as a tactic. I'm a very fidgety person. I just want things to be right. It's not that the laces come undone - just that I always like them to be tight."

Had the press coverage of the tournament affected his game?

"No, I don't think so, I just didn't loosen up or didn't warm up enough. It's happened a couple of times in this tournament when I started off slowly. At Wimbledon I'll have to be ready to start a little quicker."

"Are you worrying about your reputation?"

"You are certainly asking more about my behaviour than my tennis."

"Your behaviour was entirely different today ..."

"I thought I would just concentrate on my tennis. I couldn't afford to let other things bother me."

"Nastase's not here this year. You could be labelled the bad boy of tennis."

"I already was. I'm just going into Wimbledon to do the best I can and I'm not going to worry about that. It's the tennis that counts."

Finally, McEnroe spoke of his left thigh, which he admitted was still giving him some discomfort. "I don't realise it during the match, but I feel it the next day – now I have a week to get ready."

For John, that meant three hours' practice a day.

Sadly, the only bad call of the day went against Victor Pecci and McEnroe didn't concede his shot was out. Perhaps he didn't see it, or maybe he recalled how his challenges of authority had been distorted over the weekend.

As Frank Smith put it, "If Carter and Brezhnev had come to blows it couldn't have made a bigger impact."

* Stacy Margolin was asked to comment on her boyfriend's behaviour whilst she competed in a pre-Wimbledon women's grass court tournament at Eastbourne: "He is not a monster. Things are being blown out of proportion. I feel he has been unfairly treated, picked on. He doesn't look for trouble and he goes through many matches without saying anything. Then, out of nowhere, people are talking of a Wimbledon ban just because he ties his shoes two or three times. Really, he has tried to improve his image, but when he does blow up it doesn't seem to affect his game. John is probably a hopeless case with the British people. Sometimes I get embarrassed by his behaviour and I tell him so. He just can't ignore bad calls.

"He'll have one friendly face at Wimbledon – mine."

* According to a chauffeuse who drove John to Queen's Club, he "fiddled with the radio, rubbed his chin, picked his spots but didn't say a word."

Tuesday, June, 19 1979

"I do try to have manners – I'm really working on them, not swearing and all that. Maybe I'm not succeeding so well, but I get so angry with myself when I play a bad ball, I show it, and there's nothing much I can do about it. People keep saying I'm nastier than Ilie Nastase, but it's a different thing with him. I'm very fond of Ilie, but he really does set out to upset people. I don't copy him, I don't aim to annoy people. I just can't help getting mad with myself …

"Sure I like to be praised and liked. Who doesn't? A lot of people say I don't care about anything but my tennis. I can't argue with writers who say that, but it's just not true. Tennis isn't the end of my world. I do care about my family and friends and I'm an easy-going guy off court." (Talking to Jean Rook, 'Daily Express')

Saturday, June 23, 1979

"These people who recognise me – I go into a restaurant and they give me the best table, or do things for me that they wouldn't do for anyone else – that's not fair." (Talking to Paul Theroux, 'Radio Times')

"A lot of times I say things to myself that people shouldn't have to overhear. That's bad. But I don't consciously try to embarrass the linesmen or make fools of them." (Talking to Adam Edwards, 'Woman')

Sunday, June 24, 1979

On the Sunday preceding the 1979 Wimbledon fortnight John was at Fulham's Hurlingham Club, along with numerous other tennis players and celebrities. Incessant rain proved the bane of the occasion, although when it finally stopped he tried his hand on the putting greens.

Yet if he found that a welcome respite from the criticism being heaped on him from all sides, comments made by the late Arthur Ashe, player representative of the Men's International Professional Tennis Council (MIPTC), would soon bring disappointment.

"As a fellow American I am concerned that he should not give the impression we all come from a land of undisciplined brats," the 35-year old Ashe said.

That remark, coupled with the fast growing name of "Superbrat", must have proved psychologically damaging for young McEnroe. Typically he tried to hide his sensitivity and exude confidence in a dry humour.

"What do you think of a Borg-McEnroe final?"

"Don't worry about Borg. A McEnroe-anybody final will suit me just fine."

"Why do you continually retie your shoelaces?"

"I don't want my shoes to fall off in the middle of the rally."

"Why do you scowl on court?"

"It's my natural expression."

"What do you like least about tennis?"

"That's easy – losing."

"Will you behave at Wimbledon?"

"I'll try not to swear out loud."

"Do you ever smile on court?"

"Sure, I remember a couple two years ago."

And finally, he jokingly added, "I'm beginning to like Wimbledon. They put Connors in the same half as Borg."

The question remained – could McEnroe survive the gruelling

two-week course? We soon learnt that this supremely talented young man had much to learn, but few could have foreseen his exit on that overcast first Saturday.

* *John McEnroe Snr. told the press that he had advised his son to calm down. "John will never be a Borg or Arthur Ashe – but he's not Attila the Hun either.*

"I've told him there are more effective ways of protesting than screaming at the top of your voice. I've also said that it's sometimes best to say nothing. John does react abruptly when it would be better if he stopped and thought, but I also underlined to him he must never allow himself to be trodden on.

"I thought he handled the situation superbly after the Queen's Club blow-up. But there could be trouble with the officials who may clamp down on him sub-consciously. I'm not happy with the treatment he has received. People are head-hunting."

Wimbledon referee Fred Hoyles was forced to refute these allegations. "There's no question of McEnroe being victimised," he countered.

* *"There were 10-year olds surrounding me and they had to call the cops to get me out of there. The English girls are a lot different from girls around the rest of the world, pulling your hair and all that stuff. They lose all sense of reality. It wasn't as if they knew who I was. One or two recognise me; then, as soon as that happens, they all flock over. You can't stop to give an autograph because if you do you have to sign a thousand of them." (Talking to Ian Brodie, 'Sunday Telegraph Magazine')*

Wimbledon

Monday, June 25, 1979

The anticipated McEnroe fireworks that illuminated Barons Court never materialised for those packed around Court No.1

The 20-year old number two seed delayed the opening game of his match with Terry Moor by walking to the umpire's chair, testing his racquet, tying his laces and taking a quick gulp from a paper cup. The slow handclap began at once, but the New Yorker trudged back slowly to serve. Thereafter, despite the odd scowl, he was as good as gold.

Rain had hindered play for eighteen minutes and McEnroe, possibly as a consequence, opened with a double fault. Nevertheless, he quickly established a rhythm and went on to win the game. With appreciative teenage girls squealing their encouragement, McEnroe, like Moor, cautious on the slippery surface, then broke and soon extended his lead to 3-0. There was a brief glimpse of a break back for the Connecticut player two games later when John again double faulted, but McEnroe maintained his chokehold to 4-1.

The conclusion seemed almost foregone and the black clouds lurking above decided to grant Moor a temporary reprieve. As the skies descended, McEnroe pulled his shirt over his curly head and approached umpire Arthur May, saying with a wry smile, "Are we playing on? If we do we'll sink."

Stacy Margolin obviously agreed, using her copy of John Irving's bestseller 'The World According to Garp' as a makeshift umbrella.

They recommenced combat an hour later, whereupon John's serve and volley forays brought him further success in the shape of a 5-2 initiative. Irked by the desperate situation, the 27-year old Moor shrugged off his nerves and in the eighth game he foiled McEnroe at set point and served three consecutive winners. Yet McEnroe made Moor's joy shortlived. From there, the Stella Artois Champion captured the power for good and in a soggy scramble that made compelling theatre, he won between the showers, 7-5, 6-1, 6-4.

After his one hour and 44 minute workout he said, "I think that any time you play a first round, especially when you lost your first match a year ago, you get a little hesitant. Now I am stronger and can stay out there longer."

John was not the only one pleased with the manner of his victory. The umpire spoke of how easy the American's performance had been to handle. "I've had more trouble with junior matches. He could not have given me an easier match. He did query a couple of calls, but once I checked that the linesmen were sure, he accepted them."

"People come to Wimbledon to watch tennis. A few might come to see if there are any antics, but the tennis is the thing," was McEnroe's explanation for his subdued behaviour.

The rain interruptions hadn't frustrated him; there had been no complications. In the main, one could only say, "So far, so good."

* *"He went to Stanford University in California for a year. We think that school and education are very important and we raised our* *family that way. I don't think either Kay or I felt he was making a mistake when he finally decided to turn professional.*

"He had done what we asked of him - that was to go to university at the appropriate age of life. He completed his studies, just general subjects. He took business, he took economics, he took psychology, he took history, and he took English.

"Over the years, we have tried to inculcate in John and the boys the importance of reasonable adulthood, citizenship, etc. and the things we believe in as a family." (John McEnroe Snr. talking to Laurie Pignon, 'Daily Mail')

Wednesday, June 27, 1979
Beat Buster Mottram 6-7, 6-2, 7-6, 6-2

The British challenger did not disappoint the Centre Court crowd. In fact he broke John in the very first game and the American saved two set points at 3-5 with a wonderful ace and a forehand volley. Mottram missed two more set points in the tenth game, but he was the stronger player in the tie-break.

20-year old John muffed a smash to trail 2-5 and a double fault left him trailing 3-6. Mottram seized the set on the next point.

It was only after two hours and forty-three minutes' play that the No.2 seed captured the third set tie-break 7-4 and led for the first time.

Finally, after three hours and 18 minutes in which he could never relax, McEnroe booked his place amongst the last 32.

* Years later, Buster would comment "McEnroe is a product of the American system which is geared to self-reliance. He comes from New York and typifies the attitude of New York itself – aggression and ruthlessness. Why does youth like to identify with rebelliousness? I can't answer that question, you should ask a psychologist."

Thursday, June 28, 1979

After a five set marathon in which Italian heart-throb Adriano Panatta saw off Briton Jonathan Smith, McEnroe and Fleming took

47

to Court No.6 and dropped a set to Australian qualifiers John Fitzgerald and Wayne Pascoe before escaping 4-6, 7-5, 6-2, 6-1.

Pascoe recalls: "I guess the turning point was at 5-5, 15 all in the second. I retrieved a lob by McEnroe with a running backwards, over the shoulder return topspin lob winner. Some people would say it was a bit lucky, but I would say it resulted from hard practice! Funnily enough, McEnroe was not too impressed – and threw his racquet down on the ground."

Friday, June 29, 1979
Beat Tom Gullikson 6-4, 6-4, 7-6

Out on Court No.2, John competently quelled the left-handed Wisconsin twin.

The contest was watched by right-handed Tim, who had brushed aside Australia's Cliff Letcher in the third round for the loss of a mere five games. Sitting next to Tim was his coach, 58-year old Pancho Segura of Ecuador, who had been a real showman on the tennis circuit in his day.

Tim and Pancho decided that the former should concentrate his attack on John's forehand as the No.2 seed seemed to be making more mistakes on that wing. But would the strategy work?

* In the last match on Court No.6, darkness halted play when John and Peter led Ray Moore and Roscoe Tanner 7-5, 7-6.

Saturday, June 30, 1979

"Court No.2 is rough and heavy. It's so slow on the baselines and the bounce is never the same. It's like a circus out there." (Billie Jean King)

It was the shock of all shocks. Once again exiled to Court No.2, McEnroe fell on this, the first Saturday, by tradition the most frenetic day of the fortnight, to outsider Tim Gullikson.

On a chilly afternoon John, who had been in a quandary since he arrived in England with not getting off the blocks smartly enough, instantaneously dropped into a predicament. He felt crushed, not surprisingly, by the closeness of the spectators who pressed in on either side. Behind the court was the main concourse, a bustling thoroughfare, and to the east lay Wimbledon's busiest walkway. As the star stumbled closer and closer to a traumatic defeat, the pernicious collective gaze from his fellow competitors on the balcony above must have troubled him.

"The cold weather here and physical problems did it for me," he was to say as he sunk into a deep depression that wouldn't be fully alleviated until he won the US Open two months later. "I've got a right cold. All colds are bad when they're yours. I was stiff from the beginning. I couldn't get started. I don't feel I was ever 100%. I felt very sore - that's what comes of playing everyday and up until nine o'clock at night in this British weather. But that's sour grapes. I'm very disappointed and I guess it hasn't really hit me yet. The fact is, he played a lot better than I did. You must give Tim the credit because he played a smart match."

By the third game of the opening set John had expressed displeasure about the general immoderate activity nearby. In the fifth he lost service and, outwardly at least, was already woebegone. His discomfort was illustrated when he changed ends whilst trailing 3-4; he treated his knee and left shoulder joint with liniment.

Gullikson served out the set 6-4, and trailed 0-1, 30-40 in the second when John disputed a service call. Umpire Ron Crickmore, an army captain, ruled in Gullikson's favour and the number fifteen seed, despite five deuces, and after five break points, successfully guarded his serve. From there, without fully appreciating it, McEnroe let the set slip helplessly away 6-2. Even changing his racquet twice and taking a tablet did not save him.

News of McEnroe's demise soon passed along the grapevine to all parts of the grounds – and it sent press and public hurrying to Court No.2 as if it possessed magnetic properties. Every available vantage point was assumed whilst McEnroe's irritation increased.

He fell behind 0-4, pulled back to 4-5, before Gullikson scrambled home on his second match point, having escaped two break points.

As McEnroe left the court with a police escort anyone could tell he was very alone and extraordinarily heartbroken. The audience had done everything possible to help the tenacious Gullikson and they showed no sympathy at the outcome. To his credit, any resentment John felt he did his best to mask.

"It [Court No.2] was very slow and I didn't particularly like playing there, but you've got to win everywhere. I felt the

Wimbledon crowd were a bit hostile. I don't think that was the reason I lost. It's just so cold, it really is.

"Now I guess Bjorn Borg has a good chance – he wins it every year. And I'm sure that's what the British crowds want – Borg to win it every year, although I don't believe he should."

John had looked flat, but at least he kept calm in the face of pressure and adversity. "I don't want to give myself an excuse. It was partially in the mind and part in the body."

In truth, it had been a rout, in which Tim had been more positive and the better player. McEnroe didn't serve well and his game was totally humdrum. He hadn't been fit; he had experienced a great deal of stress in London. Gullikson realised this: "He's a great guy and a fantastic player. He is not at all like his reputation suggests."

So what was the real reason for John's defeat? To pinpoint one factor would be difficult, although his injured upper leg, which he refused to use as an alibi, meant that he couldn't get high enough up on serve and it severely reduced his first serve ratio. Robbed of that potent weapon, McEnroe was always likely to be struggling.

In the evening, Tim and his wife, Rosemary, enjoyed a celebratory dinner. John, meanwhile, went out with Stacy and hardly said a word.

* " ... *If they know who I am they're going to expect me to react. Even if I say, 'Excuse me' they'll go back and tell a friend, 'You know what, he YELLED at me.'"* (Talking to Douglas Keay, 'Woman's Own')

Sunday, July 1, 1979

A distinct air of despondency replaced the aura that John normally possessed. In a hotel room at the Kensington Hilton the hounded 20-year old read a paperback and watched television, steadfastly refusing to practise at Queen's Club for his doubles match on Monday with Peter Fleming against Moore and Tanner.

"I just don't want to talk about anything to do with tennis right now – I don't even want to pick up a tennis racquet. I'm just trying to wash the whole business of Saturday out of my mind. I took it for granted that I could just go out and play. You can't at Wimbledon because it's like no other tournament. I've learned a lot, it will be different next time, but that doesn't take away the hurt. I badly wanted to win and I'll be back. The crowd were hostile to me and that didn't help. They badly wanted Tim to beat me. What can I do about it? Be a great guy, I guess."

Monday, July 2, 1979

'The Daily Mirror' epitomised Fleet Street's reaction to John's shock loss when they said in their editorial:

"John McEnroe suffered his Wimbledon defeat with better grace than he has celebrated victories elsewhere. He was cold, injured, distracted and, finally, beaten. But he behaved. If Superbrat wasn't so super this time, nor was he such a brat."

As for the doubles, McEnroe "combined happily and forcefully with Peter Fleming" to quote the then editor of 'Top Tennis', the late Clarence Jones. In the first match on Court No.6, they completed their win over Moore and Tanner and in the fourth game on that court, the young Americans saw off Van Winitsky and Ricardo Ycaza 6-3, 6-2, 6-4. Ycaza, exactly a year older than John, had conquered him in the semi-finals of the 1976 Forest Hills Junior Event.

Wednesday, July 4, 1979
With Peter Fleming, beat Hewitt and McMillan 6-3, 7-6, 6-1

"For McEnroe, the difference between '78 and '79 was one of cemented confidence. A year can make a huge difference at that age. In my case, had it been a matter of walking off Centre Court one year and finding myself on the same court without an interim meeting, it would have been some revelation. The 'bud' of John McEnroe was now showing its lovely colour and form, leaving me having to grapple with its thorny stem." (Frew McMillan)

Friday, July 6, 1979
With Peter Fleming, beat Brian Gottfried and Raul Ramirez 4-6, 6-4, 6-2, 6-2
Amazingly, the crowd applauded John enthusiastically throughout this final and at the last changeover he smiled in acknowledgement.

At the subsequent press conference, McEnroe was asked how he would play Borg if he was in Roscoe Tanner's shoes the next day.

John said he would attack, and a reporter asked "Where?"

"At the changeover!" piped up Fleming, and everyone, McEnroe included, burst into laughter.

But gaining his first Wimbledon trophy proved a hollow achievement for the tense New Yorker. "It's better than winning nothing," he said, intimating that the title didn't take away his unhappiness.

McEnroe's low period continued. Lamar Hunt, the driving force behind World Championship Tennis, had organised an event for the week after Wimbledon at the West Side Club in New York and in the American's state of mind it was probably the wrong place to go.

As it happened, all his irritation at his setbacks of the time suddenly simmered over. John Parsons, the then tennis correspondent of the 'The Daily Mail', told me: "Basically what happened was that John McEnroe, then 20, had just returned from Wimbledon where he had suffered a pretty rough time at the hands of papers like 'The Mirror', 'The Sun', 'The News of the World', The People' etc, and indeed BBC television.

"Clearly McEnroe was not in the best of moods by the time he reached New York and the situation was not helped when he and Peter Fleming were quickly beaten in the first of their round-robin doubles matches by the Mayer brothers, Sandy and Gene.

"The next day he lost 3-6, 7-6, 7-5 to Pecci. It was a great match, but McEnroe hates losing. When he walked into the Press tent and almost the first person he saw was me – the only British journalist at the event – all his frustration and pent-up anger seemed to come to a head.

"For several minutes he launched into a fierce verbal tirade during which I was blamed for every single word written about him in London during the previous three weeks or, as he put it, "all the garbage written about me in the English press."

"It was an astonishing attack which led, quite without my knowledge or approval, to the officials suggesting he should give me an apology (which he didn't). In a way I could understand how he felt. He had been through a rough time and had to let off steam and I didn't really mind."

Benson & Hedges Championships

Monday, November 12, 1979

"It would have been nice to get a medium type of draw and then get down to the rough stuff a bit later. But I've drawn John and that's all there is to it. I'll just have to hope I play well." (John Lloyd, on hearing that he had to play McEnroe)

Wednesday, November 14, 1979

McEnroe began his defence of the £90,000 Benson & Hedges Grand Prix event with a fifty-five minute rout of John Lloyd. Although the challenger, urged on by wife Chris, rattled McEnroe in the early exchanges, his gutsy effort soon lost its bite and 6-4, 6-1 was a fair portrayal of events.

With both men hitting the ball faster than 100 mph, it was impossible to tell that this was the World No.2 and US Open Champion against a player lingering in the 200s. Lloyd dropped just one point in his first three service games, but the number one seed was pacing himself well and edged ahead 5-3 with his own serve to follow. The eager Englishman continued to probe for weaknesses and his reward was a break back, much to McEnroe's displeasure.

But with the crowd settling in anticipation of a tie-break, Lloyd relinquished the momentum by opening the tenth game with a double fault and the American's velocity and accuracy on return proceeded to earn him the set.

McEnroe's play then became a delight and Lloyd needed four deuces just to avert a 0-3 deficit before fading badly.

McEnroe finished the match in grand style, courtesy of two aces, a service winner and a fierce backhand volley. Lloyd later gave vent to his desperation, saying, "You can't pick out what he's going do. He cuts it, spins it and it's devastating."

Thursday, November 15, 1979

"I do remember finding it extremely difficult to pick the direction of his serve. It was undoubtedly the best serve I have ever played against – not necessarily the fastest, but certainly the most difficult to return because of his ability to swing the ball very wide or put it down the middle off the same swing and ball toss. A couple of times I had him 15-30 or 30 all on his serve, but he always gave me no chance at that stage by coming up with an unreturnable serve. The rest of his game was obviously also outstanding. In particular, his ability to take the ball exceptionally early and his control of the racquet head made him capable of shots that other players cannot match. Anything else about the match is really a blur. There were no incidents with the umpire and McEnroe behaved pretty well, although there was no reason for him not to as the match was not very close!

"That is all I can remember except the final thought that McEnroe was the best player I ever played on a medium-fast surface and is probably the best there has ever been on every surface except European clay." (Robin Drysdale)

Comments made by McEnroe in the mandatory press conference cast his 6-2, 6-2 dismissal of Drysdale into the shade …

According to the US Open Champion, he hadn't enjoyed Wimbledon. "I don't want to go through what I went through this year again. It was unfair, it was negative all the time. Court No.2 is a joke with people milling around and constant noise."

The American continued: "Grass is on the way out. With Australia losing its importance, the only place still using it is Wimbledon. The most important tournament of the year should not be played on grass. It may have been okay years ago when they played on it all the time, but now we don't play on it enough to prepare ourselves."

And what about the state of British tennis generally?

"During the Braniff Doubles Championship at Earls Court I was asked to coach some kids. There was snow on the courts and they were in shorts. How could you expect to get any good players that way? I don't see how anyone can come on in Britain. You have just as many players, but you don't give them anything. No chance, no help. The Vanderbilt Club is supposed to be the best indoor club, but it's 20 degrees below freezing there and Queen's is terrible."

Wimbledon secretary Chris Gorringe was forced to reply: "Rest assured, Wimbledon will keep its grass for the foreseeable future, though Court No.2 will be made safer for the next Championship."

Six years on, when the question of Wimbledon digging up their grass again surfaced, McEnroe had, perhaps due to greater maturity, changed his mind. "At the time of the French they talk about clay and around here they talk about taking the grass out. I haven't heard any players talk about taking the grass out."

Friday, November 16, 1979

Wojtek Fibak's bid to wrestle the Benson & Hedges crown from John's grasp began well before he disintegrated and the American prevailed 6-2, 6-1 in a typically stormy display.

In the first set, the spectacular tennis was overshadowed by an incident in the fifth game. Although Fibak had already dropped serve, he was still finding some immaculate returns to spurn John's deliveries. After nine deuces the tension in the cadaverous arena was palpable. Then came the explosion of emotion. McEnroe hoisted a lob, which fell on the line, accompanied by a cry of 'out'. At first it seemed to have come from a linesman, but eventually everyone realised a mindless spectator was responsible. But why hadn't Fibak bothered to play the ball? John was incensed by the interruption and only after a heated four-minute discussion did he continue to play.

By then it was too late. The Wembley Arena crowd gave John the slow handclap and when, two points later, he double-faulted to lose the game, they applauded with great vivacity. However, John, well versed by now with hostile audiences, endured the criticism well. A young lad with a limitless court vocabulary brushed Fibak, articulate in six languages, aside.

In her book 'Sportsmen under Stress', Angela Patmore recalled speaking to John during the 1979 Benson & Hedges event. John had complained about crowds "booing and clapping" when "they don't even know what's going on." So had John been speaking to her after the Fibak match?

It's possible that the Pole made use of the spectator's call of 'out' – it gave him an excuse not to play McEnroe's tricky lob. Some players would still have played the ball, even in the knowledge that they were going to lose the point. So in those circumstances I think McEnroe was justified when he said to Ms. Patmore: "They [the crowd] should understand what's going on before they make their decisions [about my behaviour]."

Saturday, November 17, 1979

Having already claimed the scalps of Peter Fleming and Tomas Smid, Gianni Ocleppo, who had only been discharged from the Italian army six months earlier, could reasonably have suggested that McEnroe didn't present an insurmountable obstacle. As it transpired, of course, the precocious New Yorker wasn't overtaxed, bringing Ocleppo's brave run to a halt with a brutally stylish 6-3, 6-0 win. In this way he merely underlined the fact that the Italian still had much to learn.

"I would prefer to play Borg," the vanquished challenger admitted. "Borg doesn't serve like him. McEnroe doesn't let you play at all. He hits unbelievable shots. I am playing well, but you don't know what he's going to do next."

The 54 minute semi-final looked like being one-sided right from the outset. John's cunning mix of shots threw Ocleppo off balance and once he'd established a chokehold on the match the 22-year old pin-up boy never recovered, typified by his three foot faults …

A few hours later John's helpful attitude behind the scenes stamped him as a true professional. By this time in the tournament there was little else to see except the American – and because his singles was designated for the afternoon, John could have expected to play his doubles semi-final in the same session. But that would have left a capacity Saturday night audience without the chance to see the undoubted star attraction of the whole show. When referee Colin Hess explained the problem to McEnroe, the player promised without hesitation to return in the evening, knowing full well that he faced a best of five sets singles the following afternoon.

After McEnroe had won his doubles with Fleming 6-3, 7-6

against Fibak/Okker, Hess said: "He was superb, really helpful. There are a lot of players I know who wouldn't have agreed to do that."

Sunday, November 18, 1979

In a lacklustre final against hardworking American Harold Solomon, John won a two and a half hour tussle 6-3, 6-4, 7-5 and in doing so took his earnings for the year past £280,000.

The New Yorker quickly learnt he had a fight on his hands against Solomon, a man who had enjoyed three Grand Prix victories in 1979, and the McEnroe rhythm was disrupted by shrewd tactics and dogged retrieving.

Experts had forecast a lengthy duel because of Solomon's gritty baseline qualities and so it proved. The eventful first game lasted twelve minutes as McEnroe served an ace, two double faults and saved two break points before taking it after a traumatic seven deuces.

Solomon, whose main characteristic was his fabled stamina, soon caused his sluggish rival to fret and the number one seed needed to summon up every ounce of aggression to survive three points that would have left him trailing 1-3.

John typically struck back. A forceful counter-surge gave him a 5-2 lead. The set shortly became his 6-3.

Solomon, who once drank 22 bottles of water during a match on a blistering hot day and still lost 13 pounds, grafted on, but when he failed to capitalise on three break points in the second game he faded slightly and one minor slip let in McEnroe.

Despite the cushion of a two sets advantage, John could never relax and on one occasion he gave way to frustration by hurling his racquet to the baseline when Solomon had outmanoeuvred him. The New Yorker sprinted to a 3-1 lead, but he took a breather and found himself twice within two points of losing the set. The second time the danger arose he won six consecutive points for a 6-5 initiative.

Seconds later the match was John McEnroe's by virtue of an ace and two service winners. The break in the eleventh game of the third set had been vital, said the winner. "I knew if I didn't break through then, I'd have been stuck out there for another hour. Solomon was playing well and I knew he could keep going all day if he had to."

1980

Masters[5]	Semi-Final	Borg	67 63 76
US Pro Indoors	Runner-up	Connors	63 26 63 36 64
Richmond	WON	Tanner	61 62
Boca Raton	Third Place	Vilas	87
US National Indoors	WON	Connors	76 76
Milan	WON	V. Amritraj	61 64
Monte Carlo	Quarter-final	Vilas	61 64
Las Vegas	Quarter-final	Solomon	64 61
WCT Finals	Runner-up	Connors	26 76 61 62
WCT New York	Runner-up	Gerulaitis	26 62 60
French Open	3rd Round	McNamee	76 67 76 76
Stella Artois	WON	Warwick	63 61
Wimbledon	Runner-up	Borg	16 75 63 67 86
South Orange	Runner-up	Clerc	63 62
Toronto	2nd Round	Van Dillen	John led 43 ret'd
Atlanta	1st Round	Austin	76 64
US Open	WON	Borg	76 61 67 57 64
San Francisco	Quarter-final	Kriek	76 63
Brisbane	WON	Dent	63 64
Sydney	WON	Gerulaitis	63 64 75
Stockholm	Runner-up	Borg	63 64
Benson & Hedges	WON	G. Mayer	64 63 63
Milan	Third Place	Noah	64 63
WCT Montreal	WON	V. Amritraj	61 62 61

Davis Cup:

V Mexico beat Ramirez 64 64 62; with Fleming beat Ramirez/Lara 63 63 10-12 46 62

V Argentina lost to Clerc 63 62 46 14-12; lost to Vilas 62 46 63

[5] Part of the 1979 Tennis Year

26 64; with Fleming beat Gattiker/Cano 60 61 64

In January 1980, when the late Vitas Gerulaitis (in the round robin) and Bjorn Borg (in the semi-finals) both defeated him in the 1979 Masters event, John found out just how tough the new season was going to be.

Connors soon bettered him in Philadelphia and Dallas; Solomon did so in Las Vegas. Vilas then stunned him in Monte Carlo and John collapsed to Paul McNamee in the French Open.

But the New Yorker excelled himself at Wimbledon, pushing Borg all the way in a classic five set battle, and he dashed the Swede's Grand Slam hopes when he won their Flushing Meadow final 7-6, 6-1, 6-7, 5-7, 6-4. At the end his parents hugged each other and he put his arms around girl friend Stacy Margolin, saying, "This is probably the most satisfying win of my career. If I can't beat Bjorn at Wimbledon this is the next best thing, even though I know he wasn't at his best."

Although John went on to pick up two titles in Australia and one each in London and Montreal, his November loss to Borg on a slow indoor court in Stockholm meant he remained the world's No.2 at the year's end.

Nonetheless, in the Swedish capital McEnroe had displayed improved quality from the back court. Yet it was still clear that slower surfaces concerned him. When he faced Vilas, then Clerc, on Argentine clay in the Davis Cup, both players overcame him, in four and a half and six and a half hours respectively.

Saturday, June 7, 1980

"I like to give autographs to kids because I can remember when I idolised sports heroes. I still idolise top athletes in other sports." (Talking to Tony Burton, 'Daily Mail')

Stella Artois Championships

Monday, June 9, 1980

"I wasn't unhappy about missing today's match. I don't like playing on Mondays. Maybe it's psychological, but I prefer to start tournaments on Tuesdays."

John, back in the country for the first time since the previous November, issued a message to British tennis fans: "I'm going to try to stop the little things from bugging me.

"I seem to get most of my problems in England and would like to relax and just play well. Maybe it will be impossible for me to get all the British people on my side, but it would be nice to know they're not against me."

McEnroe didn't have to play on this day due to the withdrawal of his first round opponent Roger Taylor. The 38-year old Yorkshireman had been taken ill the previous weekend complaining of pains in the chest and abdomen which doctors later described as a "mystery virus". These events were somewhat fortunate for John, who himself was suffering from a troublesome ankle and a blistered racquet hand.

"The ankle's easier than it was. It's up and down, depending on how I'm playing. It hurts more when I'm losing!" he told reporters.

This light-heartedness was not shared by ATP trainer Bill Norris. "John can't expect to be more than 85 per cent fit for Wimbledon," he claimed.

Tuesday, June 10, 1980

Taylor's place in the draw was taken by Tom Leonard, a 31-year old Californian, but still John's first round match was delayed – this time by the rain.

Throughout the morning and early afternoon spectators huddled under umbrellas with nothing to watch but the show court's hot air balloon cover.

Finally, the rain eased a little, although, according to the late John Oakley of the Press Association, "Had either player refused to go on no-one would have blamed them … " As it was, McEnroe, with Leonard's approval, agreed to start.

They both had trouble keeping their feet and twice John fell heavily to the ground. After an hour's play with John leading 6-3, 3-4, the court was deemed too dangerous to continue.

"Either one of us could have slipped and pulled a muscle," confirmed John, "but if these people can wait all day I can play a few games so as not to disappoint them."

For his kind co-operation, Tournament Director Clive Bernstein labelled McEnroe "a really true professional."

Wednesday, June 11, 1980

The hapless Leonard could not win another game against the No.1 seed, going down 6-3, 6-4.

McEnroe, however, was pensive. "I know that mentally I've got to work harder. I fully expect to be back on Court No.2 during Wimbledon and it's not something I'm looking forward to. I know I won't enjoy it.

"But the ten day rest I have had since Paris has been a big help. I forgot about tennis for a while and just relaxed."

McEnroe also reported that the blister on his racquet hand was healing and that his left ankle was responding to treatment. This was all good news since his next opponent was none other than Paul McNamee, his conqueror in the French Open. John felt that the match would be "very different" from their Paris encounter. "He won't be able to keep me on the baseline with his topspin."

Thursday, June 12, 1980
Beat Paul McNamee 6-4, 7-5
Beat Brian Gottfried 7-6, 7-6

John, true to his word, exacted revenge on the exuberant Australian.

But he turned his right ankle in the first game and limped for a few points. However, by the fifth game he was stepping up a gear, breaking McNamee's serve, and he finished the first set with a stylish ace.

Brian Gottfried put up stern resistance to McEnroe's blitzkrieg style, though there were no tantrums from John. Nonetheless, Gottfried would say two weeks later, in what was possibly a veiled attack on McEnroe, that players "cannot honestly expect every call by an umpire or linesman to be perfect. I know some decisions appear abominably bad, but the player must remember that the line judge makes his call in all sincerity and usually in a split second.

"Surely the time is not far off when some brave tournament director will say to an offender: 'Thank you and good-bye – you are out.'"

But John Ballantine of 'The Sunday Times' countered, "I think John McEnroe has a point in that many umpires and linesmen DO make mistakes and this irritates some players more than others – particularly types like McEnroe who are perfectionists and fly off the handle.

"I asked him once if he welcomed the invention of new electronic line equipment which might one day make errors non-existent. He said yes, he would. So electronic umpiring in which there was no possibility of error would help him reform.

"Off court, he can be charming, although he finds it difficult to communicate with people because he is suspicious of how they will treat him – and not without some cause."

Friday, June 13, 1980
Beat Vijay Amritraj 6-2, 6-2

McEnroe delivered six aces and dropped just six points on his serve in a devastating rout, yet words of advice from ATP trainer Bill Norris still rang in his ears …

"He can carry on playing without causing any further damage, but the only cure is a complete rest for a minimum of a month. And I mean a complete rest.[6] No exhibition matches. Nothing," said Norris.

"If it were any other sport, he would have to stop competing. He is in a lot of pain and a lot of discomfort, but I'm sure he will battle on.

"John realises more than anyone the need to have a break, and I think that is in his mind. Until then, he must suffer."

McEnroe admitted that his injury problems had arisen "from playing too much tennis."

Saturday, June 14, 1980
Beat Victor Pecci 6-4, 6-0

"I'm feeling good. The weather here has been warm so far and that helps – I tend to stiffen up when it's cold."

---

[6] After Wimbledon, John took three and a half weeks off before competing in South Orange, USA.

Sunday, June 15, 1980

John McEnroe produced arguably his best tennis of 1980 thus far with a resounding victory over surprise finalist Kim Warwick.

"I think I have a far better chance at Wimbledon this time," declared the victor. "Last year I was knocked out in the fourth round, but now I'm playing better and feel more relaxed."

And with Wimbledon just a week away, the American added, "Borg doesn't like my game on grass – he likes pace and I don't hit the ball that hard."

After 61 minutes of misery at the feet of a master, Warwick, ranked 58th in the world, also recognised McEnroe's threat to Borg's supremacy.

"He was not serving as well as he can, but he volleyed so many winners. Looking at him, he doesn't seem fit enough to run 100 yards, but he's deceptively quick and has a long reach. Everything I hit above the net he volleyed away for a winner."

John showed no signs of injury throughout his majestic display and said, "I feel comfortable on court. I'm serving well and moving around better. If you feel physically good you've won half the battle. If I feel as good and can play as well at Wimbledon, I'll be pretty happy."

His temper was held firmly in check. When noise from the clubhouse meant that the umpire could hardly be heard, McEnroe simply put his fingers to his lips, blew a loud "shush" and amazingly the noise subsided.

Later, he reiterated his policy of politeness: "I don't expect everybody to start clapping me, but as long as they are fair, like they were today, and applaud good shots by either player, that's OK. I realise people come to watch the tennis and don't like to see the match stopped. I'm trying hard to change my image and I think the public appreciate that."

John was "fed up with always being the bad guy. This week I'm a goodie." Queen's Club 1979 "was terrible. I know I did things wrong but I didn't think they would have such a reaction."

As for 27-year old Australian Warwick, he didn't have the necessary bombardment to worry McEnroe. He was broken as early as the fourth game, but then to everybody's surprise he moved to 40-30 on the New Yorker's serve three games later by virtue of a net-cord. McEnroe volleyed with conviction to deny Warwick and, once he had won the first set, he moved into top gear, quickly taking a 2-0 lead. Warwick saved four break points in the next game, but that proved to be his last success as McEnroe continued with unswerving dedication for the £8,435 title.

John was so relaxed after the match that he told the press, "You know, you guys aren't so bad as I thought you were!"

Thursday, June 19, 1980

In 'The Daily Mirror', Nigel Clarke disclosed what he had gleaned from the driver who chauffeured John before Wimbledon '79 – that, after reading criticism, the great American player was left "crying his eyes out."

Wimbledon

Monday, June 23, 1980
Beat Butch Walts 6-3, 6-3, 6-0

"It's nice to be cheered all the time instead of being booed. I guess I could grow to like it.

"My father has often lectured me about staying cool and keeping out of trouble and now I believe it will take something really bad to make me lose control.

"If I get a really bad call, I'm still going to be upset inside. That's my nature, but I'm trying to keep calm.

"I'm not saying I'll never blow my top again or start screaming at umpires but I honestly don't want it. I want the English public to see there is another side to John McEnroe, that I'm not just the big bully they all believe I am." (Talking to the late John Oakley, 'Evening News')

Thursday, June 26, 1980

Terry Rocavert and John were locked at 2-2 on Court No.3 when rain stopped play.

Friday, June 27, 1980

"I thought at the time that Rocavert was going to win. However, when he lost the tie-break in the fourth set he fell apart and the final set was easy for McEnroe." (Umpire George Armstrong)

The Championships thus far had been a miserable affair, with little to placate the suffering wet crowds, but on the first Friday Wimbledon's enchanting flavour at last surfaced.

John McEnroe caused much of the excitement, almost inevitably, in his match against Terry Rocavert. As the Australian moved closer and closer to a sensational upset, hordes of fans congregated around Court No.3 and at two sets to one down and 2-1 behind in the fourth set tie-break, it looked like another crushing disappointment for the No.2 seed.

Having scraped home 4-6, 7-5, 6-7 (4-7), 7-6 (7-3), 6-3 in three hours and 50 minutes, John gulped, "That was almost the end I guess." The 25-year old Rocavert had played the match of his life, even though his wife Kay wasn't there – she was buying air tickets for their return flight to Sydney.

That lack of confidence was Rocavert's failing, as he agreed. "I should like to be ambitious, but I'm not. I suppose I played a good game, but a lot of good losses don't really do me much good. At no stage did I convince myself I would win. If I had been a confident person I would have said to myself, "I am going to win this match." Instead of which all I said was, "Keep winning one game at a time." Anyway, I intend to stop tennis at the end of the year and do something else."

It wasn't Terry's day. In the morning his Wimbledon courtesy car failed to arrive at his rented Bayswater flat. His subsequent taxi got lost. In the end he arrived at The All England Club just ten minutes before he was due on court.

But if Rocavert had an excuse to be muddled, so perhaps did McEnroe. Court No.3's distractions niggled him as he hit trouble against an on-song opponent.

McEnroe's problems all stemmed from a low first serve percentage and his service returns, against a firm but not particularly difficult delivery, were well below par. He lost his serve in the third game of the resumption, the seventh of the match, and Rocavert seized his opportunity, taking the set.

The Australian didn't cease to hit the ball sweetly in the second set and he broke in the third game. McEnroe, whilst still appearing far from comfortable, settled down and levelled the issue at 7-5, saving two break points at 5-5. But a warning for slashing a ball in the net after missing an easy volley soured his pleasure.

John's anger couldn't increase his efficiency for the conditions were by now almost intolerable. The damp court was so soft that the New Yorker dug a hole with his dragging left foot when serving.

"But even that wasn't the biggest problem. The ball never came through at a consistent height. Sometimes it came up six inches and sometimes it was shoulder high. And the distractions on that court made concentration almost impossible. Perhaps other courts may be worse, but certainly No.2 was better than No.3 and after last year I never thought I would say that."

McEnroe not only found difficulty with Rocavert's challenge, but also in keeping his temper under control with noisy sections of the crowd. Youngsters kept crawling under the stop canvas and several times John had to stop play as his calm crumbled. Once he went up to umpire Mr. Armstrong, who admitted the disturbances were unsporting, but added there was very little he could do about it.

In the third set John built up a 3-0 lead and from there moved to a 5-2, 40-0 advantage, with Rocavert serving. The Australian suddenly rediscovered his touch and composure. McEnroe couldn't make any impression on any of his four set points and was forced to a tiebreak, losing 7-4.

McEnroe quickly went ahead 2-0 in the fourth, knowing he had to press if he was to scramble through the minefield and stay in the Championships. Rocavert withstood the pressure, and then mounted his own onslaught. Twice the American served to stay in the match – at 4-5 and 5-6 - and a double-fault in the tiebreak left Rocavert 2-1 up with two serves to follow. But nerves attacked Rocavert on the brink of victory – he netted an easy forehand followed by a difficult volley. The importance of these errors didn't go unnoticed by John. "All the time I was hoping I wouldn't lose, but that miss of his at 2-1 in the tie-break was vital." Rocavert could only confess, "I always play my best tennis against the world's best players – and lose."

After three hours of high drama McEnroe levelled the match and his relief was palpable as he went to the changeover. McEnroe's father sensed that John had found new purpose and left to take his youngest son Patrick to the airport. Mr McEnroe's judgement was correct, for in the sixth game the Australian twice double-faulted and John, watched by Stacy Margolin, won the set 6-3.

"I suppose I took him a little for granted and didn't feel happy until the fifth set," said John. "Bjorn Borg might have a lot tougher time if he had to play on the outer courts. I don't want it to sound sour grapes, but I would be happy if he played outside occasionally."

Although John had survived, this wasn't the form of a man supposedly gunning for the title.

Saturday, June 28, 1980

6-0, 7-6, 6-1 over Tom Okker. "I know I can improve quite a lot," reports perfectionist John.

Monday, June 30, 1980

McEnroe led Kevin Curren 7-5, 7-6, 3-3 in a Court No.1 contest dominated by serve.

Tuesday, July 1, 1980
Beat Kevin Curren 7-5, 7-6, 7-6

"It was really cold out there and even raining at times. I guess they're going to throw you out on court whatever it's like because they must be getting desperate now."

Wednesday, July 2, 1980

The following is chair umpire Bill McDonald's account of the Fleming/McEnroe quarter-final, won 6-3, 6-2, 6-2 by the latter:

"At that time this was the biggest match I had been appointed to at Wimbledon. Standing in the wings awaiting the signal to go on Centre Court I felt a little bit nervous, so I counted to ten. When the players came on court I said, "Good afternoon, gentlemen," which is the thing to do. John ignored me but Peter did give me a nod of the head. At the spin of the coin I asked John if he would like to call. He replied "No." I then turned to Peter and asked him to call. With a smile on his face he replied, "I am not calling either." Peter, I am sure, just did it for sheer devilment. What a predicament, I thought, and the game has not even started.

"Without batting an eyelid I said, "Right. Mr McEnroe: heads it will be your choice and tails it will be Mr. Fleming's choice." While the coin was in mid-air Peter shouted, "Tails," and the coin duly fell tails. By the time I climbed into the chair I was quietly saying a prayer to my maker.

"The match duly got under way and the first set was won rather comfortably by John who was playing really well …

"But when John served at 40-30 and 3-2 in the second, he banged down an ace with chalk flying everywhere. Peter did not even see the ball. The service line judge called, 'Fault,' and a quick glance at my monitor confirmed the call. John said to me, 'How much chalk has there got to be for a ball to be in?' I replied, 'One fault, Mr. McEnroe – the chalk was beyond the line.' John put his hand up in acknowledgement of my reply and started to walk back towards the baseline. He then turned round and came back towards my chair and said to me, 'Does that machine never make a mistake?' In those days we had to believe the service line monitor was infallible, otherwise there was no point in using it. I replied, 'It never makes a mistake,' to which he replied, 'You must be some kind of idiot to believe that.' I promptly issued him a warning for 'abuse of official' under the Code of Conduct and told him to play on. This he did by banging down another ace (which was in) and then saying to me, 'How about that one?' 'Game to Mr. McEnroe' was my standard reply. John went on to win with no further problems for which I was eternally thankful."

Thursday, July 3, 1980

John and Peter defeated Heinz Gunthardt (Switzerland) and Frew McMillan (South Africa) in a tempestuous quarter-final doubles clash.

McEnroe argued endlessly about the absence of a net cord judge.

Friday, July 4, 1980

"You would think Borg would let up and forget all this talk about winning again. Is the fellow never going to be satisfied?"

January, '80: Connors beat McEnroe 6-3, 2-6, 6-3, 3-6, 6-4 (Philadelphia)
March, '80: McEnroe beat Connors 7-6, 7-6 (Memphis)
May, '80: Connors beat McEnroe 2-6, 7-6, 6-1, 6-2 (Dallas)

Psychologically the match against Connors was tricky. McEnroe had never surpassed the semi-final stage at Wimbledon and he knew that Jimmy had beaten him twice in the year already – so if he wanted to retain his No.2 ranking he just couldn't afford another loss to his foe.

In actual fact McEnroe was wound so tight that his serenity ultimately snapped when serving at 4-2, 40-15 in the first set.

In that fateful seventh game the number two seed served viciously down the centre line. An explosion of chalk accompanied the ace. But the linesman could be seen at the far end of the court, his arm outstretched, signifying a fault. John approached umpire Pat Smyth from Essex with a querying expression.

"The call came before the ball was played," said Smyth.

"He never even called it."

"Well, no, yes, he called it."

"He didn't say anything."

"He called a fault."

"He didn't call a fault, he just went like that." (McEnroe extended his arm.)

"And he called a fault. Play a let, please."

As the slow handclap duly gathered momentum, the facts began to register. Whilst Smyth was agreeing that John served an ace, he also believed the centre line judge had signalled <u>and clearly called</u> the ball out. John thought there was no call (or one that was too inaudible to distract Jimmy). If McEnroe's interpretation was correct, Smyth should have awarded an ace because the linesman's error didn't interfere with Connors' effort to play the ball.

The crowd, however, seemingly had no time to understand the details of John's argument. When Smyth refused to alter his verdict, McEnroe, trying to make himself heard above the rowdy din, politely asked, "Can I have the referee, please?"

"No," came the reply from the chair.

"I'm not playing on until I have got the referee. I aced him and I want the referee out here right now. How can you award a let when I have won the point? I'd like the referee."

"You must play on," replied Pat Smyth curtly.

"I feel I have a right to get the referee."

"Mr. McEnroe, you are getting a public warning, now *please play on.*"

The Centre Court cheered their approval.

69

Eventually, John returned to the baseline. The throw-up was deliberate. The racquet head met the ball at its apogee and the follow-through was sharp. Ace! It was the perfect gesture following the lengthy altercation.

"How's that, umpire?"

Connors, ever alert for a chance to win the spectators, went up to McEnroe, wagging his finger. The crowd loved it and applauded him wildly, perhaps forgetting that this was the same man who regularly picked up fines for audible obscenities and rude gestures.

"Don't start anything. I'm telling you – shut your mouth out here. You just play the match, son. My little boy behaves better than you do. You're both the same age," Connors, the self-appointed schoolmaster, warned the weary, tormented McEnroe.

"Come on you two, act like gentlemen," intervened Smyth and with that referee Fred Hoyles came on court. He said later: "I thought I could help restore some confidence between McEnroe and the umpire. I did not feel my presence was needed as the umpire had sorted out the problem according to Grand Prix rules. I was trying to keep out of sight, but McEnroe saw me and came towards me."

TV viewers protesting at John's conduct jammed the Wimbledon switchboard. They, and those who booed him, would have done much better to try and understand why he appealed with such passion.

With the crowd's sympathies lying firmly with Jimmy, McEnroe courageously fought on to take the opening set 6-3. In the second set, at 4-2, Connors warded off eight break points in a ten deuce and twenty-six point game. The set was soon his.

But McEnroe's liveliness was unremitting. In the third set Connors lost momentum a little and his right knee appeared to be giving him some trouble. John stopped trying to out-hit Connors from the baseline and one break was sufficient to snatch the set, 6-3.

Sensing that their hero was fading, the crowd strengthened the 27-year old's resolve and he replied with a 2-0 lead. McEnroe scuttled to 2-2. Connors forged ahead 4-2. John abruptly discovered his full potential and in a period of outstanding brilliance and stupendous concentration, he caught Connors napping. The classic quality he had lacked deluged Jimmy. Thunderstruck, Connors took just eight points in those last four games.

At the press conference Connors fulfilled his role of a mature married man who had reformed his ways. "He said something to me," (not surprising after Connors' sanctimonious words), "that wasn't exactly ethical by British standards. The nastier he gets the bigger left hook he is going to get."

McEnroe said, "It's an unwritten law that players don't talk to one another."

"Not so far as I'm concerned," retorted Connors.

When McEnroe was told it was the first time the Grand Prix Code of Conduct had been used on Centre Court, he replied, "I'm not ashamed to be publicly warned. What the hell is a public warning anyway? Is it something you broadcast over BBC Radio?"

"You'll be the underdog tomorrow, John."

"So what? Surely they don't want Borg to win again. At least I'm new. I fancy my chance against Borg on grass because I don't think he likes my style of play. It's tough to beat him. He has a lot of momentum and confidence."

Even Connors believed John was in with a shout. "If McEnroe gets his serve going then there could be an upset."

కఁఴ

Such was the bad weather's effect that the subsequent scheduling made McEnroe's retention of the doubles title almost a physical impossibility. In the evening he and Fleming always played second fiddle to Peter McNamara and Paul McNamee, and the Australians' 6-3, 6-2, 6-3 result said as much about their abilities as John's exhaustion.

After McNamara and McNamee had taken the first set, they captured eleven of the next thirteen games to lead 6-3, 6-2, 5-0. John was so tired he sat down at 0-4, but at least he maintained a sense of humour. When the umpire's telephone rang during the match, John quipped, "Is that call for me?"

The next day, whilst McEnroe fought Borg on Centre Court, the Australians calmly won their own final against Bob Lutz and Stan Smith on Court No.1.

Saturday, July 5, 1980

"The only match of note that I umpired involving John McEnroe was the 1980 Wimbledon Singles Final when he played Bjorn Borg

and lost in the fifth set. The match was described as a classic and extracts have been repeated on TV in the '100 Great Sporting Moments' series.

"It lasted nearly four hours and is remembered mainly for a marathon tie-break game in the fourth set.

"McEnroe had saved two match points when Borg led two sets to one and 5-4, 40-15 in the fourth. In the tie-break there were a further five match points to Borg and seven set points to McEnroe. It brought the house down. The crowd was almost uncontrollable.

"When McEnroe came onto Centre Court to start the match he was booed by sections of the crowd because of his bad behaviour on the previous day. But when he went up to receive his runners-up prize and when he left the court, the crowd gave him a standing ovation.

"The whole match was free of incident so far as behaviour by the players was concerned and I overruled only one line call – in the tie-break game.

"I shall never forget the experience, which really was the culmination of twenty years' umpiring at Wimbledon." (Peter Harffey)

It was indeed justice that after Borg and McEnroe had struggled through two frustrating wet Wimbledon weeks, both they and the spectators, who had always waited stoically, were rewarded.

For the players, there was the recompense of having taken part in probably the best ever Wimbledon final. And the onlookers had the chance to savour two of the game's greatest players confronting each other with determination, skill and nerve. Never before had such defiance and galvanism beset the Centre Court and we will be very fortunate to see such brilliance again. At home, 17.3 million fans watched the match on BBC television.

The final began at 2.17, following on as it did after an unexpectedly long mixed doubles final in which John and Tracy Austin beat the Australian pairing of Mark Edmondson and Diane Fromholtz.

McEnroe then fell into a productive crowding game very quickly. At 0-3 Borg changed racquets and although he held serve, McEnroe took the first set 6-1. This wasn't the McEnroe who had striven mostly unsuccessfully all season, plagued by injury. It was one on peak form. John's serve was consistently devilish, his volleys firm and sure and on return he missed little, allowing the anxious Borg to commit the mistakes.

2.46: The second set. Still McEnroe held serve comfortably and Borg once again wobbled on his. In the fifth game Borg overcame a break point and four deuces before surviving narrowly. At 4-4 he was under further threat and John, envisaging a two sets advantage, was eager to take the opening. But on all three break point occasions the unflappable Borg resisted the challenge. He saved the game and suddenly felt on a par with McEnroe. The early nerves that had afflicted him so severely were flowing away, the concentration was becoming complete. And one break was all that was needed.

Not surprisingly, it was John's sense of adventure and desire to win every point with perfection that caused the problems. Owning such a dazzling array of shots can, you see, sometimes be a handicap. At 5-6 McEnroe served to save the set. 15-0: all looked well. Then an over-ambitious attempt at his favourite featherweight drop volley went wrong. Annoyed by this flaw, McEnroe stubbornly tried it on the next point, not reckoning with Borg's uncanny powers of anticipation, which helped Bjorn to latch onto John's ball for a winner: 15-30. The right-hander, sniffing a chance, timed a service return exactly, nullifying a McEnroe first serve: 15-40. On his first set point the Swede lapsed back into a lackadaisical error. On the second a precise pass was sufficient.

The sudden transfer of initiative acted out in front of the crowds must have made them blink. McEnroe, dominant for over an hour, was now back to square one. The wily Borg, a superlative escapologist, had outsmarted John in the twinkling of an eye. Persistent defence of his serve from the baseline had given Borg his confidence.

4.05: Two sets to one in Borg's favour. During this third set the McEnroe serve, so sharp and effective in the initial stages, gradually lost its sting. Borg was determined to hit out and the difficulties of McEnroe's swinging serve to the double-handed backhand he coped with by either slicing the ball low or running round to clout a forehand. John worried more and more about placement and his deliveries became increasingly tentative. In the second game Borg broke with a forehand-down-the-line winner. John, behaving well and a little conservative in his play, could only close the gap slightly before Borg won the ninth game and set 6-3.

The standard had dramatically increased. Borg's contribution was now as it should be in such a final and both were handling the odd bad bounce with a brand of scintillating improvisation rarely conjured up. If there was one sad note, it was that the American was no longer so fresh. Questions were even being asked about whether his heavy schedule on Friday was hindering him.

In the fourth set John's serve picked up. Alas, Borg marched on and John understood the number one seed would soon make a surge for the title.

It came at 4-4. Having tested McEnroe all set in order to form a plan, the Swede now put it into motion. The New Yorker was fortunate in his defence against one break point. A second was too much – Bjorn hit a whipped backhander past his ankles. Was the Scandinavian's move perfectly timed? Would the title soon be his?

Borg served for the Championship. Keeping his nerve as was vital, he moved to 40-15 and two match points. The 21-year old at the other end stood on the brink of defeat. It wasn't possible to play safe – the circumstances called for daring. And John answered that call.

Prior to this instant, McEnroe's skill had never been doubted at Wimbledon, but his courage in the face of peril had. So the blinding backhand and a forehand pass that rocked Borg back on his heels will never sink into oblivion.

Outwardly Borg remained authoritative. Only a forehand miss betrayed his emotions and John assured a tiebreak when he took the next ball very early to fire a backhand winner.

And what a tiebreak! The two combatants pushed themselves furiously, demanding more than their best. Rising passions meant markedly fewer unforced errors and the crowd was ecstatic as John's face turned from dejection one moment to jubilation the next and then the other way. Even Borg seemed transfixed, in awe of the excellence.

For twenty-two and a half minutes and thirty-four points the tension soared. Borg saw five match points come and go and McEnroe seven set points until the most fascinating 'battle of wits' sequence came to an end. McEnroe hit a cruelly dipping shot and Borg finally cracked, misjudging a forehand drop volley that didn't clear the net. "I knew that if I made one stupid mistake it would be two sets all. It was not too clever to make a drop, but I tried it anyway. There was more topspin on his return than I had expected and the ball came down too quickly for me."

The Centre Court burst out in sound. McEnroe, half-stunned, was clenching his fist and like everyone else, he was in a trance. He peered skyward, seeking confirmation that this wasn't fantasy.

The scoreboard wiped away the seemingly endless catalogue of numbers. 7-6 McEnroe. Back to earth, on with the game.

A crushing disappointment must have been weakening Bjorn in the fifth set, the thought of what might have been haunting him.

He immediately fell 0-30 down. Yet somehow he excluded the past from his memory. No way was he going to give this one up – he'd come too far. He won four successive points and it tranquilised him powerfully.

Mature McEnroe held to 1-1. On and on the battle royal stretched, these two athletes fighting non-stop. No quarter was given. The fatigue and pressure mounted.

It couldn't continue forever. And it didn't. The Borgian metronome kept ticking away: "It was the best set I ever played on my service game. On almost every ball I hit my first serve in and John was missing the return. I was thinking, 'Don't get tight,' because I did in the fourth set and lost it." But McEnroe, too vibrant to stay patient for too long, broke mentally. At first it didn't matter. Twice he served to save the match, but in the fourteenth game Borg produced two perfect returns and a volley error gave him an eighth bite of the cherry. Tired John, heavy in heart, couldn't do anything about it. The curtain fell on a titanic struggle. Sadly, John had failed.

"I played some great shots, some unbelievable tennis, but it only kept me level in the match. No matter what I did, it was never good enough to beat him."

Asked what he thought of Borg, John replied, "The epitome of the tennis player, perfect, I guess. There's no doubt he's a great player. I still can't understand why he has not yet won the US Open as well. I am disappointed, but I tried hard and it was a good match. I can't complain for I never had a break point in the fifth. I didn't get a good hand from the crowd at the beginning but eventually I felt a change in attitude. But they always wanted Borg to win. You'd think that after four wins he'd maybe let up and forget it, but no such thing.

"I guess this is kind of a new start for me."

* In June 1996 the Wimbledon Men's Final of 1980 was the subject of the BBC2 TV programme "Clash of the Titans". Stacy Margolin recalled: "You pick up everyone's energy in the [players']*

box. Every time Mariana [Simionescu, Borg's then fiancée] would light up a cigarette, I would get more nervous plus I could feel some of what John was feeling."

And John said on the programme: "I got physically tired and he [Borg] took advantage of it. It became a battle of fitness and will as opposed to who was the better player."

November 1980

In an article entitled "Tricks of the Tray" in 'Tennis Today', Stacy Margolin tells Linda-Marie Singer that she gained eight pounds after Wimbledon 1978. "They could have rolled me out of there!" commented the 21-year old left-hander.

Stacy revealed, however, that she was "a 3" (the USA's smallest size). The five foot three inch girlfriend of John McEnroe was reported to keep fit by jogging three to four miles a day and maintaining a 800-1,000 daily calorie intake. Oils and fat had been virtually eliminated from her diet. In addition, Margolin's stretches included splits: "I was a gymnast in school. So that really helps me warm up."

Stacy believed that John's company was not good for her figure. "He just eats and eats and I wind up sharing everything until I realise that I don't want to share the pounds. Oh, I tell you, it's hopeless when I'm with John."

Benson & Hedges Championships

Wednesday, November 12, 1980
Beat Trey Waltke 6-1, 6-1

The talking point in John's post match interview was his 6-3, 6-4 loss to Borg the previous week in Stockholm.

"Everything was against me," he said defiantly. "The spongy carpet made it impossible for me to play my natural game. I couldn't hit any winners – I just had to hope that I could somehow keep Borg mixed up. The problem was trying to end the rallies. When you can't end the point against Borg you're in trouble. On top of that, they didn't want me to win."

John had a right to be bemused about the Stockholm surface since the usual special tiled court at the Kungihallen had been incredibly fast. But the expensive tiles had apparently worn out after 25 years' use and an Italian-made rubberised carpet, called Sportsflex, had been used instead. For John, that was a nightmare!

So it was suggested to him after this quiet, low-key one hour win that Wimbledon's fast grass was tailor-made for his game.

"Wimbledon!" he responded. "That has to be one of the slowest grass courts in the world. That's why Borg's always winning it."

Neither could John envisage a hot British summer which would harden the Wimbledon courts and thus make them quicker.

"Don't even pray that's going to happen. That is not within the realms of possibility," he laughed.

But McEnroe had done enough to shellshock Trey Waltke. Journalist Patrick Collins bumped into the 25-year old from Missouri in a Wembley Arena corridor and was told, "He's just so good. He does all the things you don't want him to do."

Thursday, November 13, 1980
Beat Bob Lutz 6-2, 6-1

Despite feeling an awkward twinge in his left thigh, John dropped just ten points on his serve in this 51-minute match and five of those were double faults!

All in all he was in fine spirits. Stacy flew in from Amsterdam to spend some time with him and the relationship seemed secure.

Nothing appeared to have changed from June of the previous year when, in 'The News of the World', John had described the blue-eyed Californian as "the most reliable person in my life, except for my parents." He added, "It's tough because we don't see each other that much," but he said Stacy appreciated "why I am the way I am.

"That kind of understanding is more important to me than constant companionship."

Friday, November 14, 1980

Qualifier Rick Meyer surprised John in a gallant afternoon session display before the No.1 seed, relishing his task, came through impressively.

At the outset Meyer blitzed his way past John, but the world No.2 staged a solid rearguard action, winning 6-3, 6-3.

It was when behind 1-3, 0-40 that John first took measures to extricate himself from the doldrums, a state of affairs that stemmed from a late night doubles which had kept him up until 3.30 a.m. And just two games later McEnroe's sluggishness further retreated when umpire John Parry gave him a warning for "unsportsmanlike conduct" following abuse of a ball.

The punishment acted as a catalyst for John's competence and afterwards he opened up, passing comment on both his offence and opponent.

"I know I did it more than once, but I don't think they should give a player a warning for hitting a ball into the net. It wasn't vicious or anything – I was just angry with myself and not at the linesmen, whom I thought made mistakes, but were doing a pretty good job. Because they had taken away a practice court at Queen's Club it was difficult to get a hit to loosen up and it took me a while to get moving in the match. Meyer is always a difficult chap to play. I've only met him once before and I was 15 at the time, in a college team. He beat me then and my mind flashed back those six or seven years. But I got a grip on myself and after my public warning I played well."

Saturday, November 15, 1980
Beat Harold Solomon 6-3, 6-2

John found no trouble in dispatching Solomon, but inevitably he was maddened by spectator Betty Albone who clapped his double faults.

Her applause, which is taboo in tennis, exasperated McEnroe. Thus play was held up for two minutes in the second game of the second set whilst the New Yorker walked over to her and yelled, "Who the hell do you think you are?"

Umpire Mike Lugg appealed to John to continue the match and finally gave him a warning for time delay.

Mrs. Albone said her actions were caused by John arguing "over every little thing." She did, however, admit she was wrong to clap double faults.

Sunday, November 16, 1980
Beat Gene Mayer 6-4, 6-3, 6-3

From 1-3 down in the opening set, John took command and said afterwards, "I was able to pick up my game when I most needed it. I had beaten Gene in our five previous meetings and I was fully confident of this one."

Immediately John agreed to compete at Wembley the following November. In the meantime, Dennis Cunnington would write in the January 1981 issue of 'Tennis Today', "Once again, his cooperation with the organisers of the recent event could not be faulted. And there was a flicker of a grin on his face when he told me that the umpires there, the professional lot, you know, were not such a bad crowd after all."

Saturday, December 6, 1980

John refused to compete in a lucrative exhibition match against Bjorn Borg in the tax-haven resort of Sun City, Bophuthatswana, South Africa. The match had been set for today, but McEnroe told Richard Evans in 'The Guardian', "Both my father and I got the distinct impression we were being exploited by white promoters of a so-called black state in South Africa and it just did not feel right."

Instead, John played free on this day in an exhibition to raise funds for the Hunger Project Charity.

1981

Challenge of Champs	WON	Connors	62 64 61
Masters[7]	Round Robin		
	Lost to	G. Mayer	36 76 62
	Lost to	Borg	64 67 76
	Lost to	Clerc	63 60
Toronto	Runner-up	Gerulaitis	64 64
Boca Raton	WON	Vilas	67 64 60
US National Indoors	1st Round	Waltke	63 64
Milan	WON	Borg	76 64
Frankfurt	WON	Smid	62 63
Los Angeles	WON	S. Mayer	67 63 63
WCT Finals	WON	Kriek	61 62 64
WCT New York	2nd Round	Kirmayr	57 76 62
French Open	Quarter-final	Lendl	64 64 75
Stella Artois	WON	Gottfried	76 75
Wimbledon	WON	Borg	46 76 76 64
Montreal	3rd Round	V. Amritraj	57 76 61
Cincinnati	WON	C. Lewis	63 64
US Open	WON	Borg	46 62 64 63
San Francisco	Quarter-final	Scanlon	36 76 62
Mazda Cup	Semi-Final	Teltscher	67 61 63
Sydney	WON	Tanner	64 75 62
Seiko Classic	Semi-Final	Van Patten	63 75
Benson & Hedges	Runner-up	Connors	36 26 63 64 62
Brooklyn Masters	Runner-up	Lendl	62 26 64

---

[7] Part of the 1980 Tennis Year.

Davis Cup:

V   Mexico beat Lozano 63 61 63; beat Ramirez 64 63 60

V   Czechoslovakia lost to Lendl 64 14-12 75; beat Smid 63 61 64

V   Australia beat Edmondson 63 64 62; beat McNamara 97 60; with Fleming beat McNamara/Dent 86 64 86

V   Argentina beat Vilas 63 62 62; beat Clerc 75 57 63 36 61; with Fleming beat Clerc/Vilas 63 46 64 46 11-9

A year in which one becomes the greatest lawn tennis player in the world should not be remembered as anything less than sublime, but for John McEnroe 1981 possessed both bitter and sweet experiences.

At last the unique promise that had first surfaced in 1977 reached fruition as McEnroe brought an era to a close when he deposed Bjorn Borg at Wimbledon. A wavering volley, which seemed to drift timelessly before landing just within the baseline, marked the realisation of the young man's dream.

"It took me a while to realize that he wasn't there, then I knew it was all over, just a great feeling," John recalled.

McEnroe's ascendancy over his great rival was completed on a breezy September afternoon at Flushing Meadow. With Borg leading 6-4, 2-6, 4-3, 15-0 in a final of fluctuating fortunes, the American suddenly produced four stunning shots and he never looked back. The Swede's confidence, not to mention his career, was scythed.

"Suddenly I felt I could hit pretty much, or at least attempt, any shot," was McEnroe's awe-filled comment this time.

But the unblemished skill that won the United States the Davis Cup came with an errant temperament. McEnroe fell foul of the umpires at Wimbledon, where on the first day he received two penalty points from Welshman Edward James. The problem, in my opinion, was poor officiating coupled with a misunderstanding of American vernacular. But McEnroe was contrite. "Things go on out there that are terrible," he conceded. "If the others can manage to keep calm, why not me?"

Wimbledon retaliated by first refusing to elect him an honorary club member (normally a routine formality) and then recommending a $10,000 fine for "aggravated behaviour." John's appeals were long and drawn out. By the end of 1981 a three-man arbitration panel was still to meet.

The imminent hearing affected McEnroe's play and, added to fatigue, explains why he lost a bad-tempered five set Benson & Hedges final to Jimmy Connors.

The year had also started poorly. In the January Masters (part of the 1980 tennis year) the left-hander fell to Gene Mayer, Borg and Jose Luis Clerc in his round robin group and thus failed to qualify for the semi-finals.

Finally, Ivan Lendl was to dominate McEnroe in 1982, an intention he signified in 1981 by conquering John in the French Open and in the Davis Cup quarter-finals.

Yet no one can deny that John McEnroe was the Player of the Year in 1981. Incidentally, he cut down on beer and junk food – with dramatic results. Between January and late March he lost 23 pounds from his five foot eleven inch stature. But at 158 pounds he felt "a little too light" and thereafter he stabilized at a playing weight of 170.

There was no great change in the way the media behaved towards McEnroe. His psyche and his relationship with Stacy Margolin were always treated shabbily. As John pointed out after his semi-final Wimbledon win over Rod Frawley, "I can't get any worse press than I receive here."

Friday, March 20, 1981

Signing a five-year racquet contract with Dunlop in London, John said he hoped his links with the company would endear him to British crowds. He added, in a slightly wistful comment, "I'll take any possible reason to get a few people on my side."

Dunlop had hired a suite at the Waldorf Hotel and one hundred journalists were treated to a lavish buffet reception. Asked about exhibition matches, John defended them, saying they were "a reward for doing well in major tournaments."

Earlier, in November 1980 at the Benson & Hedges Championships, it had been Slazenger who'd put on a presentation that no doubt pleased the New Yorker. They displayed a new range of equipment bearing his name and the colours red, white and blue were prominently featured. "The presentation was made at the offices of the Slazenger advertising agents in London," John Barrett, the company's International Tennis Promotions Director, told me.

"At that time it appeared that John would sign a contract to use Slazenger equipment so we produced a range of McEnroe racquets, including the John McEnroe Personal, plus headcovers, holdalls and an outline of the advertising campaign we had planned to launch the range and then sell it."

But Slazenger then encountered serious problems. Dunlop in fact owned them and when boss Alan Lord saw the proposals, he wanted the bigger name to gain the deal.

McEnroe was just glad that his 'change of racquets' bother was over. His father told Tracy Leonard of US 'Tennis Magazine': "There was a point when John was practising with a different racquet every day and it started to affect his timing and concentration."

The player's equipment transfer came about because a new contract could not be agreed with Wilson. Before eventually signing with Dunlop, John passed up another more lucrative package since, "I couldn't play as well with that company's racquets."

In the end, he kept coming back to the racquet he used as a junior – Dunlop's Maxply Fort. But the artist within him was troubled by some intricate details. Firstly, the grip had to be made more angular. Next, he found the Maxply faster through the air compared with other wood racquets so lead tape was added to both sides of the bow. But as the Masters in January '81 drew closer, John was still not happy with the racquet's flexible head.

Dunlop agreed to design a new racquet in association with John, and it was decided he would play with modified Maxply Forts in the interim. The company also allowed John to compete in the Masters using his Wilson racquets, as they understood the psychological difficulty of playing such an important event with new equipment. In return, McEnroe signed a $600,000/year contract.

Stella Artois Championships

Tuesday, June 9, 1981
Beat John Feaver 6-1, 6-2

John Feaver has the same birthday as McEnroe, but received no gifts in this first round, 48-minute encounter.

Nonetheless, Feaver, seven years' McEnroe's senior, remembers the match well: "We hardly talked on the way to the court, although we greeted each other in a friendly manner and there was a nice atmosphere. He was very good and did not allow me enough time to settle down. His serve was incredible. The crowds were behind me, but he was the better player."

That was true enough. John did not lose a point on his last two service games in the first set and quickly broke serve in set two. Only at 5-2 did McEnroe momentarily let up. He had to save three break points before he finally put the Englishman away.

McEnroe explained afterwards that the wrist strain he had suffered in Paris was now cleared up. He added, "Many people think this is going to be my year, especially at Wimbledon. I hope so. Borg's record is fantastic but he must lose sometime."

Three years after their Queen's Club clash, Feaver would tell me, "On fast surfaces he [McEnroe] is the best player ever. His serve, in particular, is the best because of its movement through the air and spin off the ground. He can also spin it both ways. John is a good and clever tactician."

Wednesday, June 10, 1981
Beat Mark Edmondson 6-3, 6-3

John's single-mindedness was underlined when he told umpire Georgina Clark, "We can't play with these balls. They are not round and won't bounce straight."

Later, McEnroe said, "Maybe I was imagining things. The umpire said the balls were all right, but I wonder if she even plays the game."

Thursday, June 11, 1981
Beat Bill Scanlon 6-3, 6-2

McEnroe was annoyed with a drunken section of the crowd. "Can you close your mouths during the point?" he asked.

When his request was ignored, John shouted, "Can't you hear me up there?"

"It happens everywhere," explained the star. "You get a noisy section. You ask them once to keep quiet and after that there is not a lot you can do."

Friday, June 12, 1981
Beat Hank Pfister 6-2, 7-5

Poor umpiring marred this quarterfinal. But don't take my word for it. 'The Guardian' believed "some of the officiating [this week] …has been dubious enough to drive the most sensitive souls to distraction."

And John was baited by sections of the crowd. Indeed, spectator Vicky Gilbert wrote to 'Tennis' Magazine and pointed out that " … certain members of the audience were there purely to see McEnroe versus the umpire and their applause and comments were directed to this end …"

John's main complaint against umpire Ian Stirk was triggered in the third game of the first set when Stirk talked to the players with his microphone switched on. Remarked John, "It fuels all the problems and I asked him not to do it, but it happened again in the second set."

Saturday, June 13, 1981
Beat Brian Teacher 6-3, 6-4

"If I can play this well at Wimbledon I won't complain," conceded McEnroe. "I'm seeing and hitting the ball well and the best way to practise is by winning matches."

John found time to question authority - "Get with it" he snapped at the net-cord judge – whilst he enquired of another official, "Are you watching the line?"

But he concentrated well and won the first set with a superb back-to-the-net backhand winner.

Sunday, June 14, 1981
Beat Brian Gottfried 7-6, 7-5

Gottfried gave McEnroe a tough workout, holding three set points before he relinquished the first set in an 8-6 tie-break.

John rarely settled and in the last game of the match he slammed a ball at the canvas backstop rather near a female line judge, to whom he shouted, "Good call, lady."

He was upset with her decision and received a warning from

umpire Georgina Clark.

"I don't see any reason why a woman should umpire a man's match in this class. I am not saying they are any worse than the men umpires, but it is more difficult to get upset with them," remarked McEnroe, perhaps feeling slightly guilty at the way he had treated the umpire.

Nonetheless, Mrs Clark declared herself 'a McEnroe fan' and added that he was 'a very gifted player.' "I feel he gets into those situations to fire himself up," she commented. John may be surprised to learn that she said she was "very glad" to have "been chosen to umpire the game."

* During the final Gottfried had asked John if he was having woman trouble. "Me?" replied John. "No, I've got a nice girlfriend."*

After overcoming Gottfried, McEnroe received a solid silver replica of the 96-year old singles trophy in recognition of his three Stella Artois titles. The New Yorker confided, "This was the toughest of the three because Brian served the best he ever has [against me]."

Wednesday, June 17, 1981

"I met John McEnroe at an evening reception at the Royal Westminster Hotel in Victoria. It was a pre-Wimbledon 'Meet the Stars' type of evening arranged by the Dunlop Sports Company. At the time John struck me as being quiet, shy and a little apprehensive of such gatherings. When he spoke, however, he was self-assured and gave the impression he would not suffer fools gladly. He talked about Wimbledon and hoped that he might do better than in 1980. Basically John is a very pleasant young man, but in a fight I would prefer to have him on my side. As a tennis player he is the most naturally gifted competitor since Ilie Nastase and a truly outstanding match player who produces the most brilliant of shots with consummate ease." (Coach Paul Douglas)

Thursday, June 18, 1981

At Madame Tussauds, a wax model of John McEnroe is revealed. "He looks healthier than me," quipped John, adding, "but he's a bit quiet for the real McEnroe."

Canadian-born sculptress Judith Craig added, "He really is a pet. He was most co-operative and patient during our sittings and as you can see he's charming."

Wimbledon

Monday, June 22, 1981

"I remember parts of the match ... I have not seen it on television. It was a sad match ... I felt it brought the game of tennis into disrepute." (Edward James, Umpire: Gullikson/McEnroe)

2.00: McEnroe trod onto the green grass of a sunny Court No.1 with opponent Tom Gullikson by his side. McEnroe had never lost to the left-handed Wisconsin twin but he was more tense and tight than usual.

2.06: John launched the first ball and survived the early danger of three break points. In the seventh game he again deals with a break point. They went into a tie-break and he won it seven points to five.

3.07: The second set started. When Gullikson went ahead 4-3, McEnroe smashed a racquet as a measure of his disbelief. Umpire Edward James from Llanelli had no alternative but to make his presence felt and issue a public warning.

3.54: Despite too many double faults, McEnroe arrived at 7-6, 7-5.

Incidentally, it must be said that the standard of officiating in this match seemed rather amateurish.

At one stage, McEnroe appeared to serve an ace which actually landed inside the centre-line. Gullikson certainly wasn't quarrelling and he immediately started moving to the other side of the baseline in order to assume his position for the next delivery. There was no call, but suddenly James said that the ball had hit "a spread" of chalk.

"You can't be serious, man," yelled John. "You cannot be serious! That ball was on the line. Chalk flew up! It was clearly in. How can you possibly call that out? How many can you miss? He's walking over, everyone knows it's in in the whole stadium and you call that out. Explain that to me, will you?"

87

On another point, the linesman called McEnroe's serve out and James provided an overrule, saying into a live microphone: "We'll play that ball again. That ball was good." Irked by the authoritarian tone, John bowed down to James and the crowd laughed.

But it was no laughing matter at 1-1 in the third set when the serious trouble occurred. At 0-30 Gullikson won a ten shot rally off a serve that looked long. McEnroe queried that call and James responded firmly: "The serve was good, Mr. McEnroe."

The irritated New Yorker retorted: "You guys are the absolute pits of the world, you know that?" As he returned to the baseline, there was silence, then James declared, "I am going to award a point against you, Mr McEnroe."

Another penalty point left the 1980 Wimbledon runner-up 0-15 on his serve in the fourth game. He remembers, "The two penalty points I lost were the result of a bad call. I complained to the umpire and said, 'This is just the pits,' and I demanded the referee be called. When he arrived I said the whole situation was ridiculous. If I'm incompetent I expect to be told so. The referee told me that if I didn't deserve a penalty point before, I deserved one now. I got more angry and said something which you couldn't print. The whole thing was a farce."

And so it was. Later it would be revealed that whilst in John's earshot, referee Fred Hoyles had ordered the umpire: "Dock him another point if he does it again." The "it" Hoyles was referring to was McEnroe's innocuous "pits of the world" phrase. It was after that erroneous command that McEnroe swore at the referee and received the second penalty point. Furthermore, James had only issued the first penalty point because he had wrongly believed John had said "piss" rather than "pits."

The mix-up meant that McEnroe stood on the verge of a melodramatic disqualification.

Either John had to emerge from his miseries or create the most sensational headlines ever. Breaking Gullikson at 3-3 and 5-3 he thankfully won through, 7-6, 7-5, 6-3.

Such shameful happenings weren't going to go unnoticed, though. John showed genuine sorrow at his alarming excesses.

"I suppose it was my fault because I was feeling very jittery. I think I was definitely wrong in what I said, but I feel justified in calling the linesman an incompetent fool. I will no doubt pay for it tomorrow. In the main I am treated fairly."

Of his future conduct he could promise little. "It is never going to change until I change my methods. Things go on out there that are terrible. It is easier to keep my temper playing someone like Borg than against guys I am expected to beat. I get angry with myself if I am not playing well. Today there were bad things I did, but there were also bad things they did.

"Feeling the way I do is unnecessary and only hurts me. No-one is to blame but myself. If the others can manage to keep calm, why not me? I suggest the linesmen get paid more – I would even give $1000 if it could guarantee efficiency. Also they could have eye tests. I know it is a thankless job. I would be the last person in the world to want it and it's not easy with guys like me around."

Obviously, John attempted a little justification for his actions. "Officials should not treat players like kids and then not expect to get treated like a kid back. I still feel that officials should be changed if they are doing badly. If we do a lousy job we lose, so why shouldn't they be changed?

"I thought the guy made eight bad calls. People tell me I've got to accept it. If someone else can do it there is no reason why I shouldn't if I am a good enough player; it's just that every time it happens you go: 'God, I won that point and he took it away.' I hit ten pounds of chalk and the guy says that it hit the outside edge of some small patch of chalk outside the line. Who is he kidding? Six thousand people in the stands saw the ball hit chalk on the line and he is trying to explain to me that it hit a small patch of whatever it is.

"It is really important for a player to get over the hill at Wimbledon. Everybody was telling me I should win. But at the back of my head was the thought that 'Nasty' and Rosewall had never won it. When it is taken for granted that you're going to get to the semis or final, you get nervous and uptight. That was definitely the reason why I got upset."

Why hadn't McEnroe been defaulted, asked the American's numerous critics? The combined effect of the Grand Prix Code of Conduct's structure and the reluctance of Fred Hoyles to take such action accounted for John's position in The Championships after the Gullikson fiasco. Not that Hoyles was totally inactive. He penalised John with a $1,500 fine and warned that any further misdemeanours would be interpreted as "aggravated behaviour" and result in a $10,000 punishment and/or suspension.

McEnroe's test of character was only just beginning.

* *"He doesn't need groupies – I'm his only girl. Off court he's kind, gentle and attentive. He would be a big fish to catch – but I feel secure. I know I am the only girl in his life. John doesn't need groupies or any girls like them. He needs someone who is playing tennis competitively like he is and has the same love for the game.*

"We have to snatch whatever time we can together. Sometimes John may be playing on one end of the world and I might find myself on the other. Then our only link is the telephone.

"I think some spectators look for the worst side of his character on court. They seem to want to see him lose his temper and explode.

"Some spectators even bait him – and poor John reacts accordingly." (Stacy Margolin, talking to John Kay, 'The Sun')

* *In June 1996, Stacy told 'The Clash of the Titans' programme, "I just wanted to hide a little bit [as I watched the Tom Gullikson Wimbledon '81 match] – I was so upset that it was hard for him [John] to let a linecall go... I didn't want him to get defaulted."*

* *Ironically, an another BBC TV documentary in June 1996 entitled "Chalk Flew Up!", McEnroe would say, "My luck was always good there [on Court No.1]. I'll be sorry [when there's a new Court No.1 in 1997]. I think there was something about [the original] Court No.1..."*

* *Shortly before John's display of temper earned him those two penalty points, he showed spectators a gentler side to his personality.*

According to 'Top Tennis', "McEnroe approached the ground on foot giving thousands of queuing tennis fans a welcome treat after many hours of waiting in the steamy conditions.

"Needless to say it was only a matter of seconds before he was enveloped by crowds of besotted schoolgirls and anxious autograph hunters all trying to get a closer look at their hero.

"They were not disappointed and neither was a young Greek schoolboy who asked him to pose for a photograph just before the mob arrived on the scene.

"After the snapshot McEnroe asked the boy if he had a ticket to get in and when the reply was negative, he gave him his own Competitor's Centre Court ticket for that day."

Tuesday, June 23, 1981
With Peter Fleming, beat Carlos Aguilar and J. Edwards 6-1, 6-2, 3-6, 6-3.

Did John provide the man in the chair, Bill Pickup, with similar angst? Pickup says 'nothing happened' during this Court No.2 clash, except that: "McEnroe would not shake hands with me before the match commenced, did not look at me when I spoke to him and refused to call either heads or tails when asked to do so."

The contest began at 5.46 with Fleming and McEnroe quickly capturing the first two sets in 48 minutes. Yet there was a small hint of problems to come in the third when in game eight of set two Mac scrambled to save two break points. Sure enough, blond Fleming was broken in the sixth game of that third set, but from there the number one seeds played with increasing confidence and by 7.21, with the light fading, the match was theirs.

* Meanwhile, Stacy lost in the first round 6-0, 6-7, 6-3 to 23-year old Swede Nina Bohm. The media requested a press conference and she answered questions meticulously: "I have a cold and a temperature. I must have picked it up from some of the girls who have it also. I tried as hard as I could on court and had a couple of bad bounces in the third, but even so I had chances to go 2-1 up. Of course I am aware of being John McEnroe's girlfriend. The publicity bothered me a long time ago, but not now. I don't mind as long as I am known as John's girl and a tennis player. I do get upset when, after last evening's incidents, so many newspapermen and photographers bothered me while I was trying to practise. I realise I have said that John had calmed down more. He probably thought so, too. He doesn't know when it is going to come on. It is no good either his coach or myself telling him – it is up to him. I tell him it doesn't help and he agrees with me, but he is a normal man and a loving person. When away from tennis he is completely relaxed. There was a lot of pressure on him this week with many people wishing him good luck in the final even before the start of the tournament. Each round is like a ton of bricks on his shoulders. He puts the pressure on himself and the people around him. Maybe if he is fined it will do him some good. Perhaps he will realise that it is no good getting mad and fighting the system."*

* John McEnroe Snr. declared, "I frequently broach the subject [of his son attempting to curb his temper] and John agrees with me. We have had this type of conversation more than once. I believe there is no place for vulgarity on the tennis court but I fear that some day, some time, somewhere, he will do it again."*

Wednesday, June 24, 1981

"I do not recall being given any extra instructions for the match – in fact I am sure I would have remembered because I would have taken great exception to such instructions." (Bob Jenkins, Umpire: Ramirez/McEnroe)

In the knowledge he'd overstepped the mark on Monday, John retreated into a protective shell and gave a listless performance for the Centre Court crowd.

Although Ramirez conceded serve quickly in letting slip the first set 6-3, he thereafter put McEnroe's delivery under fierce pressure. The Mexican's fight reached its climax when he earned two set points in the next set, but McEnroe somehow clung on for 5-5, and was rewarded by a rain break that rendered the court unplayable for the rest of the day.

* Peter Fleming told the press, "I have never seen John as down as he has been over the last couple of days. You can tell this when you talk to him. He is not enjoying himself, although I don't think it will hurt his play. It is no fun to have to go out there with all that intense pressure on him."

Thursday, June 25, 1981

McEnroe's lethargy hadn't disappeared by the time he took to the court again and Ramirez had a point for two sets all before the American's 6-3, 6-7, 6-3, 7-6 success.

"Having to play a match and keep my temper was a very difficult experience," reported John. Asked if he was surprised about his treatment at Wimbledon, he said, "I am not surprised about anything that happens here." He thought the people who had applauded him were "mainly the kids and maybe they don't know any better."

"I don't even want to talk about the experiences of the last 48 hours; I would prefer to talk about the tennis and this was the best he has played against me ever. I seem to have missed my rhythm on the service and everything. I just wasn't into the match. But every day you can stay in a tournament the better it gets.

"I was pretty down, I guess, but you have to roll with the punches. As long as I feel well in myself I don't care too much about public reactions. I am a fighter."

He complained bitterly about reports that he had incurred a speeding fine in London's West End, because Peter Fleming had in fact been driving. "When I watched on TV that I had got a speeding fine and this was announced on BBC, I was surprised that a respectable TV station should do this to me as I had never driven in Britain."

Going back to the match against Ramirez, John said, "I have to find a happy medium. It just wasn't me in the first two games. I was concentrating but I'm just not acting myself. I wasn't myself and you have to go out there and be yourself. It wasn't just the conditions. There were certain balls that I knew I should go for but didn't. The bottom line is all about winning and it is nice to get better during a tournament."

Friday, June 26, 1981
Beat Bob Lutz 6-4, 6-2, 6-0

"I feel a little better today. At least the court was good. There may only be one other seed left in my part of the draw, but there are still some good players there. I have already had some tough matches. Hopefully I will play better as the tournament goes on. I don't really object to playing every day although sometimes after a tough match it is good to have a day's rest. In the second week here when you play every other day it is good, because you need the rest more. I got a little angry with myself on court today and that helps me. I am a good deal lighter than last year and at times I feel I am moving better on court. I have more or less cut out all junk food and having a beer.

"There were some line call mistakes today. I believe I am 100% right when I query a call. I have played tennis for most of my life, so I should know and see better than an elderly person with glasses. I know one serve I made was out, but it was not called. I can also *feel* when a ball is out – not exactly perhaps, but 90 per cent of the time."

Saturday, June 27, 1981
Beat Stan Smith 7-5, 3-6, 6-1, 6-2

"The first two sets were pretty close. I hit the ball much better in the third and made him work for his points. Maybe he got a bit tired. I am hitting and returning the ball better now and my game is starting to come round. But I am not serving well enough and you can't win big tournaments unless your service is good. It is tough to concentrate on Court No.1, but I do the best I can. It doesn't worry me that I don't have long rallies. I am not going to hang back and will always come in a lot. There are not going to be many long rallies with me. My next opponent Kriek, and Borg, are probably the quickest guys around the court. He is sometimes erratic but I will have to work for my chances. I was having a problem with my returns in the early rounds but if I have any serious weakness it is that I can lose patience on clay. That doesn't apply here. Before I play in singles again I will have to practise my serves. I saw some bad calls today, but I am trying not to say anything. I don't have the answer to the problems of line decisions. You just can't change a century of thinking."

Tuesday, June 30, 1981
Beat Johan Kriek 6-1, 7-5, 6-1

John won in 97 minutes and then spoke about how the Centre Court was playing. "I'm not saying it's no good, just that it could do with rolling more to make it faster. It is too slow and there are too many bad bounces," he said.

Wednesday, July 1, 1981

'The Sun' was far more interested in John's relationship with Stacy than reporting his match with Kriek; they felt that "all was not well" with the young couple's romance, citing the fact that Stacy had been booked on a midday Tuesday flight to New York. Although she hadn't left England, she looked "miserable", they added.

Asked if she would be staying for the rest of the tournament, McEnroe had responded, "It's none of your business."

And Stacy, battling with a heavy cold, said, "Everything is all right between me and John."

Mr. McEnroe solved the riddle when he disclosed that Stacy would be leaving London because she "has been sick for some time. She wants to get some sun and she can't find it here."

* Out on Court No.3 John slipped into more trouble. He was fined £375 for telling Sikh linesman Ragbhir Mhajan, "You're Indian, you're biased," during his doubles match against the Amritraj brothers.

The flare-up came when McEnroe claimed Mhajan was upsetting his game by standing up during play. The fiery American told umpire Jeremy Shales, "I told him to sit down. He keeps talking to me." But Shales told John to get on with the match and the linesman continued to get out of his chair.

Interestingly, McEnroe's opponents were in deeper trouble with the umpire – Anand Amritraj was deducted a penalty point and Vijay received a warning.

Thursday, July 2, 1981

By this stage of the tournament several factors were troubling John: an awareness that any further outbursts would be accompanied by even more vicious press criticism; the knowledge that semi-final opponent Rod Frawley, given his standing on the computer, wasn't supposed to present him with a serious challenge and press speculation that he and Stacy Margolin had broken up; all these factors gnawed away at his already incredibly fraught nerves.

Under overcast skies Frawley opened by unexpectedly breaking McEnroe – an action that did nothing to reduce the New Yorker's apprehension. The 28-year old Australian continued with his sharp consistency, whilst McEnroe switched from level to level – fitfully brilliant, but more often than not muttering about his failure to dominate his unfancied rival.

Finally, at 5-4 and deuce, McEnroe, having often glared unbelievingly at linesmen, exploded when umpire George Grime overruled a call. "I get screwed by the umpires in this place," groaned John, and he promptly received a warning for 'unsportsmanlike behaviour.' As the atmosphere became more fiery, his fragile application was restored in time to forget the early crises and at 3.13 he went ahead 7-6.

Frawley, slowing the tempo down whenever possible, remained taciturn compared with John, who refused to settle down. The second set, a relatively peaceful affair, was seized 6-4 by McEnroe and at 4-4 in the third set the earlier matters seemed to have been well buried.

However, as so often when things appeared to be going well, a major incident occurred. Another line call dispute arose and McEnroe approached the umpire's chair, again appealing plaintively for justice. Wing Commander Grime stood his ground. As McEnroe walked away, he uttered, "You're a disgrace to mankind," and the umpire awarded a penalty point.

Now 5-4 down, John felt the resounding weight of another injustice. "I was not talking to you, umpire, do you hear me? I was talking to myself. I would like the referee called before you call the score. What did I say? Please tell me!" The intensity of his plea made it sound all the more honest, but when referee Fred Hoyles appeared, he upheld the decision and announced the score must stand.

Umpire Grime would recall a decade later, "I observed that he [McEnroe] was looking across at me. The words themselves were innocuous and certainly did not constitute an audible obscenity (although the Code did not have this specific category at that time). However, believing them to be directed at me, I deemed them to be abusive."

Indignation swelling inside, John somehow turned his attention back to the tennis and resurrected his cool well enough to complete a 7-6, 6-4, 7-5 score-line in three hours and twenty minutes.

The match, however acrimonious a battle it was, represented nothing more than a curtain raiser to the chief trial of the day – the press conference. It could be argued that McEnroe shouldn't have gone, but that would have meant another fine and still more ammunition for Fleet Street. Yet, not surprisingly, John gave the press more than they bargained for by deciding to field questions.

"It was a tough match," he agreed. "I played pretty well, but it took a long time. Frawley took something like thirty seconds between each serve and that is why the match took three hours. My complaints probably took about two minutes although I have no idea how many I made. I thought the umpire was provocative and this has been general. I can't remember what I said when I had the penalty point against me. It was like 'I am a disgrace,' or something like that. I was talking to myself. I don't know what I said the first time he pulled me up. I have enough problems. I can't even breathe. It seems that the umpires want to show their force. They don't give me a chance. I was a little tense and he played better than I thought."

A newsman then asked if he and Stacy had split up and suddenly all the stored rancour rushed forth from the young man as, amid obscenities, he fumed " … the answer is no. I shouldn't even tell you that because you're such trash. Some of you write a lot of lies."

Following this altercation a tennis writer asked McEnroe for an assessment of his game. "Great question," laughed a news hound and John departed, albeit not before he gave the person concerned a piece of his mind.

At the same time a scuffle erupted between an English reporter and an American radio broadcaster. Nine people soon lay on the floor and the whole scenario was so unprecedented at Wimbledon that the late Roy McKelvie, the man in charge of the press, swiftly announced a ban on all news reporters until the end of the Championships. The true tennis scribes prepared an official apology to give to McEnroe.

Rumours abounded that Wimbledon wouldn't grant John membership if he won the tournament, though an aide of Chairman Sir Brian Burnett said, "He cannot comment."

Part of the match had been watched by Lady Diana,[8] who had been diplomatically ushered out for tea when omens of trouble first arose. Friday's headlines picked up on this:

SUPERBRAT PLAYS UP FOR LADY DIANA

DIANA SEES McENROE UPROAR

BEAUTY AND THE BEAST

Not for the first time McEnroe was seeing his behaviour obscuring his good side. The American media were dismayed by their British counterparts, with the 'Washington Post' saying that " …the nefarious Fleet Street comics whipsawed the already frazzled McEnroe into a public rage by buzzing him with questions about a long-time girlfriend."

---

[8] After the Frawley match John was asked for his opinion of Lady Diana and he replied that she was "a terrific person." And when Diana, Princess of Wales died on August 31, 1997, McEnroe, a TV commentator at the US Open, declared, "It's hard to watch a match right now. I feel sick along with the rest of the world. It's beyond tragic."

As for George Grime, he refuses to harbour a grudge against McEnroe. His abiding memory of 1981 is of John, "a superb tennis player who spoke his mind in a very direct way and expected perfection in officiating as well as in all departments of his game."

* In the other semi-final, Borg took three hours and 18 minutes to overcome Jimmy Connors 0-6, 4-6, 6-3, 6-0, 6-4.

Friday, July 3, 1981

On Centre Court the richly talented combination of Bob Lutz and Stan Smith cracked under constant pressure as Fleming and McEnroe regained the title they had previously won in 1979 with a 6-4, 6-4, 6-4 result.

"I don't think this doubles win helped to improve my service, which has not been going well this tournament. It was just nice to win. We lost our title last year when the tournament was more cramped. Today's game will not matter that much for tomorrow's singles. I feel Smith and Lutz didn't play that good a match. It is impossible to say how tomorrow's final will go. I have gone through a lot this year and it has been really tough. I am just going out to play the match, but it is not easy to relax. The title is there for me to take. Everything else is sour grapes.

"Every year I say Borg is going to lose sooner or later. It probably helps to have played the final last year. I don't think I have been playing well in this tournament, just enough to get by. Tomorrow I hope to put it all together. My mother is here for the first time and sometimes in a big match I look at the stands to see if my family and Stacy are there. Stacy is not here now. On other occasions I don't look at the stands at all. On occasions I go out on court determined not to say anything and I get angry with myself when I do lose my temper. Tomorrow morning I will practise for about 15 to 20 minutes. It would be nice to win on 4th July."

Saturday, July 4, 1981

The Centre Court's digital clock proclaimed 5.29 p.m. as the time John McEnroe finally brought the curtain down on Bjorn Borg's marvellous five year reign at Wimbledon. The US Open champion beat the Swede 4-6, 7-6 (7-1), 7-6 (7-4), 6-4 in a nerve-tingling three hours and twenty-three minutes. In the end, two weeks of confrontation were symbolised by a vacant place on the top table at the Champions' Dinner.

❧❧

Having watched Borg recover from a two-set deficit in the semi-finals, John was certain of one thing on entering an excited, tense Centre Court – his game plan. Of Connors' brave fight, he said, "It was great, good to watch, but like clay court tennis on grass. That's exactly what they both like. I went out determined to hit the ball softer, chop, come in and dink, because that's the way I play."

The source of McEnroe's stirring victory lay in the extra pace and consistency his serve carried – something that had been missing throughout the fortnight. Borg, in contrast, was particularly frail on his and both he and John were swift to realise it. Borg got 53 per cent of his first serves in, to John's 62 per cent. In the tie-breaks, where it could be argued the holder really let the title slip, the combined effect of a misfiring delivery and a confident opponent was lethal. John missed one in ten first serves, Borg five in nine.

2.06:   On an afternoon of intermittent sunshine each held to 2-2, but in the fifth McEnroe double-faulted to go 0-40 down.

Three heavy serves helped him to get to deuce. Borg responded with a typical forehand winner and a backhand volley error meant John lost his serve.

The Swede held easily to 4-2 and at 5-4 served for the set ... and suddenly hit trouble. He went 15-40 down, recovering to deuce. A double-fault let John in again, but the American netted a backhand. A fourth break point failed when Borg served a crisp winner down the middle. A McEnroe miss at another backhand provided Borg with the temptation he needed – and a forehand volley winner gave him the set 6-4 in thirty-six minutes.

In the first game of the second set John served a double-fault at 40-30. He won the next point with a drop volley, and then missed his first serve again.

Unexpectedly, a yell rang out from the packed standing area: "Get the referee, John." The spectators shushed sympathetically, especially after the troubled McEnroe then hit another double-fault. "Thank you very much," he snarled towards the gallery, though he held serve moments later. At 0-1, Borg survived two break points as, not for the first time, he felt a real threat.

By the fourth game John was in a groove. Any earlier sluggishness had disappeared and Bjorn was having to summon up every shred of athleticism and anticipation to cling on. Channelling his full resources into the match, McEnroe's temper never surfaced. When he had break point, the Swede passed him with a forehand that landed extremely close to the line. The American pretended to throttle himself, somehow managing not to let a word pass his lips. The crowd applauded and he held up both hands to show he'd conquered his ire.

Together the two men drifted tie-break bound – a tie-break McEnroe knew he could take.

3.43: The New Yorker's self-belief was well justified. One set all.

Realising his superiority was being gravely disputed, Borg wrapped himself even tighter into his own world, concentrating single-mindedly on breaking the McEnroe serve. He nearly did so in the second game and in the fourth he found the range with his whipped topspin drives and broke serve accordingly.

4-1, Borg. Would the American's one lapse of diligence be enough? Applying himself solely to his serve, McEnroe held to 2-4 and resolved to do all that was possible as the number one seed came to serve again.

And in that game came John's *coup de hasard*. One of his backhands struck the net-cord before dropping irretrievably on the server's side. In another rally, this time on break point, Borg ended up hitting thin air as a McEnroe backhand slice fell on a dead patch of dry grass: 4-3 Borg.

The Swede, irrepressible as he had been at Wimbledon since 1976, gamely fought to 5-4. Now it was his turn to test the server's mettle. At 15-30 it looked as if McEnroe would detonate right on Centre Court. He opened up the whole court only to hit a deep volley that bounced in dusty chalk around the baseline. The linesman said nothing. Borg looked hard at him. And umpire Bob Jenkins reversed the call. For John, it was a catastrophe after his superhuman effort to climb back from the precipice.

Agitated by such injustice, positively steaming inside, he hit a

John McEnroe – Please Play On

superb smash and quickly got to deuce courtesy of a service winner. Twice more he saved set points before two spiteful volleys made another tie-break a virtual certainty.

When the tie-break duly arrived the Centre Court understood Borg would be under persistent assault. Both took points off each other's serve and at 4-3 McEnroe, it was Borg's turn to serve. An angled forehand crosscourt pass followed by a sweet backhand down the line rewarded John with three set points. The defiant Borg played aggressively: 4-6. But another corking first ball backed by instinctive forehand volleying closed the tie-break and McEnroe was ahead for the first time.

Could Bjorn raise his game?

No! Burdened by the thought he'd let go a set that was his, disturbed because his game was only mediocre by his exceptional standards, he began to give way.

First there was time for one more offensive – what was to become his last ever at Wimbledon and one that will always haunt the rafters of the staid arena. But after he had missed two break points at 1-1 it was effectively over.

Seven games on and the prize was in McEnroe's reach. This had been his destiny since that far off first shot at the Douglaston Club.

McEnroe netted a backhand return: 15-0. Then likewise on the forehand: 30-0. The tentative Borg mistimed a crosscourt backhand and it flew out: 30-15; a volley too long: 30-30.

First serve – fault. John moved in for the attack. Under pressure the champion wasted a backhand: 30-40, Championship point. Recognising this as his greatest crisis, Borg knew no alternative than to take risks. A serve-volley raid: deuce. Forcing Bjorn to defend another weak second serve, John buried a smash for a second Championship point.

The first serve went wide of the service line. McEnroe returned the second on the forehand and he quickly blanketed the net. Borg tried to pass, but McEnroe cut off his attempt and the forehand volley, as if arrested by time, finally bounced out of Borg's despairing reach.

"It took me a while to realise that he wasn't there, then I knew it was all over, just a great feeling. As I felt myself go down on my knees I thought, 'You have got to get up because Borg always does that!' You've got to give it everything to be able to beat him. A couple of times I said 'Come on,' to myself and then said, 'Don't

101

even do that, you have got to conserve all your energy. Just use everything you have got for hitting the ball.'

"I feel great because I so wanted to win Wimbledon. I feel especially good because I've beaten a great champion who is one of the finest players who ever lived. I couldn't have picked a greater guy to beat and I'm very proud to be Wimbledon champion."

And of the incident where Jenkins overruled a linesman on a crucial point, John said, "I had to force myself to keep calm. When people say that a few bad calls don't mean winning or losing a match, they should think about that one."

Borg, of course, was as dignified in defeat as he had been whilst ruling SW19 for those five long years. He called the outcome 'good for tennis' and agreed McEnroe had served too well for him. "But we are very even. We have good matches and we really show the people some good tennis."

As one writer concluded, John McEnroe "had finally had the last laugh."

Or had he?

❧❧

Shortly after accepting the golden trophy from the Duke of Kent, Wimbledon's new holder received a verbal invitation for the Champions' Dinner from club secretary Chris Gorringe. The two spoke again after the press interviews, when McEnroe requested eight tickets for friends. Gorringe replied that this might be tricky and later in the day John's father, on his son's request, agreed to phone the All England Club from his hotel for information regarding the exact details. He got in contact with the then assistant referee, Alan Mills.

Mr. McEnroe found out about the matters of dress and venue and although the subject of John's eight friends wasn't raised, he did ask if John could arrive half way through. My view is that Mr. McEnroe probably made this request given his son's shyness as regards any social gatherings. The star's father also asked if an Irish couple, guests of himself and Mrs. McEnroe, could come along. Mills promised to check up and subsequently informed him that the invitation was for the family only and if they couldn't be there by 10.30 p.m. when the dinner was due to start, then the invitation was 'respectfully withdrawn'.

When his father made his thoughts clear, McEnroe, considering whether to face a group of people with whom he was less than friends, or have his own party, chose the latter option.

Two questions emerge: firstly, why wasn't there room for McEnroe's friends? Secondly, if the invitation was, as Mills says, 'respectfully withdrawn' (albeit conditionally), why weren't guests at the dinner told?

Whilst saying, " ...I think it would be a pity to stir up old controversies unnecessarily, as the difficulties were finally sorted out and he did attend the Dinner when he was again champion two years later," the then Chairman, Air Chief Marshal Sir Brian Burnett, agreed to answer my queries:

"For various practical reasons the Champions' Dinner has always been restricted in numbers, with the champions being invited to bring one guest and parents. The Lady Champion in 1981 had already been told this and accepted and the Committee felt that it would be difficult at such short notice (i.e. after the Men's Final and only a few hours before the Dinner) to depart from the normal procedure which had always been very acceptable in the past. In the end, however, to try to meet McEnroe, it was agreed in this case to fit in five guests for him – more than this would have been unreasonable and would have disrupted seating plans at that late stage. There was no final agreement as you say 'to withdraw the invitation if McEnroe was not there by 10.30 p.m.'. It was left open and we hoped he would turn up before 10.30 p.m., when we would have to start dinner.

"As the then Chairman, I said at the beginning of my speech at about 11.15 p.m., 'We are not sure whether or not John McEnroe is coming, but it seems unlikely now.' Later in my speech, when finally proposing the toast of the champions, I said, 'I am sorry John McEnroe is not yet with us here this evening.' Throughout the dinner, my wife (whom he was to sit next to) and I kept watching the main door half-expecting him suddenly to arrive. Seats had been kept for him and his five guests."

So, somewhere along the line Wimbledon's famed efficiency had collapsed. Mills told Richard Evans, author of 'McEnroe: Rage for Perfection', that the invitation 'was respectfully withdrawn' after the 10.30 p.m. deadline. Burnett claimed otherwise to me ...

If Chris Evert had been aware of the complex events that culminated in McEnroe staying away, she might not have said quite so pointedly, "I think if you win Wimbledon you have to attend." Sir

Brian Burnett had suggested she make two speeches – one for herself, the other for John. She replied, "I'll stick to one because I don't think I have his vocabulary." (This amused Evert's former boyfriend, Jimmy Connors. He remarked to Peter Bodo of US 'Tennis' magazine, "I've practised on the same court as Chris enough times to guarantee that she can match vocabularies with John any day.")

Wimbledon was full of speculation after The Championships. Some held that McEnroe would never return and John kept everyone guessing by refusing to deny it. There were rumours, too, that in the summer of '81 an offer to help formulate a truce, made by Mr. McEnroe through ATP Executive Director Butch Buchholz, was rejected by the All England Club. Buzzer Hadingham, who succeeded Sir Brian Burnett as Club Chairman in 1984, seemed to believe that this involved McEnroe receiving membership to the club, which he hadn't been given, for he told me:

"The truth of the matter was that the All England Club Committee voted unanimously that John's election would be deferred for at least a year and really there was nothing that John or his father could do to change this. The following year John behaved well and the Committee thereupon elected him. There was no conspiracy of silence and the action was taken because of his poor behaviour at the 1981 Championships. I think I should add that although a player does normally become a member when he wins Wimbledon, this is always at the discretion of the Committee.

"I am – indeed we all are – a great admirer of John's wonderful tennis, but I think that both he and his father would agree that his tantrums on the court could not be allowed to go unnoticed. I am glad to say that in 1984 he not only played magnificent tennis, he also behaved perfectly. You will find there are some people who maintain that we are being pompous and over-officious in all this. On the other hand if we were to let bad behaviour pass, there are ten times as many people who would be critical. There is an agreed Code of Conduct and Wimbledon observes this whilst reserving the right to take more drastic action if in our judgment this is called for in the best interests of preserving the sporting traditions of the game."

At the time when the new champion would usually be receiving news of his membership to the club, McEnroe instead heard of a recommended $10,000 fine for 'aggravated behaviour' throughout the fortnight. Under the Players' Code of Conduct this sanction could possibly be allied to 'suspension from play for a period not to exceed one year.' According to the report, the fine was levied:

"After previous warnings, constant querying of line decisions, bad language and verbal abuse of the referee, the umpire and linesmen ... If it is claimed that some of these remarks were made by McEnroe to himself, they were made loud enough to be heard on television by members of the Press, Committee of Management and the public. This behaviour, which amounts to a pattern of conduct bringing the game into disrepute, is unacceptable and a maximum $10,000 fine is recommended."

McEnroe, as is his wont, intended to appeal.

Monday, July 6, 1981

"Tennis is lucky to have a temperamental, salty-tongued Wimbledon champion such as John McEnroe and the tiresome little men who run the championship will never understand that. That is why they have cheapened the event of the year with the reign of terror they directed at McEnroe. That is how they can turn the world's greatest tournament into the worst." (US newspaper 'Daily News')

John flew out of Heathrow by Concorde, leaving behind the sound of breaking cups and glasses as reporters chased him for a few last comments. Wisely, John had checked in only five minutes before take-off.

Safe from the British press at last, the sight of journalists in New York must have angered McEnroe immensely. Had he heard that Wimbledon wouldn't give him membership? John was stunned; it was the first he knew about it. But they were right. At 5.25 a.m. a release from the All England Club read:

"This year ... the committee have decided not to elect John McEnroe a member at the present time in view of his behaviour on court in certain matches, which, in their opinion, brought the game into disrepute."

Will you be defending your title next year?

"Would you honestly ask any other champion that?"

Speaking later from his home in Queens, McEnroe said his exclusion from becoming a member "really does show what kind of people you are dealing with at Wimbledon. But nothing surprises me now. Whether the people over there like it or not I am still the

John McEnroe – Please Play On

champion and they can't take that away from me. Wimbledon isn't about going to dances or anything like that. To me, it is about playing tennis and winning the title."

Jimmy Connors remarked, "I feel sorry for John. The Wimbledon authorities feel they have almost divine rights. I am sure his best answer is to go back next year, win the title again and see if they dare refuse him membership then."

McEnroe also strengthened what Mills said – that the invitation was withdrawn. "I didn't go because I wasn't invited," were his words.

In the States John opened up to Peter Bodo of US 'Tennis' magazine. "It got so out of control," the Champion lamented. "It was like I'd say something and then something else and I'd keep going and there was no way I could stop. Man, was I tense.

"Wimbledon's a weird place, it's such an institution. Maybe it brings that rebellious part out in me. I wanna change that – I gotta change that. But it's hard. You never know who to turn to.

"Maybe I oughta take up meditation or something like that, something that can cool me out. Can you see me going through one of those self-help things? Man, the people would look and laugh and say, 'Hey, look who's here – John McEnroe.'"

John's friend Mary Carillo was intrigued by the fact that he seemed more interested in how she'd spent the infamous fortnight back in America. Carillo stated, "I know this for sure: John's got morals, standards and ethics. I've never seen him sell himself out – for anything."

Tuesday, August 11, 1981

"A guy showed me a picture taken when I'd won [Wimbledon] and was on my knees. When I saw it I just thought how tough a time it was over there. Not the tennis, but everything else. But if you have any brains in your head going through a bad experience helps you. It has helped my attitude already. It's a little more enjoyable to play now. I feel more at ease." (Talking to Rex Bellamy, 'The Times')

Tuesday, September 8, 1981

"Friends tell me how unchanged and unaffected he is by success. Fame has absolutely not gone to his head. If there is anyone with a great deal of humility, it's John McEnroe.

"My wife and I always kinda felt that it was the American way not to be content with giving less than your best effort. If you give that, then you've nothing to regret." (John McEnroe Snr. talking to Sue Mott, 'Daily Mail')

Benson & Hedges Championships

Monday, November 9, 1981

John arrived at Heathrow and with a dry sense of humour he told reporters, "I have got a great image, why should I change it?"

Tuesday, November 10, 1981

Twenty-five spectators demanded their money back after McEnroe failed to make his scheduled evening appearance. The organisers had in fact switched John's match to Wednesday without notifying any newspapers or press agencies. It was hardly surprising, therefore, that tournament director Len Owen was quick to point out that the American should be viewed as "the innocent party."

In truth, the player's father had agreed in a telephone conversation with Owen that John would play his first singles on the Wednesday. Owen had thought at the time that McEnroe might only be competing in the singles event. When he learnt that his star attraction was also teaming up with Peter Fleming, Owen allowed McEnroe to be scheduled for a Tuesday singles start. He explained, "I felt that if he were playing in both events we should start him on the Tuesday." But Owen admitted he had erred from what had been agreed between himself and Mr. McEnroe.

John was dismayed. "I'm in trouble again and I've done nothing," he commented.

Wednesday, November 11, 1981
Beat John Feaver 6-1, 6-1

John's tennis was "all gold" according to Rex Bellamy of 'The Times'.

And that opinion was backed up by a player in the stands who announced during the match: "He's making Feaver look like a sick dog. Mind you, McEnroe always makes most players look like sick dogs."

Feaver could only say, straight-faced, "He's very good, isn't he? If there is such a thing as having a ball on a string he's got it. You can hit a hell of a shot and he seems to have half an hour to send it back with interest. I have never played anybody who anticipates so well. He's there before you've even hit the shot. It's uncanny. He didn't let me get my nose into it."

The Feaver duel only took fifty-five minutes and less than an hour later John was back on court, partnering Peter Fleming in a 6-3, 6-4 defeat of Sandy Mayer (United States) and Frew McMillan (South Africa).

But umpire Roger Smith warned McEnroe for merely deflecting a ball on to the adjacent court. "People get nervous when they officiate me," declared John later. "They are jumping out of their pants at my matches." Yet once again his sense of humour surfaced. In the press conference, John commented that Japan might be the only place where the press didn't give him a bad time. "I can't read it, anyway," he joked.

Thursday, November 12, 1981
Beat Stanislav Birner 6-2, 6-2

John seemed a worried young man during his game with Birner, and he told the press that the $10,000 fine recommended by Wimbledon was on his mind.

Although the Men's Professional Tennis Council had lowered the sum to $5,000, John had gone ahead with his appeal and three arbitrators were now assessing the situation. The problem was that their verdict wouldn't be delivered until the New Year.

In the meantime John was dogged by worry about the decision. John himself could pick one of the arbitrators – and he'd chosen Harry Hopman.

"I was reluctant to pick him because if he voted against me I wouldn't want that to enter into our friendship or relationship we have with him and my family," John said.

Friday, November 13, 1981
Beat Brian Gottfried 6-1, 6-2

McEnroe turned in a stunning performance and Gottfried exited shell-shocked after a mere fifty-eight minutes.

"It would be tragic if he came to be remembered in years to come as a flawed genius," 'Guardian' tennis correspondent David Irvine told me around this period. "And he is a genius, make no mistake about it. At the same time he has a great responsibility at No.1 in the world. And that is sometimes difficult. He has yet to face up to it, even though I believe he has tried from time to time. Unfortunately he seems to be going through a phase at present in which he thinks everyone's against him. It's a sort of persecution complex."

Saturday, November 14, 1981
Beat Sandy Mayer 6-3, 6-3

John won in 1 hour 11 minutes, though he had a scare in the first game when he was forced to stave off four break points. In the eighth game of the second set McEnroe won five points on the trot from 0-40.

Sunday, November 15, 1981

Ever the perfectionist, John McEnroe had declared at Flushing Meadow that the year was not over; there were, he said, many titles at stake and he intended to win them.

But that proud promise had taken a battering in the weeks leading up to the Benson & Hedges Championships because John had suddenly suffered a loss of form.

First, Bill Scanlon overcame him 3-6, 7-6, 6-2 in the Transamerican Open – "I lost and that's the bottom line," a jaded and upset McEnroe said afterwards – then Eliot Teltscher beat him in an exhibition tournament in Melbourne. There was a welcome victory the following week in Sydney, but fatigue was affecting McEnroe by the time he arrived in Tokyo for the Seiko event. Unhappily for John, Bill Scanlon caused him some trouble there. According to John Barrett in the Slazenger Yearbook, "Scanlon appeared to needle

John McEnroe – Please Play On

McEnroe deliberately... the ensuing flare-up was inevitable. When Scanlon suggested to the umpire John deserved a warning, John replied, 'You are lower than dirt.' Scanlon then said, 'Umpire! He can't say that to me. That's verbal abuse.'"

Unfortunately for John, the fact he had been goaded cut no ice with Supervisor Bill Gilmour, who told him of his $500 fine just minutes before his semi-final with van Patten. Such was John's outrage at the injustice that he could summon up no will for the fight, losing very quickly ...

It was therefore not altogether astonishing that, having slaved all week to keep his temper in check, McEnroe's touch-paper was swiftly lit at the final hurdle. In the end he departed from Wembley a broken man. Fined £350, he subsequently served three weeks' suspension following a depressing 3-6, 2-6, 6-3, 6-4, 6-2 fall from grace at the hands of arch rival, Jimmy Connors.

John played brilliantly to take eleven of the first fifteen games and from there built up a two sets advantage.

When at 0-1, 40-0 in the third, he lost the point and hit a ball into the backstop, no-one was in danger. Although umpire John Parry was technically justified in giving a warning, it was a harsh action for such an insignificant offence. After that, McEnroe fell apart, unable to direct his efforts to the match. Just two points later he queried the warning, and a courtside microphone was broken. Parry deducted a penalty point, giving Connors break-point, but John saw the incident thus: "The other thing I did was to put the racquet on a microphone and it broke."

Referee Colin Hess and Grand Prix Supervisor Keith Johnson came on court to listen to John's protests, but a six-minute conversation resulted in the backing of Parry's decision.

Connors went on to break for 2-0 and by 3-0 McEnroe's self-control had evaporated ...

In the fifth set John had two break points for 3-1, but soon went 2-3 down and hit a ball into the stands. Penalty point. With Connors serving in the next game already 15-0 up, McEnroe managed only two more points.

Still the bitter player faced the press: "I just do not understand why it all started. I just hit the ball into the back stuff. I really didn't think anything about it and the umpire's reaction really surprised me."

In the papers John was once again the villain. The umpire, who twice lost the score, received little criticism. Nor did Connors,

110

supposedly a mature married man, who was fined £200 for an "audible obscenity" (he also punctuated the match with numerous sly gestures). When Jimmy left the court for an impromptu chat with Earl "Butch" Buchholz, executive director of the ATP, he should have been defaulted, for the Rules stated clearly: *"Any player who, without the permission of the Umpire, leaves the court area during a match shall be disqualified by the Umpire."* In addition, Connors often slammed his racquet down, but John Parry never once warned him for this. Ludicrously, he declared there was a 'different degree of anger' in the two players' excesses.

McEnroe, who also lost his doubles crown, talked of the pressures and fatigue that had dogged his progress for two months. "The travelling hurts you and the price you have to pay for being number one is that everyone wants to beat you. The snowball gets bigger and bigger, and sometimes it's a mental effort to actually go out on court. I've been through a lot this year. I've won some big titles but it's tough going out there, day after day. I look in the mirror and see the black under my eyes. I need a rest."

Thus John McEnroe left the competitive arena in 1981 on a sour note. Not since the spring had he looked so sluggish, played so indifferently and felt so exhausted. And creeping doubts about his chances for 1982 were already surfacing.

* Fans mobbed McEnroe as he left Wembley, prompting him to smile and say, "I hope to see you all again next year."

Monday, November 23, 1981

"Crowds upset McEnroe more than most players. He must have felt he was playing in a Roman amphitheatre. The [Wembley Arena] crowd were out for blood and were not happy until they got it.

"As soon as McEnroe went to query a decision, which he was entitled to do, the crowd started slow handclapping. They wanted something to happen and goaded him until it did.

"I umpired McEnroe in the doubles semi-final the day before, and he was well-behaved.

"But the crowd was much kinder, possibly because it was a doubles match and they didn't identify with one person so much. I thanked McEnroe after the match and he appreciated that." (Umpire Ian Stirk)

1982

Masters[9]	Semi-final	Lendl	64 62
US Pro Indoors	WON	Connors	63 63 61
Memphis	Runner-up	Kriek	63 36 64
Belgian Indoors	Quarter-final	Glickstein	Withdrew
WCT Finals	Runner-Up	Lendl	62 36 63 63
WCT New York	Semi-final	Dibbs	76 63
Manchester	WON	Simpson	67 63 10-8
Stella Artois	Runner-Up	Connors	75 63
Wimbledon	Runner-Up	Connors	36 63 67 76 64
Canadian Open	Semi-final	Lendl	64 64
ATP Champs	Semi-final	Denton	76 64
US Open	Semi-final	Lendl	64 64 76
San Francisco	WON	Connors	61 63
Australian Indoor	WON	G. Mayer	64 61 64
Seiko Super Tennis	WON	McNamara	76 75
Benson & Hedges	WON	Gottfried	63 62 64
Antwerp	Runner-Up	Lendl	36 76 63 63

Davis Cup:

V India   bt V. Amritraj 64, 97, 75; bt Krishnan 61, 57, 64; with Fleming, bt A/V Amritraj 63, 61, 75

V Sweden bt Jarryd 10-8, 63, 63; bt Wilander 97, 62, 15-17, 36, 86; with Fleming, bt Jarryd/H Simonsson 64, 63, 60

V Australia   bt McNamara 64, 46, 62, 64; bt Alexander 64, 63; with Fleming, bt McNamara/McNamee 62, 62, 36, 86

V France   bt Noah 12-10, 16, 36, 62, 63; bt Leconte 62, 63; with Fleming, bt Leconte/Noah 63, 64, 97

[9] Part of the 1981 Tennis Year.

For McEnroe, 1982 was a miserable time. It was always going to be extremely difficult to repeat his Wimbledon, US Open and Davis Cup victories of the previous year and in fact this time even John's rare skill could manage just one of those three feats – the Cup. It was his crucial victory in the final over Yannick Noah on an alien clay court that swung the tie in favour of the United States. In the quarter-final against Sweden he had overcome Mats Wilander in St. Louis before declaring, "It was just mind over matter. It was the longest match I've played and I can tell you my body's not feeling very good. At some points, I thought it would never end. I enjoy being part of the team and I enjoy the other guys doing well. I know that sounds like a lot of bull, but I mean it. Playing for my country is pretty special for me."

Elsewhere, by McEnroe's standards, it was a dismal season. The fines recommended after Wimbledon '81 may have been finally quashed following the decision of the three man tribunal, but when John returned to SW19 he suffered the vast disappointment of a 3-6, 6-3, 6-7, 7-6, 6-4 loss to a rejuvenated Jimmy Connors in a little over four hours.

An ankle, twisted badly at Brussels in March when he stepped on some racquets at the side of a practice court, dogged him throughout the spring and his touch suffered accordingly. In truth, the injury led to dire consequences. McEnroe decided to pull out of the French Championships and instead appeared in a modest grass court event at Manchester. He won, albeit with difficulty, and his confidence remained impaired.

Connors was not the only player to have John's number. Lendl humiliated the New Yorker in the '81 Masters, in a stormy four setter at the WCT Finals, in straight sets in the Canadian Open and again at the Flushing Meadow semi-final stage. The US Open loss was particularly disappointing since the preceding week John had practised for 30 hours.

In fact, after winning the US Pro Indoors in January, McEnroe didn't record another Grand Prix success until exacting revenge on Connors at San Francisco in October. The win coincided with a slight change to John's new racquet, the Maxply McEnroe. Transam tournament director Barry Mackay told me, "Bob Howe of Dunlop gave John several Maxply McEnroes at the start of the event. One of the slight changes was a decrease in the stringing tension and John's play throughout the week was superb." That was the beginning of four straight Grand Prix victories and 24 consecutive wins, which gave McEnroe some reason to be optimistic about 1983.

Indeed, Tony Palafox told 'World Tennis', "If John can serve well and return well and get his concentration going (thinking about one thing at a time), he'll be right back in there."

Wednesday, January 27, 1982

The suspended sentence that loomed over John McEnroe for six months was finally cleared after the three man independent appeals tribunal delivered their verdict in Philadelphia. Lawrence W. Kreiger and the Honourable Robert J. Kelleher found McEnroe guilty, but the player's representative on the arbitration panel, Harry Hopman, sided with him. Under the Mens' Professional Council's Code of Conduct, *"The arbitrators shall find that a Major Offence has been committed only by unanimous vote. In no case, may the arbitrators find that a lesser offence has been committed or impose a penalty different from the one designated in the charge."* So McEnroe was at last completely free.

"I am delighted," said John McEnroe Snr. "I hope this puts the sad and unnecessary dispute to bed because it has no other place to go. I am pleased to see that the one man who knows what world championship tennis is all about reinforces the views expressed by the players' representatives to the Professional Council."

And even Fred Hoyles came to see McEnroe's misdemeanours of 1981 in a different light. Speaking in October 1990, Hoyles admitted, "There was no reason why he couldn't query a decision, especially in those days long before we had the training we have for officials now."

As for Edward James, umpire of the infamous Gullikson/McEnroe encounter, he was sacked from working at a tournament in Bristol in 1983 after making a 'procedural error'. He admitted to not having seen a ball, but, instead of upholding the linesman's decision, he asked the players to replay the point.

The Manchester Open

Monday, May 31, 1982

John said, "Those two weeks [of Wimbledon 1981] were the worst of my life as a tennis player. I said afterwards that I didn't know whether it was worth going through it all again. But I'm here, so … "

Tuesday, June 1, 1982

"I did meet John McEnroe during the tournament and for the first few days found him reserved and retiring. It was only towards the end of the week that he relaxed and was easy to talk to. On two occasions during the week, he was rather aggressive on court and it would appear that this aggression was through his tremendous will to win." (Ian Stewart, Tournament Secretary)

John's preparations for defending his Wimbledon singles title began at the West Didsbury Club, Manchester, in a match against little-known South African Craig Campbell.

Obviously the American remained a little pensive about his ankle injury, but he had no more than a gentle work-out. The 18-year old student from Miami University was sunk 6-2, 6-1 in 52 minutes.

"I wasn't relaxed enough to open up and swing. I couldn't get in to the match," said Campbell, trying to explain the lack of pressure imposed upon McEnroe. Would John retain his Wimbledon crown? "As long as he gets plenty of practice on grass before the tournament," replied the loser.

That was McEnroe's reason for coming north. Promoter Harvey Demmy had acted smartly when he heard the player wanted to test out his injured ankle and, having agreed to lay on a private jet after John's opening match for him to fly to Paris to receive the World Champion's award of 1981, Mr. Demmy had secured McEnroe's appearance. Besides, John said he'd been told Didsbury was a "nice place."

Other live topics at John's press conference included his beleaguered ankle – he reported twinges but insisted it was "nothing serious". Manchester? "If all goes well, I'll be glad I came."

 * *John played against Campbell with one eye no doubt checking the adjoining court, where Stacy Margolin beat Cheshire's Belinda Thompson 7-5, 6-2. Meanwhile, Stacy's pal, Trey Lewis, was reported in the press as saying, "John is a really nice guy. I know Stacy very well and she likes him so he must be OK." (22-year old Trey would fall in Manchester's third round to Van der Walt of South Africa.)*

 * *The 18-year old Nick Fulwood had a message for the British team manager, Paul Hutchins, before facing McEnroe in the next round. "Come and watch me play tomorrow," said Fulwood, who*

had just lost his place in Hutchins' national junior squad.

The Derbyshire youngster, junior covered court winner in 1981, added, "I'm sure I can do better than Campbell. The way I feel, I've got nothing to lose so I might as well go out and go for my shots. I will not lose any sleep. We are due to play about 5.30 and I might start to worry at three o'clock. Or maybe I won't."

Rain in fact postponed their match until 12.30 p.m. on Thursday...

Thursday, June 3, 1982

On a scorching day in Manchester, John, still apprehensive about his play, won an interesting match over Fulwood 6-2, 6-0. It proved a short work-out for the 23-year old, and umpire Dan Blunt recalls, "The match was one-sided but McEnroe took things seriously. His behaviour was good and it was an enjoyable match to umpire."

Blunt continued, "McEnroe's father is a lawyer and what McEnroe does on court is to create a situation where he asks the umpire questions as a barrister would do to a somewhat nervous witness. This creates tension sometimes, but if you are umpiring you simply concentrate on the match and answer any questions McEnroe puts to you. Personally, I don't think he is a 'bad boy' – he is a perfectionist and requires all the officials to be as close to perfect as possible."

Less than two hours later John was back on court, but he produced a controversial display against fellow-American Jay Lapidus and although he assured victory in two sets, it was not before initiating such headlines the next day as "Northern Revival is marred by McEnroe" ('Daily Telegraph') and "Mac the Mouth is back in Business" ('The Sun')

Lapidus, three months younger than McEnroe and like his celebrated rival a left-hander, was in good shape. He "fancied his chances" before their quarter-final.

A former Princeton University player, Lapidus had nearly defeated McEnroe two years earlier in New Jersey and today he again started strongly against a tight opponent. John's uneasiness meant that in the seventh game of the forty-one minute opening set, angered by a double fault, then a mistake which sent him break point down, he slammed a ball which skidded up into the crowd and hit a spectator on the shoulder.

Following cries of "What are you doing about that, umpire?" line judge Roy Newton left his seat to tell umpire Stephen Winyard exactly what happened. Winyard had missed the incident as he was marking his score sheet.

"I just made sure the umpire knew what happened just in case he hadn't seen the incident," Newton explained afterwards. As the official returned to his place on the far tramline McEnroe asked, "What is all that about?"

"I told him what I said and his answer was unrepeatable," remembers Newton.

Yes, John was rude in this instance. But in the heat of a difficult battle, with things not going his way, the thought of yet another warning for the petty offence of "ball abuse" just aggravated him … and, as we know, John is not slow to voice his irritation.

Later during his 6-3, 6-4 win he shouted, "Why can't we have more linesmen? There are 20 of them watching the match." Referee Bea Seal told him to "get on with the match" to which John responded, "Get on with getting an umpire."

Afterwards the American told the press such a situation shouldn't arise. "It's not easy for an official to call half a court, so mistakes are made."

John was far from error-free himself, with nine double faults. Half his first serves missed their mark. One journalist noted, "That is not the form of a Wimbledon Champion." In truth it had been a gruelling one hour and 36 minute skirmish.

❧❧

With Peter Rennert[10] versus Brian Levine and Christo Steyn

"The match took place on Thursday, June 3, although it didn't finish until the next day as it was called off for bad light at McEnroe and Rennert's request when they were 5-6 down in the final set.

"The umpire was Mr. Neville Spencer of Nottingham, and I,

[10] 23 year-old Peter Rennert had become a friend of John's at the Port Washington Tennis Academy in New York. Like McEnroe, he attended Stanford University, graduating with a degree in Psychology and gaining the College Player of the Year Award from US 'Tennis' Magazine.

Albert Taylor, was one of five linesmen on the Thursday and six on the Friday. McEnroe and Rennert soon found they had a match on their hands. Somewhat unusually I was on Centre Service – possibly because McEnroe serves down the centre a lot and the umpire said afterwards that he was glad he had a C.S. as there were a few close ones. It was quite a good match and I wrote in my scrap book, 'McEnroe had his usual disputes with the umpire over nothing really, but he wasn't too bad.' The match was quite keenly fought and there was possibly some needle because earlier in the week – in a match which I umpired – Levine had beaten Rennert 13-11 in the final set. Levine/ Steyn won the first set 6-4, lost the second 6-4 and were 6-5 up when they came off at 9.15 after one and a half hours."

Friday, June 4, 1982

Controversy reigned at Manchester as Kate Latham, playing on the court next to McEnroe against Stacy Margolin, went across to the star to shout, "For Christ's sake shut up. We are trying to play."

The incident occurred in the middle of the American's tough 6-3, 7-6 semi-final victory over Australian John Alexander on Centre Court One.

John cursed his poor first services ("Get one in for the sake of argument"), but what really unnerved him was a bizarre altercation with chair umpire Bill Pickup from Stockport.

"The cause of McEnroe's outburst was the service linesman changing his call on a doubtful ball [and thus signifying a fault]," Pickup told me. "The change of call was in favour of McEnroe and resulted in Alexander complaining to me that the linesman concerned was being intimidated by John McEnroe. I informed John Alexander that this was not the case and I agreed with the change in the linesman's original decision. I then asked Mr. Alexander to continue the match, the score being 15-15, first service. John McEnroe then argued that it could not be first service as Alexander had already served once and I repeated, "First service." At this stage McEnroe approached my chair arguing volubly that Alexander had already served once and it could not be first service. I told him that in accordance with the rules of the game, in respect of an interruption to play, it is stipulated that the whole point must be replayed, thus it was first service. At this point Kate Latham told McEnroe to shut up,

but he retorted, "Sh.." and continued arguing with me. Kate Latham again asked McEnroe to get on with the game and let them get on with theirs, alleging he had nothing to complain about, and he retorted, "Why don't you walk over here and kiss my ...?" At this stage I repeated to Mr. McEnroe that under the rules the point must be replayed and the score was 15-15, first service. He then grudgingly returned to the baseline to receive service, but went to the wrong side of the court. On seeing this I repeated the score and McEnroe strode to the right side of the court."

After the 29-year old Latham won her way into the women's final, she told the press that Stacy was fully behind her. "I apologised to Stacy afterwards, but she said, "I'm glad you did it.""

"He's only a little boy," Latham added. "I was annoyed. I was involved in a close match and had a big struggle and could only hear his nonsense about balls getting wet and incorrect calls."

According to a spokesman for the Referees' Society, the incident that occurred in John's semi-final was a "terribly difficult one" to judge. On the one hand, if the linesman had reversed his call promptly, it could be said that there was no interruption to play and that McEnroe was in the right. If, however, a point had been played by the time the linesman indicated his new decision, Bill Pickup was correct to state that play had been interrupted.

The spokesman added that the linesman might have changed his call immediately but, given the pace of tennis on grass, the rally might have been over by the time he did so.

Thus, this was a complex incident and John's anger at seeing Alexander miss his first serve but be given two more due to an official's mistake is understandable.

With Peter Rennert, versus Brian Levine and Christo Steyn

"They restarted at 4.39 with the same umpire and an extra linesman on Near Tram. On the resumption Mac was serving to save the match, which he did. Then the next two games went to Steyn and Levine amid tumultuous applause.

"The final point was very good with Rennert making three or four outstanding retrieves and McEnroe one good one too before they went out at 8-6.

"Levine/Steyn played very well in the match and deserved to win... McEnroe wasn't of course at his best. The standard was exceptional with some superb rallies and a great deal of long exchanges." (The combined recollections of Mr. N. Spencer (Umpire) and Mr. A. Taylor (Linesman))

* At the end of the day McEnroe signed autographs for about an hour.

Saturday, June 5, 1982

Following the debate about his conduct, John behaved himself admirably in the crisis of the final day and finished out on top. The official in charge of events, Dan Blunt, said that the New Yorker "concentrated on his tennis and caused no problems to the linesmen."

One of them, Albert Taylor, recalls, "I was on the baseline for the McEnroe/Simpson final. It was a very good match and McEnroe certainly didn't have it all his own way and could easily have lost. He started off with some very good serving in the opening game, but Simpson came more into it and there were many good rallies and exciting play. McEnroe broke to lead 3-1 and took the first set 6-3.

"During this set I might have made a mistake when I called a drive from McEnroe in (I thought it just caught the back of the line). Simpson looked round as though he thought it was out, but he didn't say anything. Some of the crowd shouted, "Out." Umpire, however, upheld my call.

"Simpson took second set on an exciting tie-break and a long final set developed. I had two more very close calls – again both McEnroe drives - but this time I called them both out and was pretty confident of being right. McEnroe glared at me once from the far end. Although Simpson served for the match at 8-7 McEnroe pulled out all the stops and ran out 10-8 in the third after two hours and twelve minutes."

And that just about tells the whole story. After collecting the modest first prize of £1,200 John said, "I am not hitting the ball as I would like, but this match does not make or break my Wimbledon chances." McEnroe's slight despondency at his form was tempered by the fact that his left ankle had emerged from the tournament unscathed. "It's a matter of confidence. I didn't think about the injury so much in the final and that helped my game."

So the American moved south to renew hostilities with the rest of the professional tour, who were arriving from the clay courts of

Paris.   Perhaps his struggle with the New Zealander should have warned him all was not well.   It would be a misery of a summer.

In June 1986, Russell Simpson told me, "John was the best player I have ever seen.   On court he would do anything to win a tennis match, but off court he is charming and fun loving most of the time."

* In the March 1984 issue of 'Tennis World' Manchester referee Bea Seal was interviewed by Henry Wancke:

HW: You mentioned you refereed a tournament in which McEnroe played – Manchester – where he was well behaved.   Did you in fact speak to him before the tournament?

BS: No – no; I don't try and set up anything.   There is nothing I hate more than that.   No – I thought knowing him and his reputation I might have a problem here and there and within ten minutes of going on court (versus Campbell) I heard his mutterings or voice.   So I thought, "Problems" and walked down to the court and as soon as I got there he shouted, "I want a net cord judge."   Didn't say please, just that!   I wasn't going to be shouted at so I walked out to the middle of the court and made sure spectators could hear what I was saying.   I thought this was important.   So I said, "Mr. McEnroe, you are here to play tennis, I'm here to referee the tournament – so would you please get on and play tennis.   I can then go back and referee the tournament – and you are not having a net cord judge.   Thank you."   I never had another word out of him.   That was the end of that ..."

But Mrs. Seal allocated a net cord judge for John's clash with Simpson.

Stella Artois Championships

Monday, June 7, 1982
Beat Andy Andrews 6-4, 6-2

Andrews, a 23-year old from North Carolina, may have served more aces than McEnroe (ten compared with six), but the No.1 seed conceded only nine points on serve in this 73 minute encounter.

In the fourth game of the second set McEnroe had inaudible exchanges with the umpire regarding one of Andrews' aces.   Asked afterwards about what he thought of the official, John replied that he no longer answered such questions due to a "new sensibility."

McEnroe also remarked, "I'm not happy about my form or my fitness. I need to strengthen my ankle. I don't want to think about the injury, but I'm just not 100% right."

Wednesday, June 9, 1982
Beat Charlie Fancutt 6-3, 6-2

Five feet ten inch Fancutt had defeated Ivan Lendl at Wimbledon the previous year, but playing McEnroe on grass was a different matter altogether.

On a windy day, John lost just one point in the final three games. After the press conference, Laurie Pignon wrote in 'The Daily Mail', "McEnroe said there were one or two things about his game on which he could improve. Whatever these are, they were not strikingly obvious."

Thursday, June 10, 1982
Beat John Sadri 6-3, 6-2

McEnroe was happier with his 70 minute display against big-server Sadri.

John disclosed, "When I'm playing well I don't think about it [the injured ankle] too much. All in all I was moving well, better than I have done for a very long time and I just hope it continues."

Friday, June 11, 1982
Beat Chip Hooper 6-3, 6-4

McEnroe was relieved to have outwitted his six foot, six inch opponent from Washington DC.

Hooper had recovered from eye surgery in 1981 and had soared from No.235 to No.17 in early 1982. But the black newcomer realised the talent he had been up against. "He's an unbelievable shotmaker. I couldn't gauge either the speed or the direction. It's weird not knowing if the ball's going to come back at you hard or soft."

John accepted the only dubious decision made by umpire Mike Lugg. In the second set a Hooper serve was called out by a linesman who then reversed his call. Lugg refused to replay the point, instead awarding an ace to Hooper. Said McEnroe, "I just thought we should have played two balls. But the umpire in his judgement said the call did not affect the fact I was aced."

McEnroe was aced off court, too. On this day Peter Tory of 'The Daily Mirror' proved that neither the player nor his friends could ever feel safe from the public's gaze when he reported that he'd seen Miss Margolin in "lively form at a West End nightclub" – without John.

Saturday, June 12, 1982
Beat Chris Lewis 6-0, 6-2

The New Yorker thrashed the New Zealander, but all the time he was toiling desperately to hone his game. "I've got to hit the line," he wailed in anguish, revealing the low margins for error he set himself.

But McEnroe did admit, "I'm happy with the way I'm improving. I was pleased with my game. Chris moves well and hits some good shots. That's what I wanted."

Lewis was left echoing many players' sentiments: "Since John is exceptionally quick and has such great anticipation, you never feel relaxed. His serve is unlike anyone's in the game, I never know where it's going."

Sunday, June 13, 1982

John was routed 7-5, 6-3 by Jimmy Connors and said sadly, "My serving has been up and down for a while and I am trying to correct that. I didn't seem to be moving as well as I have been. I have no excuses for some of my shots, but it is frustrating when you've had an injury which is improving, but is not yet 100%."

At least the singles loser had fun in the doubles final. McEnroe and Peter Rennert shared two pairs of socks of different colours in a 7-6, 7-5 win over Victor Amaya and Hank Pfister.

Tuesday, June 15, 1982

"And whadaya mean he hasn't got a sense of humour? The guy's a lotta fun. Don't expect to see it at Wimbledon. How can you joke in a pressure cooker where everybody hates you? Or loves to hate you?" (Peter Rennert, talking to Noreen Taylor, 'Daily Mirror')

Friday, June 18, 1982

'The Daily Express' William Hickey column quoted 'a friend' of John and Stacy as saying, "Yes, they are apart. But they remain good friends although they have been separated now for a few weeks. They no longer have a girlfriend/boyfriend relationship."

Saturday, June 19, 1982

"I'm essentially who I am. I'm not going to be out there laughing and joking, because that's not the way I was brought up. That's not me. I'm playing to win and if I'm not fighting, then I'll lose my concentration." (Talking to Bud Collins, 'Radio Times')

"I wouldn't like to be an umpire for me, that's for sure. I'm a perfectionist. I get impatient with incompetence, especially my own! And that's why when I get mad at myself, I let it out against officials."(Talking to 'Woman's Realm')

Wimbledon

Monday, June 21, 1982
Beat Van Winitsky 6-2, 6-2, 6-1

John set off on his bid to defend his Wimbledon crown with a three sets to love whipping of fellow American Van Winitsky.

With Winitsky serving, John pounced on the first two points of the match, executing two authoritative backhand winners. A volleying error from the Junior Wimbledon Champion of 1977 presented three break points to McEnroe, but Winitsky pulled himself together and plucked the game for himself. However, it didn't bode well for the future.

In the second game McEnroe opened tentatively with two consecutive double faults. The six foot one inch Winitsky may have anticipated an early break, but McEnroe clearly thought otherwise, retaliating with three fierce service winners. At 2-2 John made up his mind to take charge. Although he missed a first break point, a low service return that Winitsky couldn't control put him 3-2 up.

Some more unforced errors caused Winitsky to be broken again two games later. At 5-2 John served for the set and stared hard after a doubtful call cost him the first point. There were no tantrums – instead he gave, according to 'The Daily Telegraph', a "toothy" grin to umpire Paul Alderson, a dentist, and won the game.

The second set was never a struggle. Winitsky conceded serve in the first and third games and in the twinkling of an eye the challenger was confronted by a two sets deficit.

The pattern was predictable by now and the Florida-born Winitsky yet again yielded serve. Then, at just past three o'clock, light drizzle followed by a heavy downpour stopped play for an hour and a half.

But a little later an eight point streak, finishing with a thunderous forehand pass, completed the one-sided encounter in John's favour.

Afterwards he revealed that he had never received the replicas of the men's singles and doubles trophies he had won at Wimbledon in 1981.

"Hopefully I'll get the trophies I won last year," he said.

The All England Club's explanation for the incident was that the trophies would have been handed over at the Championship dinner, but after the Van Winitsky match John's father was able to finally pick them up from the Secretary's office.

Dave Kindred of 'The Washington Post' was unimpressed by the Club. Why had they done nothing in the intervening twelve months, he wondered? "That means that, for a whole year, not a single member of the distinguished All England flew to New York on business. Such a trip could have included a stop at the law office of John McEnroe Snr. The traveller could have carried the trophies. Or – and this is creative thinking – the club could have put the trophies in a box, insured them and mailed them."

John, himself, was more forgiving. "The people here are attempting to make an effort," he remarked. "It might be a good idea if everyone tried to make an effort. A couple of people came up to me today trying to be more pleasant. I certainly hope this will continue." He added, "I'm trying to go out there in the right frame of mind and enjoy myself a lot more than I did last year. I had no problems today – let's hope it stays that way."

Wednesday, June 23, 1982
Beat Eddie Edwards 6-3, 6-3, 7-5

John had no easy ride on Court No.1 against 25-year old South African qualifier Eddie Edwards, but he tried hard to hide his temper.

He mentioned he was "probably backing off the throttle" to keep himself in check. "I'm trying to laugh it off a little more because I don't want to go through what I went through last year."

He added with a small smile, "I'm planning to enjoy my tennis career at some point."

But inevitably his emotions occasionally boiled over. Firstly, he found it "tough when there is so much noise. I became annoyed with the crowd who were cheering him a lot when I missed."

Secondly, "I was angry at the way I played. When you hit one ball sweetly enough and then put the next ten feet out of court you know you can't win tournaments that way."

Finally, McEnroe was irked by a warning for ball abuse given by umpire George Armstrong. The American had blasted a ball into the back netting in the third game of the final set.

Coincidentally, Armstrong had penalised John for the same offence in the second round of Wimbledon '80!

"I don't see that as ball abuse," argued John. "It should be for hitting a ball out of [the] court [confines] or aiming it at a linesman. But then this wasn't one of the world's best officiated matches."

Saturday, June 26, 1982
With Peter Fleming, beat Brod Dyke and Peter Johnston 6-2, 6-4, 6-4

"Brod and I qualified and I distinctly remember how nervous I felt when Weller Evans, the ATP representative, told us who we were to play. He had a big grin on his face, of course!

"Then the match was on Court No.1 and I was so nervous I could hardly hit the ball on the strings. I had to serve first and started with a foot fault.

"I really think McEnroe and Fleming just coasted through the match. I had no thoughts at all of winning. McEnroe was getting fed up with the umpires etc. and at one stage said, 'This is my last match,' which I thought was quite funny.

"Some other thoughts do come to mind. I remember at the beginning of the match the umpire asked who was serving first. Brod – who always served first – immediately replied, 'Johnston,' and then just laughed at me!

"The comment I made about never thinking we could win simply means that normally in a match you can envisage the possibility of victory – in this case I could not.

"Also, nerves normally last for only a couple of games. However, in this case they remained for the whole match, the reason being that I was just not used to the situation. You have to go through it a few times before you can settle down and just concentrate on the tennis. See, for McEnroe it was just another day at the office, whereas for me it was a big event." (Peter Johnston)

❧❧

" … I'm intensely proud of him. He's never disappointed me. At school he got top marks. His first teacher said he was gifted and he whizzed through every subject, especially maths.

"He's always wanted to be part of the group, just to blend into the crowd, and still does. When people talk to him, they are amazed to find that he's so shy. Sometimes he can hardly get the words out, he's so self-conscious. He'll go to a party and stand in a corner all night, not sure if people will talk to him." (Kay McEnroe, talking to Donald McLachlan, 'Woman')

Sunday, June 27, 1982

In 'The Sunday Express' John McEnroe Snr. tells Clive Hirschhorn, "He started playing tennis properly when he was eight. That's when I took up the game as well. Except I was 32. For two glorious years I was able to beat him. Then he turned ten and wiped the court with me. And even at ten he had an intensity in his game – and competitiveness – that was frightening. As soon as I became aware of it, I just knew tennis would be his life. He always played to win. Coming second was the pits. That's still his attitude today. It has to be. If it weren't, he wouldn't be the world's best player. Even when he plays ping-pong with his two younger brothers, he plays to win."

Monday, June 28, 1982
Beat Lloyd Bourne 6-2, 6-2, 6-0

Two years earlier at Wimbledon rain delays had forced John to play both his singles and doubles semi-finals on the second Friday. Borg, however, had won his semi-final singles against Brian Gottfried on the Thursday and was consequently more fresh for that epic five-setter.

127

So you might have expected John do the obvious thing and eschew the doubles when the weather ravaged the tournament this time round. But no. John declared, "Even though it looks as though I'll be playing almost every day there's no way I'll pull out of the doubles. I don't believe you should enter an event unless you plan to finish it. I wouldn't do that just to make sure I do well in singles."

Thankfully his game was coming together. "I haven't been happy with the way I've been playing for some time, but on the whole I hit the ball pretty good today. It's greater consistency on my serve that I need. I really think the last time I had a good match was against Borg at the US Open last September, but I'm pretty critical of myself."

McEnroe felt the tournament was 'difficult' because competitors were having "to practise on wet mud, although the courts here are quite different and, considering everything, very good.

"With all the stoppages it's hard to know what is happening, but everyone is in the same boat."

Wednesday, June 30, 1982
Beat Hank Pfister 6-4, 6-4, 6-4

In the words of Albert Taylor: "The match started at 12 noon because of the rain earlier in the tournament. The umpire was David Mercer and I was on Right Centre Service. It was a bad-tempered affair, both players being "niggly" with Mercer, a service line judge and the net cord judge. Pfister fought hard, but McEnroe was just too strong all round."

Pfister also found time to annoy McEnroe during this last sixteen test. When the Champion served in the third set and shouted, "That was a clear netcord," Pfister smiled and said, "I heard it, John."

"Wanna play two?" enquired McEnroe.

"No," beamed Pfister.

John later confessed, "I got angry about a let call and when something like that goes wrong you never know how important it might be in the end. I tend to float into space and lose my concentration as well.

"And I'm not as intense as I was a couple of years ago. Then, I used to get uptight about every point and that's the way you have to be if you want to stay at the top. I'm trying to get that back."

Two hours and eleven minutes after the Pfister contest ended, John and Peter began their doubles against Rod Frawley and Chris Lewis on Centre Court. Inevitably McEnroe was somewhat jaded and perhaps umpire David Howie was a little harsh to warn him for time-wasting when he sat down too long in his chair after a third set changeover.

When Howie suggested to John that he should enjoy the match, John replied incredulously, "Enjoy it?!" as if the idea had never entered his competitive head.

But it was a duel boasting high drama. John was broken in the fifth game of the final set and had to play brilliantly to save three match points when Frawley served at 5-4. After two hours and twenty-five minutes the favourites scraped through 7-6, 3-6, 8-6.

Friday, July 2, 1982
Beat Johan Kriek 4-6, 6-2, 7-5, 6-3

John battled past Kriek, but it took two hours and nineteen minutes before he recorded his victory.

McEnroe's early diffidence was exploited in the fifth game, when he dropped his serve after committing three double faults. At the changeover, he smashed his racquet on the courtside chair, earning a warning.

But in the second he levelled affairs by twice breaking Kriek. The next set saw Kriek fighting ahead, capturing McEnroe's serve to love in the first game. John recovered from that setback, but then promptly lost his serve at the start of set four. The break back came three games later and John duplicated that success in the eighth.

Yet it had been a traumatic match. And as the American prepared for a stressful and strenuous weekend, he probably wished he wasn't still competing in the men's doubles event.

His semi-final with Peter Fleming against Kevin Curren and Steve Denton had to be halted for the night when the holders led 6-2, 6-4, 2-6.

Saturday, July 3, 1982
Beat Tim Mayotte 6-3, 6-1, 6-2

"This Wimbledon is better than last year. My best Wimbledon was when I first came here in 1977. I was like a tourist – an unknown.

"I know basically how I'll play him [Connors]. You should certainly see a good match. Where I will be in trouble is if he gets his serve in a groove."

According to Mayotte, "It should be some final. McEnroe is probably the most talented player in the world, but both he and Connors are like sharks smelling blood. When they sense a weakness, they home in for the kill."

* Tempers flared in John's doubles semi when he argued too long with the umpire after his serve at match point was called out. Steve Denton and Kevin Curren took offence. Apparently Denton and McEnroe nearly came to blows in the locker room afterwards.

"There was a violent argument," confirmed Curren. "No punches were thrown, but it could have got very nasty. Steve was ready to hit him, but McEnroe appeared to pull back."

Sunday, July 4, 1982
Lost to Jimmy Connors 3-6, 6-3, 6-7, 7-6, 6-4

McEnroe kept his temper in check and battled furiously, but after four hours and fifteen minutes Jimmy Connors became Wimbledon Champion for the second time.

Jimmy's wife, Patti, declared, "I'm so proud of him, but I'm sorry someone had to lose. It was sad looking across at John and at his father."

And Jimmy himself added, "It was a life-and-death struggle in the sense that it was all-out guts play. We both gave everything we had and that is why I like playing McEnroe. He brings out the best in me because I know that he is going to fight for every ball."

And McEnroe most certainly did strain for everything. He seized the first set having countered two break points, which could have left him reeling at 0-3. As it was, he held serve to 1-2 and broke Connors to love in the sixth game. When the No.2 seed dropped his serve the next time around, McEnroe soon led 6-3.

In the second set Connors reached 2-0, lost five points in a row in the next game to concede his serve, but captured John's delivery in the fourth game and took the set in thirty three minutes.

McEnroe continued to struggle in the third set as Connors raced again to a 2-0 lead. But at 30-all in the tenth game, Connors fired two consecutive double-faults and McEnroe soon wrapped up the ensuing tiebreaker 7-2.

McEnroe came so close to winning Wimbledon in the next set. He was unable to convert two break-points that came his way in the first game, but fortunately neither could Connors in the sixth game. But when the second tie-break began, the New Yorker scored the first point against serve to lead 3-2 with his two service points to come.

But somehow Connors just reached a superb drop shot from John, and when McEnroe replied with a volley that would normally have been a decisive winner, Connors responded with an amazing reflex volley to recoup the leeway.

The holder served to make 4-3, but Jimmy held serve to 5-4 and John then dropped a service point which allowed Connors to win the tie-breaker, 7-5. Incredibly, then, John had been just three points from victory!

Perhaps it weighed on the 23-year old's mind, for he dropped serve in the third game of the deciding set and could make no further impression on the match. Connors took the title in decisive style with an aggressive serve, which sent the chalk flying.

Ten minutes after losing to Connors, disappointed John returned to Centre Court. But he had nothing left to give. Peter McNamara and Paul McNamee regained their title with a 6-3, 6-2 victory in 49 minutes. At least the final rally provided marvellous entertainment for the fans, but McNamara's winning forehand down the middle must have been a dagger in the heart for poor John.

Still, Wimbledon showed him some compassion. A club official stated: "It was an incredible thing to do. He went straight back to play again, even though he was quite entitled to demand ninety minutes rest. There is no disputing it, the man has guts."

Next, McEnroe had to face the press. It seems that the young American had been invited to become a member of the All England Club between the two finals, for the topic came up in his conference. John declared, "It's definitely a nice thing."

About the men's final he murmured, "I thought I could have played better but Jimmy won it fair and square. I have enjoyed Wimbledon more this year, but perhaps I put so much energy into my self-control that I lost something from the rest of my game."

* In the 'Sunday Mirror', it was announced that John had appeared free of charge in a TV commercial to raise funds for research into cystic fibrosis. McEnroe said, "I fight hard to win each match. These kids fight hard to stay alive."*

Monday, July 5, 1982

Said Connors: "He defended that title with pride. If I had been pushed further, that would have been it … McEnroe will be back to win again – he's that sort of guy."

At Heathrow, John told reporters, "No words, no words." Asked if he felt shattered, McEnroe just smiled and nodded. His father added, "He's very disappointed. But you can't win them all."

Thursday, July 15, 1982

John flew into England on Concorde to take part in a "Special Dunlop Day." The sports company had imported juniors from eleven countries to be coached by the American at Bisham Abbey, Buckinghamshire.

McEnroe was joined by his own coach, Tony Palafox, together with Rod Laver and Tom Okker. And so that a little pro-am tennis was possible, celebrities James Hunt and JPR Williams were on hand, too.

McEnroe was still recovering from his six hours thirty-two minutes' Davis Cup win over Mats Wilander when he arrived in England. But he made 10-year old Michelle Oldham's[11] dreams come true for the "Jim'll Fix It" TV programme, coached the juniors and played some exhibition sets so that everyone went home happy.

Saturday, July 17, 1982

A 153-year old stone-built Methodist Church at Wetherby, Yorkshire. Outside stand an expectant, screaming mob of 2,000. The reason? The marriage of Peter Fleming to English model, Jenny Hudson.

John McEnroe, best man and a childhood friend of Fleming, proved the cause of the excitement. To avoid his seething mass of admirers, John, never comfortable in such situations, slipped into the church by the back door.

Yet the fans were not the only ones to be kept waiting. For Jenny, 24-year old daughter of a local councillor, arrived quarter of

---

[11] In 1992, Ms. Oldham was playing collegiate tennis in America.

an hour late in a white Rolls Royce.

During the service, people outside the church jostled each other for vantage points. Teenage girls Janet Wright and Julie Myers, wearing John McEnroe tee-shirts and pink carnations, had an agonising eight hour wait for their hero.

Fortunately John appreciated their gesture. As he emerged from the church he noticed the two girls and rewarded them with a big grin. After posing with the bride and groom for photographers, he delighted some more fans by waving and shaking a few hands.

McEnroe was obviously bewildered by events. "What a hell of a crowd," he murmured. "I must be more popular than I thought."

Benson & Hedges Championships

Wednesday, November 10, 1982

After a decidedly depressing year for John McEnroe, in which he was knocked off his pedestal as the world's No.1 tennis player, the American returned to the venue where that cruel slump started. But if the Benson & Hedges Championships of the previous November marked the beginning of his decline, McEnroe was perceptive enough to realise that the Wembley Arena could initiate his rehabilitation.

In truth, he was all at sea for a while against young Claudio Panatta, until experience told in a rigorous tussle.

At first McEnroe was surprisingly listless and although a break point fell to him in the fourth game he was not enjoying his customary progress. As the number one seed's difficulty in gaining a discernible rhythm increased, he let in the Italian who gratefully swooped to break serve for 4-3.

However, any thoughts that McEnroe would be devoured with a predatory air were soon dispelled. The losing Wimbledon finalist quelled the Roman fires to move level in the eighth game, benefiting from two double faults.

Henceforth McEnroe surged on relentlessly and when his 22-year old opponent dropped serve again four games later, it permitted him the first set 7-5.

After being subjected to great pressure in the fifth game of the second set McEnroe finally dislodged his adversary 7-5, 6-2 in one hour and twenty-five minutes.

133

Umpire Ian Stirk had no real problems, although a linesman was accused of deliberate bias by the winner, who explained his irritation was evoked by fatigue. McEnroe had only left Australia on Sunday night, arriving by Concorde fifty hours later, and he confessed: "I don't really know what time zone I'm in."

Thursday, November 11, 1982

John underwent a stiff examination from hard-hitting newcomer Mark Dickson before securing his quarter-final berth in the Benson & Hedges Championships.

At one stage the below-par McEnroe trailed 0-3 in the second set, but Dickson failed to increase the deficit and the number one seed gratefully hung on to overcome his spirited opponent 6-3, 6-4 in eighty-eight tense minutes.

The 22-year old from Florida, who had turned pro in July and had since catapulted himself to 35 in the world rankings, possessed a booming serve, which even McEnroe found at times impossible to return.

Then at 0-3, 15-40 John produced two stunning winners. The first was a forehand and a subtle backhand pass followed.

After that Dickson barely knew what had hit him. Although he held serve in the seventh game to lead 4-3, the tidal wave emerging on the opposite side of the net soon washed him away.

For McEnroe it was a performance he would most likely wish to forget. The crowds baited him, especially in the third game of the second set when umpire Roger Smith reversed a service call after the New Yorker had hit a perfect return.

"With all the problems in the game today, you've got a nerve to call that ball out. Your logic is really sick. If I don't complain now you will screw it up when it really counts," yelled the American.

Barring his path now was the sporadically brilliant teenager Henri Leconte, who declared, "It will be a good chance to prove myself."

McEnroe's aims were slightly loftier – to illustrate the sharpness he had sorely lacked throughout the year.

With Peter Fleming, beat Richard Lewis and Frew McMillan 6-3, 6-4

"I have in fact known McEnroe since he was twelve. The great coach, Harry Hopman, took me over to his court in New York and after I'd seen McEnroe hitting a few balls, Hopman said, 'I think he is going to be good.' I shall never forget that moment.

"I also played John in San Francisco in 1982. It was a second round match and I lost 6-1, 6-1, but again it was a memorable day. John had lost in the US Open two weeks previously and was psyched up for San Francisco. He was brilliant against me. He ran the full width of the court to smash back one of my smashes. I made the ball bounce up high and he nearly ran over a linesman getting to the shot. In the final, he gained revenge on Connors, 6-1, 6-3. The final was the closest match he had all week.

"The doubles at Wembley I remember for losing my opening service game. Bad news against anyone, but against them, a disaster. I served badly that game and am surprised by the umpire's book that I got 50% of my first serves in. I remember the game being worse than that.

"The overall match was very quiet or flat, as we say. That means it was pretty poor tennis, with no long or exciting rallies to get the crowd going. I remember thinking how we were not troubling our opposition and this was reflected by the fact we never got to deuce on their services. All in all, because John never got angry – perhaps Frew and I had failed!" (Richard Lewis)

Friday, November 12, 1982

6-3, 7-5 was the score over Leconte, with a break in the sixth game of the first set and the eleventh game of the second.

"It was a difficult match – he's no slouch. These young guys are not respecting their elders anymore," joked McEnroe, who is only four years the senior. The American was entirely serious when he added, "He just went for broke and was dangerous, but he didn't always know where the ball was going. When he settles down, he'll beat some good players."

Leconte's gutsy spirit was epitomised in the first game, where McEnroe had to dig his way out of a 0-40 pit before holding serve …

For ninety-nine minutes the two gleamed with brilliant serves and outright return winners. The 7,000 lucky enough to be present saw some remarkable reflexes at the net and John was once again near his compelling best. If the going got awkward, he lifted himself by a fraction. It was his passes – "the McEnroe special – under pressure, taking the ball on the rise, counter-attacking with perfection," as the late Dan Maskell once described them, that finally marked him as the superior player.

Saturday, November 13, 1982
Beat Steve Denton 6-1, 6-4

The Texan only garnered three points as he lost the first four games and in the second set he claimed a mere five points during McEnroe's five service games.

❧

"John's good for tennis and he's a big personality. Sure, I remember beating him at Cincinnati in August 1982: it was a good feeling, but not so pleasant for him, I imagine!

"There's no animosity between us. Players only have confrontations on court.

"Personally, I think he's fine as a person. He's just trying to make a living and besides, people on court and off court are different. I don't think he's been given his privacy.

"Does he practise hard? When he gets down it it, he does; the trouble with being a great talent is you feel you can get away with things.

"But he is beginning to take better care of his body. As you get older, you have to. I think he's seen the power and fitness of the other players and now he's making a conscious effort to get back." (Steve Denton, speaking in June 1988)

Sunday, November 14, 1982

John, although still maddened by his loss of form in the summer, continued his rejuvenated spell and so took his winning streak since the US Open debacle to twenty-one matches without conceding a set.

In front of an expectant crowd he confirmed his improvement with a highly competent 6-3, 6-2, 6-4 dismissal of fellow countryman, Brian Gottfried.

John's fourth triumph at this tournament in five attempts prompted him to say of his domination, "I hope people aren't getting sick of seeing me in the final." This they were not. It was hard to tire of a man whose artistry with a racquet was so breathtaking and although critics pointed out he seldom smiled on court, McEnroe warned them not to read too much into this. "When I play well I really enjoy it. I may not smile and show it the way some players do, but I love the competition of tennis."

Gottfried lacked the necessary verve to severely trouble McEnroe and if he ever looked like challenging the New Yorker, it was countered by tennis of another class.

On the second deuce at 1-1, McEnroe suddenly applied the pressure to expose the limitations of his opponent with disarming ease. It proved a merciless spell in which the left-hander won ten points in a row for a 4-1 lead. What worried the sixth seeded Gottfried most was McEnroe's swinging serve to the backhand and he later admitted to having great difficulty reading it.

In the second set, the champion chose the fifth game to move ahead, capturing eight successive points and the inflexible Gottfried must have then known it wasn't to be his day – especially against a McEnroe brimming with confidence.

In fact, John was so pleased that he said after the match, "I'm playing much better now." Typically he didn't feel satisfied by that: "But I don't think I have improved enough."

McEnroe's only lapse in superiority occurred when he suffered a fall in the sixth game of the third set. Gottfried grabbed his chance to square the match at 3-3, but immediately dropped his own serve to love. And that, as they say, was that. We had one uneasy feeling afterwards – that John had totally dictated proceedings and, if he had so wished, could have finished the match much quicker.

* *In the 'Mail on Sunday', Patrick Collins recounted a little incident that had apparently occurred earlier in the week when John's physiotherapist Cynthia Tucker had been soothing the player's temples and probing his neck as he lay on the massage table.*

Ms. Tucker told tournament referee Colin Hess, "I'm getting him ready to play tennis." Hess replied, "Splendid. Glad you're starting at the right end." Hess told Collins, "He laughed. Had a good chuckle. I knew he would. He's a human being, you see. People tend to forget that."

Cynthia would tell me six years later, "John is one of the most charming people I've met in my life. He's very sincere and has been much berated by the media. The image he has been given is totally false and I think anyone who has met him off court would uphold my opinion."

John and Peter show off their first Wimbledon silverware, at Wimbledon in 1979, and are applauded by Sir Brian Burnett who stands between them.

1984, Wimbledon Centre Court:
John serves to Wally Masur.

McEnroe struggled during Wimbledon '82, not least because he had a troublesome ankle injury

The epitome of perfection:
John has just defeated Connors to win Wimbledon in July 1984

A pensive John returns serve during the 1985 Wimbledon Championships

Wembley Arena, 1986:
John and Peter Fleming once again displayed their doubles prowess.

Moody Mac questions a linecall on Centre Court in 1988

A picture that encapsulates the determination displayed by John at Wimbledon 1989

A press conference, Stella Artois Championships, June 1990

The last singles on Centre Court – McEnroe demonstrates his reflex skills on the volley

André Agassi calls time on John's last Wimbledon singles bid

The genius is still there – Olympia, December 1998

Wimbledon 1999 – it may only have been the mixed doubles, but John wanted the crown very badly

1983

Masters[12]	Runner-Up	Lendl	64 64 62
Philadelphia	WON	Lendl	46 76 64 63
Richmond	2nd Round	Tanner	63 57 62
Las Vegas	1st Round	Waltke	36 63 64
WCT Finals	WON	Lendl	62 46 63 67 76
WCT New York	WON	Gerulaitis	63 75
French Open	Quarter-final	Wilander	16 62 64 60
Stella Artois	Runner-Up	Connors	63 63
Wimbledon	WON	C. Lewis	62 62 62
Canadian Open	Semi-Final	Jarryd	63 76
ATP Championships	Runner-Up	Wilander	64 64
US Open	4th Round	Scanlon	76 76 46 63
San Francisco	Runner-Up	Lendl	36 76 64
Australian Indoor	WON	Leconte	61 64 75
Benson & Hedges	WON	Connors	75 61 64
Antwerp	WON	G. Mayer	64 63 64
Australian Open	Semi-Final	Wilander	46 63 64 63

Davis Cup:

V Argentina lost to Clerc 76 60 36 46 75; lost to Vilas 64 60 61; with Fleming, beat Clerc/Vilas 26 10-8 61 36 61

V Ireland beat Sorensen 63 62 62; beat Doyle 97 63 63; with Fleming, beat Doyle/Sorensen 62 63 64

"This is going to be the big year for me. I am desperate to be the top player again and now I believe I can handle the aggravation that goes with it. I am an emotional person. I can't predict what I'll do on a tennis court, but now I know that, if I am to get back to the top, I've got to change.

---

[12] Part of the 1982 Tennis Year

"I must accept I cannot be a private person and that people will want to see and talk to me. I like being nice." Thus spoke John McEnroe before trying to win back the Volvo Masters crown at the beginning of 1983.

And over the following twelve months he hit peaks and troughs. A few days after those words were spoken Ivan Lendl drubbed him 6-4, 6-4, 6-2 in that '82 Masters final, to which McEnroe muttered, "I really believed I was playing well."

But the important thing in life is to learn from your mistakes and John certainly did just that. Having defeated Tim Mayotte at Philadelphia's semi-final stage to set up another meeting with Lendl, he arrived at a press interview smiling, "because I just talked to Don Budge, who was giving me a little advice for tomorrow. He just told me I can't do worse than I have in the past. A lot of people are telling me I have to attack more and that is what I am going to do, because at least that way, if I lose, I'll lose a lot faster."

He didn't lose. Nor was it fast. 4-6, 7-6, 6-4, 6-3 was the final score in McEnroe's favour and he knew it was an important victory.

The two next clashed on May 1 for the WCT Dallas title. McEnroe won a four hour and sixteen minute five setter 6-2, 4-6, 6-3, 6-7, 7-6. Many experts felt that John's racquet, a mid-size graphite borrowed from brother Patrick, was mainly responsible for the dazzling display. John himself remarked that "if I can keep on improving like the way I have since I picked this racquet up [Dunlop's Max 200G], I might end up using it forever." And he did, for the remainder of his time on the professional tour.

The Dallas success was made all the more sweet because John had been troubled by a shoulder injury: "I have seen three doctors and I've had three different answers." It wasn't until his English osteopath Cynthia Tucker saw him in June that the problem was sorted out.

In the meantime, the circuit duly moved on to Paris and the French Open where John fell to'82 winner Mats Wilander 1-6, 6-2, 6-4, 6-0 after leading 4-2, 40-15 in the third set.

It was a strange match. John pulled a leg muscle at 3-2 in that third set and from 4-2, 40-15 he lost 23 consecutive points to trail by two sets to one and 0-1, 0-40 in the fourth. John said, "I choked the third set. I should have won it 6-1. I let up and couldn't get my concentration back again. It started when I missed a few balls. It happens to me more on clay than on other surfaces. There are no excuses. He played a lot better than I did."

McEnroe made amends at Wimbledon, becoming champion for the second time in the most one-sided final since 1974. Despite this, Wilander dispatched him from the ATP Championships and at Flushing Meadow John lost to rival Bill Scanlon.

On that occasion John remarked, "I could blame the [Flushing Meadow] crowd, the umpire, the planes and 50 other things, but in the final analysis I can only blame myself for not playing well enough." (In time McEnroe would say that his poor footwork had been mainly responsible for the result.)

When 19-year old Wilander in the Australian Open again vanquished the American, his claim to be No.1 looked a little flimsy. And the Melbourne defeat hurt John. He played with a taped right knee after straining it in practice, but he didn't mention it at the press conference. Instead, he merely stated that his performance was "shocking" and, "He taught me a lesson."

Wilander's only significant flaw was a third round loss to Tanner at Wimbledon, but when thrashed in January '84 by McEnroe at the '83 Masters, an event the New Yorker won by easily beating Lendl, he could only be placed second or third.

So, sure enough, 48 hours after dowsing Lendl's spirit McEnroe was proclaimed World Champion for 1983 by the International Tennis Federation. "This is the way I would like to play all the time," he admitted. "But don't read too much into what happened here. The year is only beginning and there's five guys capable of winning the big tournament titles."

Even allowing for this, John had re-emerged.

Stella Artois Championships

Monday, June 6, 1983

Many fans preferred to watch John practise with Brian Teacher rather than see the actual first round matches.

Tuesday, June 7, 1983
Beat Jeff Borowiak 6-3, 6-3

John was in reflective mood after falling over nine times during his success on the slippery centre court at Queen's Club.

He expressed the opinion that he still had much to achieve during his career, commenting, "I am no longer considered a younger player though I'm still only 24. Nobody will care about me in ten or maybe even five years, so I have to make the most of the talent I've got."

Cheering up a fraction, John continued, "I am looking forward to toning down. I have done some things I regret but I am not fifty. I am still learning."

Turning to consider the playing conditions, calm McEnroe asserted, "It was difficult to keep a foothold while hitting the ball and I suppose the court was close to being unplayable.

"It would be a shame if the whole of the tournament was played in these conditions, but I suppose that Wimbledon could be the same."

Wednesday, June 8, 1983
Beat Freddie Sauer 6-1, 7-6

McEnroe played very much within himself, saving three set points in the second set before holding, and losing, a match point when he served at 6-5. However, the American ace regained his composure, seizing the tiebreak 7-4.

Thursday, June 9, 1983
Beat Cassio Motta 7-5, 6-2

John again struggled against modest opposition, but by producing winners at crucial moments he managed to battle past the Brazilian's resistance.

The start of the match was delayed for an hour due to the first rain of the week, but when they got under way the American was soon protesting about the noise emanating from a two-way radio which lay "in the hands of a linesman", according to 'The Times.'

Afterwards, McEnroe pledged to defend beleaguered Argentinian, Guillermo Vilas, who faced a one-year suspension and a fine of $20,000 for allegedly accepting a $60,000 guarantee to play an event in Rotterdam.[13]

"I plan to make a stand on behalf of my friend," announced John.

---

[13] In January 1984 a three-man committee decided the fine, but not the suspension, would be enforced.

"I will do whatever I can to help him. I feel very bad about it."

McEnroe explained why he supported the concept of guarantees and therefore supported Vilas. "As long as the prize money is enough and the tournament is working within a budget, what is the difference between spending money on a player, or billboards, or advertising?"

Friday, June 10, 1983
Beat Brian Gottfried 6-0, 6-1

This quick-fire triumph met with a very modest explanation from John: "He didn't play well for him and everything went my way."

"My serve is ten to fifteen per cent harder if I hit it properly and my volleying is now more penetrative," added McEnroe, praising his new racquet, Dunlop's Max 200 G, for his improvement. "It helped my shoulder injury and it's helped my game."

John disclosed he had put on weight for added strength. In addition, his shoulder was apparently responding to daily stretching exercises.

Saturday, June 11, 1983
Beat Kevin Curren 7-5, 7-6

McEnroe became aggrieved when umpire John Parry issued a warning for abuse of equipment. Spectators and press believed John was twirling his racquet when it slipped from his grip.

The match threatened to get away from John, too. He led 5-2 in the second set and later admitted, "I lit up. I thought it was in the bag and in the end I was a little lucky."

Superstitiously, the player opined, "I won this tournament in '81 and then went on to win Wimbledon, so perhaps victory here means something and is an omen."

Sunday, June 12, 1983
Lost to Jimmy Connors 6-3, 6-3

Connors struck near-perfect returns in this 82 minute final and he said afterwards, "I don't really think I can hit the ball any better."

In contrast to Jimmy's focussed finesse, a dog barking, a man's cough and a TV cameraman all upset McEnroe and he sarcastically urged a spectator in a blue shirt to "keep moving."

At 2-2 in the second set John aggravated his left shoulder when he lunged unsuccessfully for a volley. That "was unfortunate because it happened when I was just beginning to play better. I just did not play well enough overall. I picked up my game a couple of levels but it still wasn't sufficient. I didn't play all that badly but I hope I can serve a little better at Wimbledon."

John conceded that Connors, "in great form", had to be "the favourite for Wimbledon."

* The 'Sunday People' speculated about the depth of McEnroe's love for new girlfriend, model Stella Hall.

According to a Londoner, Jenny Frost, who had been out with them, "Stella seems really good for John."

The paper also quoted an unspecified 'friend' of the couple as saying: "Something changed in John after he met Stella. He's not the most patient of men yet he spent hours coaching her to improve her tennis.

"The old McEnroe would never have done that. He'd have been bored after a few minutes.

"John's not the type who goes in for one night stands, even though some really beautiful women have thrown themselves at him."

Ms. Hall, daughter of a North Carolina tobacco family, confessed in the same article, "I want to spend as much time as possible with John."

Thursday, June 16, 1983

Connors and McEnroe practised together at Wimbledon for ninety minutes. John was later accused of swearing at courtside photographers, though he argued in 'The News of the World' that their presence "was another intrusion into my privacy – which I value highly."

He further maintained " ... until you lose the freedom to walk the street without being pestered you can't understand how annoying and restricting it is."

Friday, June 17, 1983

McEnroe was at the David Lloyd Slazenger Racquet Club in Heston, Middlesex to draw raffle winners on a charity night in aid of muscular dystrophy research.

John duly drew the raffle, posed benignly with six-year old Caroline Fick and was all set to umpire a £50 a seat charity match.

But when he was interviewed by BBC's Des Lynam, an American crew began filming them and a bitter fight broke out between the two crews. McEnroe stopped mid-sentence, jumped into a car and made a rapid exit.

Again using the following Sunday's 'News of the World' as his mouthpiece, John said, "I felt sorry for the organisers of the charity function I attended ... I felt for the children present, those who'd put a lot of work into the evening, the people who came."

Saturday, June 18, 1983

Men's tour pro Drew Gitlin dredges up a story from John's immature youth for 'Daily Star' hack Bryan Cooney.

"I've known Mac since he was a kid," divulged Drew, who had been beaten by John in the third round of the French Open. "He never grew up with any great respect for anyone or anything. When he was sixteen they were calling him to court to play in the US National Hard Courts – he was sitting in the dressing room playing poker. He sent someone to tell them he was in the bathroom. Believe me, he wasn't going anywhere until he had finished that hand."

But Briton Chris Bradnam remembers going on a six-week junior circuit with his compatriot, Andrew Jarrett, over twenty years ago. According to Bradnam, McEnroe was "very much alienated" from his fellow Americans because he was "blinkered in everything he wanted to do," It seems he was determined to be the best one day.

Nevertheless, John often chatted with Bradnam and Jarrett. Says Chris, "He was definitely looking for company."

Sunday, June 19, 1983

John tells Fred Burcombe in 'The News of the World' that he is a perfectionist to the degree that he "could never treat anything on a casual, nothing-at-stake basis."

McEnroe also revealed that his ankle had been really "playing him up" during Wimbledon '82 and that he might not have reached the final without Stella's support from back in the States.

Finally, the controversial star pointed out, "It's the wrong impression to think that I don't like England or its people. Sometime I'll come here and see all the sights and do the things I want, without any tennis distractions." He continued, "Despite any image I might have, I still receive much more fan mail from England than any other country – and I'm grateful for that support."

Wimbledon

Monday, June 20, 1983

With the 1983 Wimbledon Championship beckoning, all the usual commotion that surrounded John McEnroe was doing its best to destroy him. The newsmen were anticipating a tussle with Ivan Lendl, with whom John had collided earlier in the year at the WCT Dallas Finals.

So what did the 1982 runner-up make of the Czech's chances? "It would be wrong to say he isn't capable of reaching the final. He has a big serve, he volleys reasonably and he has penetrating passing shots and returns. At Wimbledon you don't need much more than a serve and returns."

There was the added difficulty that people wanted to see John dealt with ruthlessly at the first sign of trouble.

The late Fred Perry chimed in, "I can see it reaching the point where someone says to a player like McEnroe, 'That's it, you're out.' If you want to make an example of someone it's certainly no good throwing out the lesser players. McEnroe is very intelligent. He's got everything there is. But he's an introvert, a loner and he has strong ideas of his own about what's what. Through that, he gets out on a limb on court and then he doesn't quite know how to get back. The main problem is that he wasn't clobbered when he first played."

The previous week John had helped open The West Midlands Tennis Centre at Telford. He did everything asked of him – waving to the crowds and signing autographs. "That was great," he said later. "Now that's the way I want more and more people to think of me. I hope I can go into Wimbledon and show the people there that there really are good things about me.

"I've said it before, I know, but the time has come when I really must start enjoying my tennis and giving people enjoyment in watching me. It's been said I can play only when I have the rage inside me. I don't believe that, and so now I have to prove it.

"At Wimbledon it's autographs ... even if you slow down you're mobbed. But I used to be starry-eyed myself when I was young and I know how much it hurts to be snubbed by someone you hero-worship."

At Telford, John in fact met one of his idols, Jimmy Greaves. He told the former soccer star, "When I won the Wimbledon title in 1981 it was like a million pound weight had been lifted off my shoulders. Within hours it was plunged back on again as the row blew up about the dinner."

And Welshman Mike Davies, Executive Director of the ATP, lamenting the lack of discipline in the game, said insensitively on the eve of Wimbledon '83, "One disqualification will bring everyone to their senses and it could come in a major Grand Prix event."

Referee Alan Mills tried to deflate the uneasiness, saying he would be "firm but fair". It still looked like a 'get McEnroe' campaign.

Thus all eyes descended on the well-laundered Court No.1 for McEnroe's opening ordeal against hard-hitting Ben Testerman, in a rematch of their French Open meeting when John's temper had invariably overflown. With all the worries heaped on his shoulders, he behaved well. Typically the tabloids focused on his complaints to both foot fault judges and his sarcastic self-admonishment:

"Great, John, keep up the great tennis."

"Give up the game!"

"What's wrong with me?"

After his 6-4, 7-6, 6-2 win John half-explained why he'd been so negative. In practice he had torn a shoulder muscle and it had required treatment.

Would it dog him throughout the tournament? And if so, with what consequences?

Wednesday, June 22, 1983
With Peter Fleming, beat Chris Bradnam and David Lloyd 6-4, 6-4, 6-3

"'How are you doing?' McEnroe asked me before we went on,

though he hadn't seen me since our junior days. He obviously remembered the six-week Orange Bowl Junior Circuit we'd both played on.

"McEnroe continued, 'What are you doing now?' I told him I was coaching and he responded, "But you qualified for the dubs here, didn't you?"

In fact, David and I had won through the qualifying pretty easily. Sundstrom and Giammalva got in the draw as lucky losers and reached the quarter-finals. We'd beaten them in straight sets.

I didn't lose my serve in the entire match and I aced McEnroe once.[14] John's backhand was impossible to pick because he just used his wrist at the last moment. Peter Fleming was very good at the net. They were so tough to break – we only reached thirty once." (Chris Bradnam)

Thursday, June 23, 1983

Perhaps Wimbledon should have taken heed. After three days of sunshine, the courts fell under the shadow of stormy clouds. Conflict between players and officials grew.

No place was this troubling atmosphere more apparent than on hazy Court No.1 where John soon found himself in all kinds of trouble against the deceptive Rumanian Florin Segarceanu.

4-6, 6-2, 6-3, 6-3 was the final score and it reflected well on young Segarceanu, a stylish shotmaker, who had been a member of his country's Davis Cup team since 1979. It was his well-planned and varied ploys that rattled McEnroe and they inadvertently caused the outbursts.

The first incident occurred following a McEnroe double fault in the opening set. A vehement swipe at the turf caused a divot and a warning for racquet abuse from umpire Malcolm Huntington. Then, in game one, set two, Segarceanu put his hand up to show he was not ready to receive John's serve due to spectators in his line of view. McEnroe did not see his opponent's gesture and went through with his service. He didn't really know what was going on when he told Huntington, "If you are going to call me for technicalities I'm going

---

[14]Chris' memory unfortunately plays tricks on him! He dropped his serve in the first set and it was in fact Fleming whom he aced!

to walk off and you'll have the default you obviously want."

At 4-1 in the same set, after one of five foot-faults, John summoned the referee in an unsuccessful attempt to get Allan Higgs, the relevant linesman, replaced. As Alan Mills hastened to the scene, McEnroe passed the time by saying to Huntington, a sports journalist from York, "You are doing a wonderful job for somebody who doesn't know two plus two." Mills attempted to restore order – "I was right behind the line judge and he's doing a competent job" – to which McEnroe replied, "Do you know what the word means?"

Later, the number two seed said, "I'm not ready to become a martyr at this stage of my career. It would take an awful lot for me to walk out of a tournament, but that still does not stop me standing up for myself when I think I'm unfairly treated. I did nothing to be ashamed of – and even the referee agreed with me. I questioned one call for ten seconds and anything I did I had a perfect right to do.

"I'm serious about walking out in the sense that if people continue to make unfair decisions I won't continue the match. The umpire was edgy and made some wrong decisions. There's no doubt in my mind that people are looking for things from me because everything I do is scrutinised."

At 2-0 in the third set Mills was once again summoned to arbitrate. The umpire had given a penalty point against the young American for hitting a ball at the net. "What's going on here?" asked the bemused McEnroe. "This is no fun whatsoever. I want it to be fun." Although Huntington's decision was reversed, quite correctly in the opinion of John Parsons of 'The Daily Telegraph', Mills firmly rejected McEnroe's appeals for the umpire to be removed: "He is competent and he's staying in the chair."

John picked up on his dismay viz-a-viz the proceedings, repeating his wish for a more tranquil environment to be linked with his matches. "I don't enjoy playing here at the moment. I've already apologised for things I've done in the past and I don't claim to be the greatest guy in the world."

Saturday, June 25, 1983

"At last! Mac is getting the message," announced 'The Sunday Express.'

Certainly in checking 21-year old Californian Brad Gilbert 6-2, 6-

2, 6-2 John did his utmost to behave.

Evidence that he was toiling desperately to control himself was confirmed when he first served. He stood back from the chalky baseline to stop possible foot faults. One recalled that the French Championship had left him $1,750 worth of fines away from automatic suspension. Perhaps John was similarly aware.

For the 24-year old genius to undergo a complete transformation was asking too much. In the third game there were raised eyebrows at a late call. Five games on, what looked a perfectly angled volley was judged out. McEnroe thought it just caught the line, but after a mild word with Bob Jenkins he went no further.

Seventy-nine minutes was all the Centre Court had to scrutinise McEnroe and later he told the press, "I would class this match as satisfactory. I am more content with my form at the end than at the beginning. I am not saying that it was the best match I have ever played, but I am serving better and being more aggressive – so things are moving in the right direction. My shoulder is going pretty well. I am getting a fair amount of treatment on it. It sometimes gets sore and I have to take care of it, but it is playable, if not yet in perfect condition.

"Nothing outside the playing of tennis has worried me. My only distraction has been what I have read about myself.

"I have played Scanlon [his next opponent] once before on grass and won, but he is a tough player and must be going pretty well. He has beaten me in the past and I'm fully aware that he is a dangerous player … It has never crossed my mind that I will become the greatest player ever, nor do I worry about winning the Grand Slam. Realistically I don't think I would do it … Each year here is different, although I don't really remember too much about the past years … I have done well here and that has got to say something, although at times I haven't enjoyed myself. The line calls were all right today, there were a couple of mistakes. The big players are still left in the tournament, but I cannot worry about anything except Scanlon and the next match."

Early evening deflected McEnroe from doing that, showing as it did how hard he found it to keep quiet when he felt badly treated. The Code of Conduct report, imposing a $500 fine, said about his 7-6, 7-5, 6-3 doubles win against Bud Cox and Jakob Hlasek: "On the second to last point of the [Court No.3] match, a line judge erroniously (sic) caught a ball still in play which he shouldn't have done. After the match Mr. McEnroe was discussing this with the chair umpire (David Mercer) who agreed with Mr. McEnroe that the line judge was in the wrong. The crowd heard the discussion and a spectator started to bait and provoke Mr. McEnroe with comments (comments were inaudible) …"

These incited McEnroe and Mercer felt duty bound to report his words. It is a pity John should have been penalised due to the totally inconsiderate nature of his antagonist.

Sunday, June 26, 1983

"I don't mind having a reason for protesting at a mistake of my own, or an error I consider somebody else has made. The scariest part is when I can offer no explanation for an outburst.

"The perfect illustration of that, and why it's distracting, came in the early rounds of the US Open, only a couple of years ago.

"I sat in the locker room for an hour, talking to myself, convincing myself I had to remain calm, no matter what. Yet in the very first game my concentration snapped when somebody in the stands stood up.

"I immediately reacted scathingly. My words were directed to that one person and only about five people in the crowd heard them.

"As I played on I attempted to analyse why I should have blown and lost my good intentions. It set me back.

"Apparently, the guy's seat was wet and he'd stood up. I apologised to him later during the match – which I won. I went up to him and confessed to him that it was a mistake for me to have shouted as I did. He was pretty nice about this and accepted it well."
(Talking to Fred Burcombe, 'News of the World')

Monday, June 27, 1983
Beat Bill Scanlon 7-5, 7-6, 7-6

"I am a little surprised that Connors was beaten by Kevin Curren, but it does not make my path any easier whatsoever. It seemed there were tougher players in my half anyway … I felt I returned much better, but wasn't really able to put the ball away when I wanted to. I hope I serve better in my next match against Sandy Mayer, whose game is similar to Scanlon's. I thought today I played the big points reasonably well and I feel comfortable.

"Comparing this time now to last year, I feel much better, mostly due to the weather. Last year it seemed as though the second week was rushed, but now it seems as though everything is running on schedule. As far as the foot fault problem I was supposedly having, I decided I did not need that aggravation and so I am now stepping back about one-half inch each time I serve so that there will be no doubts."

* *'The Sun' gave 'a top psychologist's' verdict on the McEnroe psyche: "He is desperate for love and approval – and terrified that the consequences of failure are that he will not get it."*
Wednesday, June 29, 1983

When John met fellow New Yorker Sandy Mayer at Queen's Club in 1979 it was a tempestuous affair. Unaccountably, on Court No.1, his 6-3, 7-5, 6-0 victory refused to catch the imagination.

Nevertheless, the minor incidents that did occur were enough for the tabloids to feed on. "Let me fix McNasty," "I'll sort out the brat" and other headlines of that ilk filled the sports pages, dwarfing an occurrence when McEnroe served for the first set, double-faulted and whacked a ball that happened to flash past his opponent. Mayer went up to the umpire David Mercer, saying, "Next time he smashes the ball violently in my direction I'm going to take matters into my own hands. How hard do you have to hit the ball to be violent? You've got to follow the Code of Conduct."

McEnroe, who from experience wasn't surprised that Mayer had complained, said, "I was just about to apologise when I looked up and saw him at the chair." And that was all – it certainly didn't merit the attention it received.

At one stage McEnroe was penalised for 'racquet abuse' after flinging his racquet to the ground, an action that was loudly applauded by the noisy gallery. "I thought Mercer's decision was a bit hard," said 'The Daily Mail's' Laurie Pignon, echoing common sentiments that certain sections of the Code of Conduct were petty in the extreme.

The match itself didn't delight the connoisseur. Mayer achieved an early break in the second set, but otherwise underwent a miserable time, buckling under pressure.

John, as one had come to expect by now, was not satisfied with his play and spoke of injury: "I pulled a groin muscle slightly in my right leg while practising before the match. I used some Tiger Balm ointment to keep it warm. I felt a little twinge, but if the weather had been warmer I probably wouldn't have noticed it. I had a similar injury in Forest Hills, but it was not so bad this time. In general my fitness is all right. My shoulder is OK and feels a lot better and I shall be all right for the semi-final against Lendl. Whatever happens I will not use it as an excuse. The wind was also difficult out there and played havoc with some of the shots. I knew from playing him in the past that somewhere in the match I would be able to pick up on his serve and get on top."

For many the quarter-final was solely a preview for McEnroe's encounter with Ivan Lendl. A grudge match, the press believed, or "Dynamite Day," "The War Game"…

"I am looking forward to the match," said John. "You are going to see both of us going full out for a win. I have to be aggressive with my serves and volleys and attack his serve whenever possible. He seems to have adjusted well to grass and the fact that he is probably the slight underdog because of my experience takes pressure off him. Whoever wins will be favourite in the final, but that doesn't guarantee victory. You cannot take anything for granted."

* *By summer the dislike between the two had made way for mutual respect. TV commentator Gerald Williams explains: "They were both playing in Europe and McEnroe was offered a lift by Ivan Lendl in Lendl's car. Lendl drove him half way across Europe. On that trip together they seem to have discussed their differences and explained to each other how difficult it is not to feel a certain antagonism towards your closest rival and since then they've been able to become reasonably close chums …"*

Friday, July 1, 1983
Beat Ivan Lendl 7-6, 6-4, 6-4

"I served and volleyed well, but the rest of my game was not at its best. Over the whole match it was one of my best for consistent serves. He had a pretty good angle with his serves and I tried to meet the ball by moving in. There were quite a lot of bad bounces on the court ... I have still got to win another match and cannot take anything for granted.

"It was not a good idea for Lendl to hit a double fault when I had break point (in game7, set 2), especially as there had been no breaks of serve in the match. I think we will have a lot of good matches in the future. The important thing today was that he did not know where my serves were going and that forced him to guess. In the first set he had 85% of his first serves going in and that was pretty good, but he missed a few and that gave me my opportunity. Winning the first set on the tie-break gave me a good psychological boost, for Lendl knew he had to win three sets against someone who was serving well. Although I won in straight sets it was a close match ...

"I kept him off balance and put the pressure on him, but overall I think I can play better. Someone who serves like Lendl should be good on grass, but sometimes he gets a bit lazy on the volleys and that is what let him down. Even so, he proved he can be dangerous on grass as long as he can cope with the mental side ... I was aware that the Prime Minister, Margaret Thatcher, was watching me. It must have been nice for her to see two conservative guys!

"After Wimbledon I have a month off with no tournaments and hopefully I will be celebrating on Sunday."

* *In 'The Sun', John's girl Stella, a keen art student with a degree in business studies, declared, "He's teaching me to play, but I call it 'giggle tennis'.*
"We get on well. He makes me laugh. He's a lamb, a sweetheart. He's really fun to be with. I guess I see a different side to him."

Saturday, July 2, 1983
With Peter Fleming, beat Tim and Tom Gullikson 6-4, 6-3, 6-4

"Every time we lose a doubles match before Wimbledon we seem to win here, so it was a good sign when we lost at Queen's. Hopefully it's a good omen for the singles final as well, although I was not thinking about that match, only trying to win today.

"Naturally the singles is more important to me, but I am proud to have been the No.1 doubles player for the past three or four years. In fact my record is better in doubles than in singles here. The ideal is to be No.1 at both."

* McEnroe's younger brother Patrick was also in action, losing on Court No.2 in the semi-final of the junior competition to Swede, Stefan Edberg.*

"I don't consider myself following in my brother's footsteps. I'm just doing my own thing and haven't decided whether to make tennis a career yet. My first prerogative is to get into college. It feels the same for me playing in the juniors at Wimbledon as it does for any of the other young players – except that I get a lot of extra attention because of my name.

I never give John advice about his behaviour and I never would. I have learned from his experience that it is not worth getting excited on court so I try to be very calm and I think I've done a decent job of it. Right now I am nowhere near the stage of thinking I could be a top player, but I see what it means in terms of my brother. I think it's ridiculous that he is always hounded by the press and other people. He cannot even eat a meal or do anything without being bothered. I do not get any hassle at school because of John and our entire family gets along well."

Sunday, July 3, 1983

"McEnroe is an artist with the racquet. He plays so unlike anyone else." (Chris Lewis)

John regained the Wimbledon title he had let slip in 1982 by crushing unseeded New Zealander Chris Lewis 6-2, 6-2, 6-2 on a Centre Court bathed in sunshine.

Lewis, who only detained the American for eighty-five minutes, admitted, "I just lost to a player who was in another class today. Even my speed around the court was useless. He made so many cold winners."

Lewis sparked off hopes for a dramatic contest when he held serve in the opening game with great flair. McEnroe, determined to assert his authority from the start, then held to love, swiftly broke his opponent and from there the gap continually widened. The loser noted, "There was absolutely nothing I could do to halt the run of play." With a second break in the fifth game the New Yorker banked the set in twenty-six minutes. "Chris is the sort of player, who, if you let him in a match, will make you work for it. I was determined to keep all over him and make him work for every point," John said.

In the second set a thirteen point streak gave McEnroe a 4-1 lead, although Lewis had no cause to be despondent. Reaching the final had surpassed his wildest dreams and as runner-up his prize money of £33,000 doubled his earnings for the year. Whenever a rally developed the unseeded man matched John, but the champion conceded only nine points in twelve service games and returned Lewis' serve with interest, providing the New Zealander with few easy volleys.

In the end, like the seven unseeded Wimbledon finalists before him, Chris Lewis didn't even have a set to show for his commendable endeavour. Only Marty Mulligan and Wilhelm Bungert had earned fewer games. But as he pointed out, "When you have someone at the other end of the court who returns as well as McEnroe, it immediately puts extra pressure on you."

John, on the other hand, didn't experience much pressure. Never before had he played so well in a Grand Slam final. "I was clear favourite and people expected me to win a one-sided match. As long as I kept my game together it was always going to be tough to beat me."

The victory came at an important time for John, who had endured a wretched time in '82 and had not had too much reason for pleasure in early '83. His anxiety vanished, his arms were raised aloft, he shook hands with both opponent and umpire Huntington and then warmly accepted everyone.

He said later, "I feel great to have won. There is no question about that. I am glad to have been able to win in the way people wanted me to. Everything went according to plan. I knew he would be nervous and that I had to get on top of him early. I managed that and I don't think he had a chance of fighting back. I kept all over him and he had an uphill struggle all the way. I have beaten him fairly comfortably twice before and I believe I would have had a harder task against Curren. I feel pretty good physically and in better shape at the end of the tournament than at the start. I feel very good about things today. When I won Wimbledon for the first time there was a lot of pressure on me …"

As to the future, all McEnroe would say was that, "I have started controlling my emotions and in the long run I know I can play better if I learn to harness them completely. I'm the sort of person who needs to get involved in what I'm doing. I can't act like Bjorn and expect to be up for every point. Everyone has his own way of getting psyched up for points. As long as I can do it without hurting anyone's feelings I will be all right."

His intentions had been declared; he should have been a crowd favourite by the time he defended his title in 1984. Sadly, it wasn't to be.

The controversies of the following year were a long way off when McEnroe arrived, six hours after the final, at the Champions' Dinner at the Savoy Hotel – an event he had shunned two years earlier.

"It is a pleasure to be here," said John, continuing, "I would like to thank Wimbledon. They have made an effort to understand what I'm all about, when I don't really know myself. I appreciate the effort they have made and I hope the effort continues from both parties in the future."

At last the warring factions had settled their differences – Wimbledon's policy of 'firm but fair' had paid off.

* In 'The News of the World', John had said in jest, "My girlfriend Stella has seen every set of mine this championship. She's my lucky charm – I'll throw her out the window if I lose!

"I tell you – you get older quicker at Wimbledon. It's a tournament full of tension ... Stella jokes that she has some grey hairs beginning to show. And it's her first time."

* Such was the ease with which McEnroe had gained victory that just a month later British National Team manager Paul Hutchins was writing in 'Tennis World':

"John McEnroe has instinctive, natural ability. This type of talent a player is born with. It cannot be taught... The serve of John McEnroe is probably the most awkward to return in the game, as being left-handed, he hits with heavy slice, always taking his opponent wide and forcing him to virtually try for a winning return. When he volleys, it sometimes looks easy, but it is invariably due to the fact that he has opened up the court to volley into ... On grass, whenever there is a short ball, he will use the pace of the court with a short backswing to come to the net ... John McEnroe is able to dictate the rallies, taking the pace off the ball, and seemingly to manoeuvre the ball at will ... I appreciate every player wants to win every point, but John McEnroe in my opinion wants to win every point hitting a perfect shot. He is only satisfied and motivated by perfection. The court is his stage and everyone around it must have 100% concentration. This is why he reacts more than most to the atmosphere of the crowd and to close line calls. When he argues you would think he would lose concentration, but once the discussion is finished he is able to 'switch back on' to the next point and continue as if nothing had happened. All his energies are channelled into each point of each match."

Davis Cup [versus Ireland]
Tuesday, September 27, 1983

John McEnroe jetted in to Dublin 'in a most mild and gentle mood' after a fourteen-hour flight from San Francisco via London.

Guillermo Vilas and Jose Luis Clerc's wins over John in Buenos Aires, coupled with Italy's 3-2 beating of Ireland, had sent the American Davis Cup team to the Emerald Isle for a relegation tie.

More significantly, because McEnroe's paternal grandparents came from County Cavan and County Westmeath respectively, it was always likely to be an emotional time for him.[15]

In the airport VIP lounge, John informed the gathered media, "My first plans for Dublin are bed. I know that the US team is very confident of victory here in the Davis Cup, but I am not predicting anything.

"I know that I have had a few shock defeats lately, but I have been working on medical problems with my shoulder and foot and now I am back on top form. If I'm lucky I hope to win easily enough."

Looking tired, John continued, "I leave Dublin next Monday. I would dearly love to holiday in Ireland and if I get a chance before Monday I will visit country areas. I doubt I'll get to see the homeland of my grandparents. But I should be able to get back here for a holiday very soon."

---

[15]Tragically for John – not to mention all the McEnroe family – both his paternal grandparents had passed away by the time he was nine years old.

Wednesday, September 28, 1983

'The Evening Herald' began its saturation coverage of John McEnroe's stay in Dublin. The front page had a photo of Stella Hall, who is described as 'the camera-shy girl friend."

On the centre pages, gossip columnist John Feeney accused McEnroe of paging The Berkeley Court Hotel's room service for an acoustic guitar. The article finished churlishly, "It's a hard life for the jet-setting superbrat but it has its compensations."

In the sports section, there was a photo of John and brother Patrick. The Irish No.1, Californian-born Matt Doyle, was quoted as saying, "Well, it is quite obvious that if John plays anywhere near his best then we have no chance. But we have nothing to lose and I can tell you we'll be going for our shots."

In contrast to 'The Evening Herald', at least 'The Daily Mail' did some research. John Roberts was dispatched to Rathwire, fifty miles away from Dublin, to speak with McEnroe's great aunt Molly (a sister of his paternal grandmother).

The strident 85-year old declared, "He's criticised a lot and some of it is jealousy. I've always given him credit for being successful off his own back. Nobody pushed him."

She also commented on John McEnroe Snr. "Even as a nine-year old he could talk like a lawyer. He's nice, gentle, kind and understanding and was a wonderful son to a wonderful mother."

Thursday, September 29 1983

'The Evening Herald' once again featured Stella on its front page, this time next to the headline: "McEnroe sells sweaty shorts."

The accompanying story referred to a charity auction held at the Berkeley Court. John had taken over the role of auctioneer from Irish rugby international Fergus Slattery and he had to elicit offers for his own shorts! Having heard that one of his well-used T-shirts had once gone for £1,000, John opened the bidding for his shorts at £5,000! But the shorts on display were new and the bidding was slow. So McEnroe laughed, "You want a pair of sweaty ones. I'll wear these for my match against Matt on Sunday and whoever buys them can have them then."

In the end, the star's shorts fetched £550 for charity.

Not that 'The Evening Herald' was feeling charitable towards McEnroe. Their Mr. Feeney wrote a story in which John allegedly sent team captain Arthur Ashe into the kitchens of a Dublin restaurant with a request that his meal be re-cooked. Ultimately, John had no option but to speak out in a press conference. Brandishing a copy of the offending article, he said, "This is lies from start to finish. It's bullshit journalism. I'm a human and I expect respect. I will give it in return. This happens to me all over the world and of course it annoys me. Wouldn't it annoy you?"

On another occasion, McEnroe remarked that he planned to return to Ireland in the future and one wag asked, "For your honeymoon?"

"You have a good sense of humour," John flatly replied.

In the evening Mr. McEnroe invited plenty of relatives to a gathering at the Berkeley Court. Great Aunt Molly was there, and she later said of John, "We didn't say very much but I think he's done very well for somebody his age."

Friday, September 30, 1983
Beat Sean Sorensen 6-3, 6-2, 6-2

"The atmosphere was excellent and all 6,000 seats were sold. But I never really put him under any pressure. A lot of the time his anticipation was excellent and he was already moving before I knew exactly where I was going to play the ball!" (Sean Sorensen)

Saturday, October 1, 1983
With Peter Fleming beat Matt Doyle and Sean Sorensen 6-2, 6-3, 6-4

Sunday, October 2, 1983
Beat Matt Doyle 9-7, 6-3, 6-3

For the last time, the Irish crowds warmly applauded McEnroe. Doyle had been slightly put out because "at the opening ceremony they cheered louder for him than for their own team." He added, "McEnroe is more than just a tennis player now. I guess you could say he's on par with a rock star, continually in the limelight."

Before leaving Ireland, John received a silver cigar case from the

United States Tennis Association in recognition of his success and loyalty, whilst the Irish LTA handed him a cut glass bowl. McEnroe, for his part, thanked everyone for "being so nice to me while I've been here."

Benson & Hedges Championships

Wednesday, November 9, 1983
Beat John Lloyd 6-2, 6-4

"I feel that John McEnroe had the best eye-hand co-ordination of any player on the circuit. He was able to hit any ball from any position; he could also react at the last minute to hit reflex volleys and return of serves. Great eye-hand co-ordination is so necessary to do this, particularly on fast surfaces and when playing against someone who hits the ball very hard. He was the most talented player in the world and he was so difficult because you couldn't read his shots." (John Lloyd)

❧❧

Lloyd had reached the fourth round of the US Open in 1983 and he provided McEnroe with a tough ninety-minute workout.

But the New Yorker was his own worst enemy in the opening set, continually missing his first service. The fifth game also saw the Wimbledon Champion hit two consecutive double-faults to give Lloyd a break point. However, McEnroe averted the danger and saved another three break points in the seventh game.

As for Lloyd, he was on the back foot every time he stepped up to serve in the match. He faced break points against him in seven of his nine service games. But McEnroe was upset when he failed to convert his chances – he kicked a courtside flower arrangement and a section of the portable court barrier when Lloyd held serve in the second game of the second set. Umpire Bob Jenkins warned the American for 'abuse of equipment.'

Lloyd also said, "In the middle of the match I heard McEnroe say, 'It's the worst match I've ever played.' I thought, "Thanks a lot."

The result was a complete reversal of the TV commercial at that time which advertised a video system and which showed Lloyd beating McEnroe 6-3, 6-2, 6-0. Unknown to viewers, the role of McEnroe was played by 1982 Wimbledon Junior Champion, Pat Cash.

"The script didn't come true tonight, did it?" said Lloyd. Jocular McEnroe responded, "I haven't seen it, but if he beats me I'd better get paid for the advert."

Thursday, November 10, 1983
Beat Vince van Patten 7-5, 6-2

Each Benson & Hedges Championship, from the tournament's birth in 1976, had always had a dose of controversy. And since 1978, that controversy had always involved John in some way or another, but although the tradition was continued in his match today, he could take no blame for what occurred …

At the end of the one hour and twenty-nine minute contest, John ran to the net to shake hands and was immediately snubbed; van Patten gathered his equipment, wagged his finger and issued a stern reproof.

His angry march from the court was accompanied by noisy boos, and was followed by McEnroe, head lowered and imperturbable, to spirited applause …

It transpired that van Patten thought 'chicken' umpire David Mercer was biased towards the Wimbledon Champion and that John had attempted to drill a ball through him - "I'm not going to take this stuff anymore."

Yet McEnroe spoke for many and, judging by the headlines the next day, the majority of the press, when he remarked, "I really don't see what he has to bitch about after a match like that."

van Patten's claims lacked substance because (a) McEnroe was warned for "ball abuse" as early as the first game when he muffed a smash and (b) as for the alleged attempt McEnroe made to strike him, the ball was only hit at half pace. "If I tried to hit him, I'd have gone for the head," John said.

"I didn't deserve the cheers," he added with trademark bluntness. "I didn't want the cheers for the reason I got them."

Friday, November 11, 1983
Beat Steve Denton 6-3, 6-3

A comprehensive win, but John still pouts at umpire Ian Stirk, "I want a ruling to have the cigars put out."

When spectators continued to puff away, McEnroe requested the presence of the referee and supervisor.

At one point, John told Stirk, "Cigars smell a lot worse than a cigarette."

Referee Colin Hess finally resolved the crisis by arranging to have the extractor fans turned up and the service doors opened. He didn't want his sponsors embarrassed.

"Surely people should be able to do without smoking for a couple of hours?" John maintained after the match. "It can't be that difficult."

Denton added, "It was like a London fog out there."

Saturday, November 12, 1983
Beat Anders Jarryd 6-3, 6-1

"I guarantee that tomorrow there will be no repeat of 1981 when I was stale at the end of the season.

"I've got bad memories of that final against Jimmy. It was a bad-tempered match, bad for the crowd, a bad day all round. I was out of line. I lost after being up two sets to love. That won't happen again."

Sunday, November 13 1983
Beat Jimmy Connors 7-5, 6-1, 6-4

Connors virtually gave up when he received a warning for an 'audible obscenity' at 5-6 in the first set.

"It's always nice to win – but not like that," the victor remarked. "Perhaps the best solution would be to have a band of travelling professional umpires paid about £20,000 a year. They could be under the control of an independent body, so they could be fined if they were not up to standard. That way, both umpires and players would have their livelihood on the line."

As for the final itself, John declared, "I think Jimmy lost his concentration and got distracted which is a shame. But I was determined not to see a repeat of our stormy game in 1981 and I think I played well."

1984

Masters[16]	WON	Lendl	63 64 64
Philadelphia	WON	Lendl	63 36 63 76
WCT Richmond	WON	Denton	63 76
Madrid	WON	Smid	60 64
Brussels	WON	Lendl	61 63
WCT Finals	WON	Connors	61 62 63
WCT New York	WON	Lendl	64 62
World Team Cup: Beat Higueras 63 60; beat Clerc 63 63; beat Maurer 61 62; beat Lendl 63 62			
French Open	Runner-Up	Lendl	36 26 64 75 75
Stella Artois	WON	Shiras	61 36 62
Wimbledon	WON	Connors	61 61 62
Toronto	WON	Gerulaitis	60 63
Cincinnati	1st Round	V. Amritraj	67 62 63
US Open	WON	Lendl	63 64 61
San Francisco	WON	Gilbert	64 64
Stockholm Open	WON	Wilander	62 36 62

Davis Cup:

V Rumania beat Nastase 62 64 62; beat Segarceanu 26 62 62; with Fleming, beat Nastase/Sergarceanu 63 64 64

V Argentina beat Clerc 64 60 62; beat Jaite 63 64; with Fleming, beat Clerc/Jaite 75 46 63 61

V Australia beat Cash 63 64 61, beat Fitzgerald 46 62 61; with Fleming, beat Edmondson/McNamee 64 62 63

V Sweden lost to Sundstrom 13-11, 64 63; beat Wilander 63 67 63; with Fleming, lost to Edberg/Jarryd 75 57 62 75

John was superb in 1984 – so superb that Rex Bellamy in 'The Times' exclaimed, "McEnroe did not play tennis. He composed it.

---

[16] Part of the 1983 Tennis Year.

He turned prose into poetry."

The hyperbole was definitely justified. McEnroe contested 85 singles matches and won 82. He beat Jimmy Connors in the Wimbledon final 6-1, 6-1, 6-2; he dispatched Ivan Lendl 6-3, 6-4, 6-1 for the US Open crown. Only Rod Laver, who won the Grand Slam in '69, and Jimmy Connors, who lost just four of 103 matches in '74, had enjoyed such sparkling success.

Yet John really should have gone throughout the entire year unbeaten. In the French Open final he led Lendl by two sets to love with a service break in the third – yet somehow 'blew it'. The American's desolation was intense.

As for the Davis Cup in Gothenburg, McEnroe knew he would have to play with an injured left wrist. Nonetheless, he arrived in Sweden from the United States via fog-bound Heathrow at 1.00 a.m. and immediately stepped onto the practice court. Against Henrik Sundstrom he tried his hardest – as he always did for his country – but fatigue and pain got the better of him. He was also troubled by the clay court's bad bounces.

And Vijay Amritraj's win in Cincinnati? That came 24 hours after John had played three matches in one day to win the Toronto title.

On a personal level, John split from Stella Hall in '84 and at the end of the year The New York Post published a photo of the 25-year old strolling along Park Avenue at 51st Street with film star Tatum O'Neal. The paper quoted a 'tennis insider': "It's definitely a romance. They both say they're in love."

June 1984

"I suppose we [John and I] have just started to put our names up there amongst the all time great doubles players. I think any one team or any great player who is great in one era could have been equally as great in another. Some people go as far as to say that we would have beaten people like Newcombe and Roche – that's purely conjectural, but just to be in the same category would be nice." (Peter Fleming, talking to April Tod, 'Tennis' Magazine)

Stella Artois Championships

Tuesday, June 12, 1984
Beat Marty Davis 7-6, 6-2

"I should have put Lendl away in the fourth set on Sunday, but I didn't. That gave the crowd the opportunity to get involved in the match and it had a snowball effect. If you are playing well and don't put it away, then you're in trouble. I was on a high, went down and couldn't get back again."

Wednesday, June 13, 1984

"Putting that defeat to Lendl out of my mind is going to be really difficult during this tournament, although hopefully my mind will be set in time for Wimbledon …

"I was very down and very stiff on Sunday and when I arrived here I checked with a doctor that I was OK to play.

"I did consider pulling out, but I figured I had an obligation to come here and try my best.

"But it's going to be tough. I wanted to win so much in Paris," said John, once he'd trounced fellow American van Winitsky 7-5, 6-0.

Thursday, June 14, 1984
Beat Steve Meister 6-4, 6-3

It said much for John's skill and mental tenacity that he was knocking his opponents off with such ease. The French Open heartbreak had by no means dissipated; four days earlier he'd suffered "probably the worst night I had" after a tennis match. Perhaps it helped that on this day he was, biorhythmically, at his highest point in physical terms.

In 1985 he told Helmut Sorge and Teja Fiedler of 'Der Spiegel' just how hard it had been following the Lendl game: "I couldn't sleep, you know. I had about 15 beers or something and I didn't feel anything. That's how angry I was. I was so worked up …"

Friday, June 15, 1984
Beat Danie Visser 6-3, 6-4

Queen's Club's garden party atmosphere was tainted today when 'The Daily Star' served up this article for its 1.5 million readers:

"JOHN'S NEW GIRL – SUPERBRAT NETS LOVELY BETTINA" SMASH-HIT EXCLUSIVE by Alasdair Buchan.

The story started in typical tabloid style: *'Superbrat superstar John McEnroe lost out on the tennis court in the final of the French Open Championship.*

'But he came away from Paris winning game, set and match in the love-stakes.

'And the new woman in the life of the American No.1 is lovely Swiss-born tennis player Bettina Bunge.

'Bettina celebrated her 21st birthday this week, keeping her friendship with Mac the Mouth a close secret. But some of her friends and rivals began to suspect that love was in the air during the French tournament.

'Bettina is always a happy-go-lucky girl," said one of the top women players last night.

'But in Paris she suddenly started acting like a giggling school girl whenever anyone asked her what she was doing each evening after the tennis was over.

'Everyone tried to get out of her what was happening. But she wouldn't say anything."

'And although John and Bettina took great care during the tournament to avoid being seen by the ever-inquisitive Continental pressmen, they finally let down their guard at the prestigious Champions' Ball.

'The exclusive event was thrown by the French tennis authorities, in honour of John and women's champion Martina Navratilova.

'McEnroe skilfully drew the crowd of photographers away from Bettina's table as he posed for happy smiling photos with Martina.

'But the moment the speeches were over, the New Yorker left his seat of honour and went straight over to chat to the new lady in his life.

'Ignoring all the other revellers around them, the two remained deep in conversation for twenty minutes – and Bettina was obviously entranced by his every word.

'But although Bettina and McEnroe left the ball at the same time, they carefully made sure that several friends surrounded them – and they left in separate cars.'

The then chief tennis correspondent of 'The Sun', Hugh Jamieson, who at the time was conducting a series of exclusive interviews with John, said to me: "No-one knows how the rumours linking McEnroe with Bettina Bunge came about until 'The Daily Star's' front page story.

"McEnroe angrily denied it at a Press Conference during Queen's week and challenged 'The Daily Star' reporter to produce evidence which he refused to do!"[17]

"I had previously asked McEnroe about the story and I certainly had no reason to question his denial."

Bettina denied the allegations, too. Speaking at a women's tournament in Birmingham, she said, "I have known John for two years and I suppose we are good friends. But that's as far as it goes. I'm not his girlfriend.

"He hasn't been in touch since I got to Britain and I suppose the next time we'll meet is at Wimbledon."

* When Rick Parrott of 'Inside Women's Tennis' reminded Bettina of the rumours some years later, she responded, "Well, what can I say about that? None of that stuff has been true – typical English papers."

Saturday, June 16, 1984
Beat Jimmy Connors 6-2, 6-2

"McEnroe the real master" – 'Sunday Telegraph'
"It's not that I have a different strategy this year – it's just that I am hitting the ball better, hitting with more authority."

Sunday, June 17, 1984
Beat Leif Shiras 6-1, 3-6, 6-2

McEnroe led 6-1, 2-4. At 30-40 Shiras bounced the ball twice – he had decided where to place it. Fault. John edged in just behind the baseline. Another long pause. At last Shiras served. McEnroe replied with a hard forehand that landed on the dusty baseline. Leif played a weak backhand due to his doubt about the ball and the pace

---

[17] McEnroe told Mr. Buchan his story was 'a 100 per cent lie'. "You make me sick. You should be embarrassed to call yourself a human. You write crap."

of McEnroe's shot. It landed invitingly in the service court and so John finished the point off with a greedy crosscourt forehand. It appeared to flick the side-line, too. Yet as McEnroe walked to change ends, Leif stared hard at the umpire. He pointed to the baseline and mouthed the words, "The ball was out." The crowd joined in with shouts of "Out". And then, suddenly, the temper of John McEnroe was most certainly ignited.

Umpire Roger Smith hurriedly said, "The ball was out, the ball was out." He pointed, though, to the sideline – not calling the ball out that Shiras had questioned. John, dumbfounded, went up to the chair with his arms outstretched.

"She (the lineswoman on the sideline) called it in. Why did you wait ten seconds? She called it in, she went like this." (John put his palms down, signifying the ball was in.)

"I saw the ball out," replied the umpire.

"Why didn't you call it then? How could you wait that long?"

"The ball was out. Play on."

"Play on? I'm not playing on. She called the ball in, you didn't say a word. Why the hell did you overrule her? I want the referee out here."

"Call the referee," said the worried Smith after a while, as the slow-hand clap gathered momentum.

By now the crowd was stamping its feet in joy. They had got what they wanted. They continued to clap and kept shouting out. That partly explained why John felt the need to raise his voice. The accompanying din also added to his frustration.

"Ask her, how did she call it. Just ask her what call she made."

At last the referee, Jim Moore, and Grand Prix supervisor Kurt Nielsen came to the court. Neither was to get much chance to speak, as John continued to argue his case in voluble terms. As Moore began talks with Smith to establish exactly what happened, John broke in, adding, "I just want to know three things. Number one: he [Shiras] didn't even question that call, he questioned the one on the baseline. Number two: she called the ball in. And number three: nothing happened for twenty seconds. Why all of a sudden did he decide to call it out?" Nielsen broke in, speaking very quietly. "What the hell difference does it make?" John replied to Nielsen's inaudible comment.

Moore and the Supervisor merely listened to John and this clearly dissatisfied the player.

"There's nothing anyone can do ever. You guys sit here like two bumps on a log and say nothing, because some idiot in the chair does nothing. It's unbelievable."

By now John knew that the call wouldn't be changed and he reluctantly started to make his way to return the next Shiras serve. He could not, however, resist telling Moore, "It's overruled and so it's a great decision? So f------ what! What is the great thing about it? He's no reason to overrule – she called it in, he didn't question it. Why the hell did he overrule? Ask him! Ask him why he overruled."

Moore did so and then said, "He saw it out."

"He saw it out. Yeah, and this racquet is purple," John shouted, pointing to his racquet and walking to the deuce court.

"The score is deuce," announced Roger Smith. John trudged to the baseline, still fuming his disapproval and disgust ...

Grand Prix rules stipulated that an umpire must overrule a call 'promptly' and so John was perfectly justified in feeling hard done by when Mr. Smith's overrule came when he was sitting in his chair having changed ends.

What could not be justified, however, was the completely insensitive press coverage of the incident. Ian Wooldridge in the 'The Daily Mail' declared "Ban Him Now" and some MPs called for John to be deported.

With the trauma of the French Open still fresh in his memory, this latest controversy was one John could well have done without. And few bothered to hear the reasoned explanation he gave to Harry Carpenter of the BBC: "It just had to do with the fact that I think you need consistency and you have to make a decision very quickly – that's what the players look for in an umpire. What happened was that Leif had thought the previous shot I hit [the baseline shot] was out and really kinda wasn't playing it, and then I hit that shot that the lineslady called in, and I think that the guy in the chair thought he [Leif] was questioning that call, when in fact he was questioning the shot earlier. He wasn't even questioning the call that this guy waited twenty seconds [on] and I just think you need a person that does the job and does it spur of the moment, and he didn't do it. It was just an incorrect decision to make at that point, I felt."

"John and I have known each other since we were 12; we played the same tournaments.   Right from the start he was something special.   He isn't arrogant like the media say, but he's always been an argumentative type of guy.   He prefers the honesty of his friends to being patronised.

"He's a bit of a perfectionist, too, and sometimes the pressure gets too much....

"It's true that after the Queen's Final we went to the Hard Rock Café together – we had a few beers and talked about music and mutual friends.

"We also discussed the match.   The umpire had been late in overruling – he wasn't authoritative.   John was right to argue; I wasn't put off.   He likes to raise the intensity of a match as he operates best when things are boiling over.   He finds peace in madness.

"Playing McEnroe is quite different to playing anyone else.   He beats you with guile and deception.   You don't hear the ball on the strings because his racquet is strung so loose.   Then the ball is on you so quickly.   He has quick hands; his use of the court is artistic and creative…

"John's very into his family right now – he's dedicated to them.   I still have dinner with him sometimes.   He likes a beer and to get a little bit loose. We often talk about the future.   Off court, you see, he's happy.   Being a father has given him peace…

"Basically John has brought tennis to a peak.   It'll hurt the game when he retires because we need him.   He's dynamic, interesting and finds time to do a lot of charity work.   He gives a lot back.

"He's a good man." (Leif Shiras, talking in June 1988)

❧

Meanwhile, to Neil Amdur of 'World Tennis', John's mother Kay declared, "He's seen somebody with their eyes closed sitting on a line on a hot summer day.   He wants them to perform the way he believes he does - well."

Wimbledon

Tuesday, June 19, 1984

Speaking at a press conference to reporters highly critical of him,

John declared, "What I regret is that I come to places like this and have to deal with people like you."

He added that hopefully one day he would be able to talk about other things besides court behaviour.

"It's all I have been asked about for five years – and there's nothing new in any of the questions. It's incredible to me that that's what still happens – it's embarrassing. Maybe I do go a little further than I should. But rather than criticising me, shouldn't you look for the reasons?"

* According to UK 'Tennis' magazine, British television showed biased coverage of the event. "ITN's Carol Barnes kept asking, 'How long do you think you can get away with your on-court behaviour, Mr. McEnroe?' When he rose to the bait and snapped back after only a few hundred repetitions, that was the clip that was shown on the evening news." (McEnroe was aware of the technique. "They just take out the little clip that they want," he said.)

Monday, June 25, 1984

John entered the Centre Court arena on a day of cloud and occasional sunshine.

Predictably it was a slightly restrained performance against the lively Paul McNamee, and that certainly explains why the Australian gleaned a set, going down 6-4, 6-4, 6-7 (7-9), 6-1. David Mercer, the umpire, received none of the emotion that Roger Smith had encountered at Queen's Club and the match never did more than spark now and then.

"I've decided to let my racquet do the talking. Over here you people have no sense of caring about human beings and I think it's sad. I don't understand it. So many of you don't even care to talk about the tennis. I do not think my thoughts on this conflict with what I am doing with 'The Sun' because although I am not writing the stories myself, I have approval over what is written. The other articles are not true – like what they said about Wimbledon – the new Chairman has been fine and extremely fair to me. He is very nice – comes into the locker room and talks to the players. Wimbledon said they would go by the rules and that is exactly what they should do. I am doing this bit with 'The Sun' because I am able to get my point across and I am getting paid for it.

"As for my play today, I am satisfied that I won and I just want to get better with each match. The court played fairly well considering this was the first match and I'm sure it will get slower as the days go by. Paul played well and brought some good points out of me. First matches are always tough, but here, with all that is going on, every match will be tough. I thought there were a few bad line calls, but it is not in my best interests to say anything at the present time. The crowd today was all right and my attitude is not as positive as I would like it to be. After losing the tie-breaker I wanted to get a quick start in the fourth because I felt Paul was relaxed. I did not play as well today as I have been playing."

McNamee was asked who could overthrow the holder. "I honestly can't think of anyone," came the prophetic reply.

Thursday, June 28, 1984
Beat Rod Harmon 6-1, 6-3, 7-5

"I felt I was in control, but for some reason I just stopped returning. Although I have served better, I was getting pretty good placement, but he returned better than last time and besides, I usually serve better indoors. I lost a little rhythm because of the wind and things like that. Also, I felt a little stiff, but it just went away and I seemed to loosen up.

"I feel I am a better player than I was a year ago, but I don't think I am playing that great yet. I don't feel I am playing as well as I did in some tournaments in the early part of the year.

"Yes, it's true that I don't think they should have microphones on the court and then you would not have the problem of hearing bad language, or microphones should also be used on other sports, but at the moment I think tennis is the only sport they put it on, for some unknown reason. I fully intend to bring this up with the ATP. I have been doing it for years at the Open, but unless you get the support of everyone nothing is going to happen …

"The pressure for me is pretty much everywhere I go now and Britain is the worst country to have problems with the media. I have been lucky enough to win this tournament two times and that is something that cannot be taken away from me. Anything else I do here is icing on the cake …

"I don't really go out very much because it's not enjoyable to go out. I don't want to deal with the whole scene. It's tough, but makes you appreciate the other times more."

Saturday, June 30, 1984

John continued in his new, almost serene manner on Centre Court against the hard-serving Australian Wally Masur. He cruised into the last sixteen 6-0, 6-4, 6-3 in one hour and thirty-four minutes. Top gear was seldom required.

His behaviour was impeccable. Umpire Bob Jenkins overruled three decisions, but John refused to be ruffled, just muttering his displeasure, staring hard and shaking his head once or twice.

It was a solid effort with McEnroe at times opening up his full repertoire. A few points stuck in the memory – one being when John passed Masur with a beautifully disguised forehand drive, letting his wrist do the work. On another point he again angled the racquet head at the last second to hopelessly wrongfoot the Australian.

Serving at a set up, 2-2 and 0-15, McEnroe showed his touch, playing a delightful drop volley on the backhand side. Masur went on to break serve that game, but John later unfurled a couple of powerful crosscourt backhands – one when he trailed 2-4, 0-30. Masur, who ended 1983 at 66 on the computer, held three points for a double break, yet McEnroe went into overdrive to evade the gathering crisis.

His wish for perfection led him to say, "I'm still not satisfied with my play. I have had some good sets, but have not been consistent and have not been putting it together. Not that I am playing badly, but not as well as I can. On clay there is more time to play shots, but grass is a different game and every shot is important for often there are just one or two shot rallies. I didn't have a good rhythm on my serve. I had trouble with my toss."

That was true – twice John lost balance as he prepared to serve and the second set was touch and go for the most part. At that time McEnroe seemed to be having trouble with his left knee, though he dismissed suggestions of injury.

On several occasions the Champion's temper could have been stirred. In the last game of set two, Jenkins overruled the service judge who called a Masur serve out. Two games on there was an identical occurrence.

McEnroe also questioned the state of the balls; he "suspected one of them to be defective – out of balance in fact. I therefore checked the nap of each ball and found them to be satisfactory. He did, however, find a ball with a nap defect in Ireland during the [1983] Davis Cup," said Jenkins. In addition, the American shook his head when a Masur drive was called out. Finally there was another overrule – this time in John's favour.

So much for the petty controversies. Whatever derogatory comments that could be levelled at this southpaw genius, a lack of courage was not one of them. In the final game of the match he was behind 0-40 on serve, but he gritted his teeth and produced a quick onslaught for victory.

And so the thrashing of Masur put Bill Scanlon in the firing line. Would their contest break the uneasy calm of John's encounters thus far? McEnroe had some harsh words to say about the Texan.

McEnroe: "Things are starting to get interesting now. There are some tough matches to come, including the next one … Scanlon tends to get under everyone's skin."

Journalist: "Is there a particular reason why he gets under yours?"

McEnroe: "I think he goes out of his way to attempt to do so. He realises that he has a lot better chance of winning if he does. Some people don't realise the subtleties Scanlon uses. When you play me, it's sometimes easy to get the crowd against me, if you know anything about… er… how to work with crowds, and that's one thing he does. Those types of people, you know… er… *(he fidgeted and nervously fingered his hands)* look like they're your friends from the outside, but are stabbing you in the back in the meantime when you're not looking. You know, that's one thing you can't accuse me of, because when I go out there it's very obvious how I feel. So you know that's why when someone like himself does things like that… you know… I personally don't respect people who do things like that. I respect his tennis ability. I don't worry about what he does. I'm not saying he does it all the time and I can't speak for everyone, but I believe the majority don't respect him. I expect a hard match, but I expect to win."

Scanlon had struggled against 16-year old Boris Becker before the junior retired with torn ankle ligaments and he mockingly told the press, "Let's just say I haven't been out to dinner with McEnroe since we've been in London. He didn't call me when he got into town. He does not like people who are tough on him. If I would just roll over to him every time he would love me. I don't care. No, I've done nothing to bridge the gap between us. Do you think I'm dying to be his friend?"

Scanlon spoke of McEnroe's outbursts with officials. "Half the time it's planned. If you notice, he tends to cause more of a scene when he has lost a little momentum."

However, McEnroe has always claimed, and I believe him, that nothing he does on court is premeditated. Furthermore, umpire Bob Jenkins has said, "I do not think McEnroe's arguments with officials are calculated to disrupt his opponent."

Sunday, July 1, 1984

The worst example of Wimbledon's press coverage was the build-up to John's match with Scanlon, a fact that was confirmed by Hugh Jamieson who told Charles Arthur of 'Tennis' magazine that during the tournament:

"All the other papers were waiting for McEnroe so they could come down really hard on him. 'Just wait,' they were saying. Obviously any misdemeanour would negate what McEnroe had said in 'The Sun' about wanting to behave well and so on. In the other papers, his matches were always previewed with words like, could, might, possibly, promise to … and so on, all hoping for bad behaviour since there was none to actually report. Mac and Scanlon were shown on TV, cleverly edited to make it appear that they were talking to each other. This was widely used to fuel speculation about possible clashes, tantrums, etc. Yet they didn't just leap up on the dais and begin declaiming. It is misleading, to say the least, when TV and Press don't include the first, leading question."

Given all this, John would probably have welcomed a short respite from dealing with journalists, but his wish was in vain. On Sunday, whilst practising at Queen's Club, the 25-year old star was asked if romance could affect his game. "That's possible," he replied. Had McEnroe dined with the model who appeared in chocolate commercials, Janis Lee-Burns? "I haven't even met here."

The short, irritable responses signified John's tension. His mind was fixed, gazing into the near future. Scanlon was lying in wait, poised to ambush. Of that, John was sure.

* *McEnroe could "thank" 'News Of The World' journalist, Geraldine Hosier, for the questions about his love life. Hosier's story alleging John had visited Janis' Regent's Park home appeared on this day, under the headline "Mac's New Sweetie: Chocolate Flake Beauty Makes Champ Crumble."*

A week later Janis sold her revelations to the same paper. According to the 20-year old, they dined at London's trendy Ma Cuisine restaurant; drank camomile tea at John's 'shabby' Chelsea flat and had a telephone argument over a white tracksuit top that she did not return quickly enough to him.

She reported John as terminating the row with the words, "Please forget the last few minutes."

Monday, July 2, 1984

At 11.30 a.m., two and a half hours before John McEnroe and Bill Scanlon were due on Court No.1, referee Alan Mills informed Georgina Clark that she was umpiring the match.

The Oxford housewife needn't have worried, because, to use her words, it "went very well." "Both players were good-humoured and tolerated a rather extraordinary interruption – from a member of the public who craned his neck through a small aperture at first floor level and shouted directly at John McEnroe – with great patience."

That McEnroe had not done anything out of place against a player with a history of needling him couldn't obscure the most significant fact – Scanlon didn't play badly and yet the 6-3, 6-3, 6-1 score wasn't a fair illustration of McEnroe's phenomenal superiority.

"In all the times I have played him I would say that, without a doubt, this is the best he has played," confirmed Scanlon. "He returned serve very well and if I didn't hit a good serve I felt a little bit defensive. It is hard to say who could beat him. A player who is capable of hitting hard enough, a Lendl for example, who will serve strong enough to neutralise his return of serve, but really it's going to have to be a case of whether he has a few loose points and his opponent puts it together."

On this day McEnroe's consistency enabled him to score numerous points off Scanlon's serve, breaking it six times. It was the second game of the second set before he first had to save a break point himself and from 3-3 in the second John took absolute control and nine of the next ten games. Such a bout of power and accuracy made his loss to Scanlon at the '83 US Open all the more remarkable. John said he liked to think he'd improved since then, "but I think he was playing better at the Open. I just go out there and play a match which is what I hope everyone wants. I thought I played pretty well and concentrated well. If I can keep this level up I think I have a good chance in the next couple of rounds … It's pretty noisy out there, but if you put your mind to it, it doesn't matter …

"I don't remember hitting a volley that hard, I was a little bit tentative volleying. I thought it was one thing I didn't do very well. I need to keep up a high level. I played the best match of the tournament for me and hopefully that will continue. I feel reasonably comfortable about the way I'm playing. Sometimes I play well and beat a guy easily and sometimes I will struggle.

"If I play well though, I feel I am going to win. What matters is me trying to win the tournament. That's the only thing that matters at this point … I didn't really do anything yesterday, I just worked on my own, mentally getting prepared. It wasn't going to matter who was in the chair. It didn't matter to me one way or the other.

"It's good to give a little bit of my side of the story to the papers; it's better than nothing. Everybody was trying to make a big deal out of my playing Scanlon and I just wanted to get my mind on the tennis and just concentrate when I was on the court and think about the right things. As I said a couple of days ago, on grass you have to be ready for every point because everything happens so fast."

* In September 1985, I asked commentator Gerald Williams to address John's feud with Scanlon. He replied, "Bill Scanlon has been seen by McEnroe as an irritant, but McEnroe is irritated by many people, isn't he? You don't see Wilander being "niggled" by anyone, do you? It's in the eye of the beholder, and in the mind.

"Essentially I see John as a perfectionist and perfectionists are difficult people to live with. They also find it difficult to live with themselves. I long to see John at peace in his heart and, speaking as a Christian, I know where that peace is to be had."

Wednesday, July 4, 1984
Beat John Sadri 6-3, 6-3, 6-1

"I thought I played pretty good today. The toughest match I've played against Sadri was in college [when McEnroe won the NCAA

Championships in June 1978]. I think I have improved since then, but I think that was probably the greatest match he will ever play. He served about 30 aces and it was a really close match. I've had a couple of other close matches with him, but none that have been as close as that one.

"I feel I am playing better than I was at the beginning of the tournament. The last couple of matches turned out to be easier than I thought they would be. If I play well I think I will win against Cash, but he has beaten some good players to get this far and he must be playing as well or better than he ever has. I'm looking forward to meeting him. He's been around at least a couple of years and as I said in the first days of the tournament, I think he is one of the few young guys who have a chance of doing anything.

"For some reason I feel pretty good and relaxed. Maybe because all this crap was going on before and I felt really good about getting onto the court because that's the only place I can escape it and show people what I can do. If anyone is getting more than enough hassle, I am. I don't think I should be criticised so much for what I have done and I don't think they should say I'm the greatest in the world just because I don't do something for a few weeks."

Friday, July 6, 1984

Valiantly though young Pat Cash fought, still John had yet to relinquish a second set as he went into his fifth Wimbledon final with a 6-3, 7-6, 6-4 win. Now it was Connors in the 25-year old's path.

"I'm looking forward to playing Jimmy since we have played so many times and have had so many great matches. I think we both play our best against the best players and the key for me is not to get overly emotional. Jimmy likes to build it up to that pitch because he plays his best then. My emotional level was bad in '82 and I was just not ready for a long match. Jimmy can tell when a guy is not at his peak and he takes advantage of it. I will definitely need to play more aggressively against Connors than I did today. I will need to keep him off balance and if he returns my serve well I could be in trouble."

As for the match with Cash, the Australian kept even with John before artistry and confidence became decisive. McEnroe, his Max 200G like a magical wand, controlled the ball beautifully, always making it dance to his tune. One break was enough to give him a 4-3 lead in the opening set. Then, in the ninth game, Cash double-faulted to 30-40 and netted a low volley on set point.

Cash had a break point at 4-4 in the second– "he really began to get on my serve" – but in the tie-break he led 4-1 and lost it 7-5. "I thought Cash had control and probably could have won it – which might have made the match a different story," said John.

"In the third set," he continued, "my right leg hurt a little – maybe a strained hamstring. It hurt a bit the other day, but I didn't think too much of it. I started to have trouble with my serve because the sky was so clear that without a cloud I could not judge where the ball was and I was hitting it on the way down. My right leg slowed me down." But John recovered from a 0-2 hurdle and eventually served out successfully after 2 hours and 8 minutes.

"He's a great player," realised Cash. "The better I returned, the better he sent the volley back. He's just got amazing touch. His serve is his big weapon, but I don't think he served that well today."

We weren't to know then, but apart from the McNamee match, this was the one, against the Wimbledon Junior Champion of 1982, that tested John's mettle the most.

Saturday, July 7, 1984
With Peter Fleming, beat Pat Cash and Paul McNamee, 6-2, 5-7, 6-2, 3-6, 6-3

"Playing doubles helps me. Both times I have won the singles here, I have also won the doubles. It's good practice for the return and serve which basically on grass are the most important shots. It's worked out nicely this year because I've played singles one day and doubles the next."

Sunday, July 8, 1984

"I just came here to try and be the best tennis player I can. Hopefully they will see that. I think actions speak for themselves."

"HE'S THE GREATEST"

"MASSACRE IN THE SUN"

"CHAMP MAC'S FINAL BLITZ"

"MAGNIFICENT McENROE PAINTS HIS MASTERPIECE"

Jimmy Connors' belief that he could win his third Wimbledon title at 31 broke up into fragments on a parched Centre Court.

In the most one-sided final since Donald Budge beat Bunny Austin for the loss of four games in 1938, John McEnroe devastated the world No.3 6-1, 6-1, 6-2 in 80 magical minutes.

McEnroe attained the £100,000 first prize with a flawless display, made all the more remarkable since it was achieved in the Centre Court's 102 degree heat. Humiliated Connors surrendered quicker than Chris Evert had the previous day to Martina Navratilova. "There was a lot of heat out there," he joked, referring to both McEnroe and the searing conditions.

After all the controversies he had endured over the previous four weeks – his French Open disaster, the Queen's Club quarrels and general press roughness – McEnroe not only wanted to win, he intended to leave Wimbledon on a high, showing exactly why he'd scored 56 singles victories and picked up nine tournaments in 1984.

"Last year when I played Chris, people were saying that I could not do the same to Connors or Lendl. It was nice to be able to go out and do it. I am sure Chris feels better."

As in John's previous six rounds the officials were hard pushed to hear a word from him.

"It's a good feeling to play well and keep cool. It's better for me in the long run this way and certainly I hope it's something I can continue to do. But it's not something I can guarantee." He also said officiating hadn't improved.

What of Connors? He realised how Ken Rosewall must have felt ten years previously. In 1974 the arrogant youngster had felled Rosewall 6-1, 6-1, 6-4. Against McEnroe, the now ageing left-hander salvaged only 42 points.

The 25-year old's serve was singled out by Connors. "He served as well as he ever has and didn't give me a chance to jump on my return. I've been seeing the ball as big as a basketball, but today I couldn't find it." No wonder: McEnroe put 75% of his first serves into court and not once allowed Connors to extend him past 30. In actual fact John recorded four love games, three to fifteen and four to thirty. Five of Connors' eleven points off John's serve came in the first set, four in the second, two in the third. "I got into a good groove and mixed it up a lot. I had a whole variety of serves going – and that made it difficult for him."

What made it even more difficult for Connors was that he abandoned his familiar baseline haunt to gamble at the net. "I just felt that Jimmy could not hurt me. I overpowered him, which is something I have not done too often before. I really kept the pressure up well," remarked McEnroe.

Desperation struck the prey from the very first game. McEnroe served out to love and included the first of his ten aces. The 31-year old was then broken. Had Lendl's inflexibility in the semi-final deprived Connors of the chance to hone his game?

"I would have loved to have made a better match of it. I did the best I could on the day. He played well and I did not even get started. Hence the result," said Connors despondently.

Definitely, McEnroe's was an extraordinary talent, that of a "genius at work" according to the late Don Budge. Perhaps his greatest asset was deception, the ability to knock an opponent off guard by taking the ball early or late. His shot variety, with infinite combinations of pace and spin, bemused all but the most hardy opponents. At the net McEnroe's touch was unrivalled and his astonishing reflexes saved him if the approach shot was ever indifferent. Never did he try to bludgeon himself out of trouble – instead he found imaginative angles hitherto unexplored.

McEnroe's service games raced by and Connors, who won the fourth game of set one and the fifth game of the second, could only remember one small spell on par with the illusionist John – when he tied the champion to 2-2 in the third set.

In the end John took the trophy and went on a lap of honour around the Centre Court, before bowing extravagantly to an empty Royal Box.

Talk that he belonged among the most glorified names in the game thrilled him. "It's an honour for me to be mentioned in the same breath as my idol Rod Laver and Bjorn Borg," he commented, smiling. "When I'm playing well there is nobody who can beat me. It was the best I've ever played, but I can still do better."

The only moment John let himself be remotely sidetracked was at the close of set two, when he briefly recalled the French final and being in the same position against Lendl. "I purposely tried to stay calm and save all my energy for the match. I wasted a lot of energy in Paris, getting angry with myself and that hurt me. That is something I learned."

He had never broken his promise of Day One: "I'll let my racquet do the talking. I just want to get in and out with the title – without any problems."

❧❧

On that idyllic July evening the victor again went to the annual Champions' Dinner. For once at total ease, McEnroe was full of charm, beginning, "I shall try to keep this speech as short as the match."

John expressed his sincere thanks to the All England Club Chairman Buzzer Hadingham, who had declared at the beginning of the Championships that there would be no witch-hunt against the American.

"On the Friday before Wimbledon, I myself got a long telephone call from John McEnroe Snr., ringing from New York," Hadingham recalls. "He knew what a hostile press John got as a result of the Queen's Club incident. I told him that the Code of Conduct would be enforced for all competitors and that John would be treated in exactly the same way as anyone else who violated the Code. Incidentally, this Code is laid down by the Men's International Professional Tennis Council, on which the players have three representatives, so it is a Code agreed by the players themselves.

"John had such a critical press which continued right through the week before Wimbledon, that obviously his father was anxious. I had been interviewed by about twenty lawn tennis journalists on the Sunday, during which I emphasised that we would enforce the Code of Conduct and that, as the new Chairman, my head would be on the block if we did not act when players broke the Code. I remember one of the tennis journalists saying, 'What are you going to do if the Code of Conduct is broken and you fail to take action?' To which I said, 'Then the AELTC would have a headless Chairman!'

"On the Monday of the beginning of the Championships, reading all the many press comments, I came to the conclusion that John,

184

seeing my name rather strongly featured, might think I was gunning for him. So I wrote a personal letter wishing him luck in the Championships and emphasising that all players would be subject to the Code of Conduct and that I was not in any way gunning for him.

"At ten to two on that first Monday I went into the changing room and said to John, 'Did you get my letter, John?' He said, 'Well, I haven't actually opened my mail, it's all in my locker.' I said, 'Don't worry John, I've got a copy in my pocket, but I'd like you to read it.'

John took the copy and I left him to talk to some of the other players. Then I came back and said 'OK, John?' He said, 'I appreciate it,' and shook hands. He behaved well throughout the fortnight – and I breathed a sigh of relief – not just for myself, but for John too!"

Of his relationship with referee Alan Mills, McEnroe joked, "Alan told me before dinner that he had not seen me since before the tournament. I had to say it was a pleasure."

The conclusion was one of a cheery, hopeful nature – "I just hope I can share this honour with you a couple more times in the future" – and it made one wish John could display such a well-developed sense of diplomacy on a tennis court. However, the comment was still a fine, gentlemanly way to conclude what had been, all in all, a very successful 1984 Wimbledon Championship.

Monday, July 9, 1984

"Let us note, in passing, that throughout the tournament McEnroe's court conduct was almost exemplary ... This made nonsense of the popular argument that he cannot play unless he makes a fuss. He can. He did. Indeed, he has never played better."
(Rex Bellamy, 'The Times')

The Wimbledon Champion left the country with younger brother Patrick by Concorde, to join the rest of this family who were grieving for the death of William Tresham, McEnroe's maternal grandfather.[18]

---

[18] Kay McEnroe's father, British-born William Tresham, had hoped to see John play at Wimbledon in 1984. It would have been the ex-miner's first visit 'back home' since emigrating in the 1930's," 'The Sun' said. In 1979 John told Fiona Macdonald Hull of the 'News of the World' that grandfather Tresham sent

"MAC HID TRAGIC SECRET" declared 'The Sun', explaining that John had struggled through the early rounds with the death a closely guarded secret. There was known to be something wrong when his parents, Kay and John, weren't present to witness their son's spellbinding win. After the final, whilst talking to BBC's Gerald Williams in an interview, McEnroe said he was sure "they enjoyed it." Yes, it was true he dedicated the triumph to his mother – "she knows the reason why." McEnroe told Williams he did not want to disclose the cause. No doubt it would become common knowledge "in the next month or two, or maybe year, or day or hour."

Despite his sorrow the American agreed to sign autographs and he waved to cheering passengers. Reporters questioned him with regard to his good behaviour and 1985 plans, but they received no reply. McEnroe's silence was only broken when talk turned to more immediate plans. "I just want to get to Gate Two," came the muttered reply.

* *'The Sun' editorial said:*
"Yesterday John McEnroe won Wimbledon in devastating style… We shall long remember his destruction of Jimmy Connors with some of the finest tennis ever seen. With almost equal pleasure, we can recall the delightful incident when, as the 'old' veteran of 25, he showed newcomer Pat Cash how to make a gracious deep bow to the Royal Box. 'The Sun' presented John McEnroe's own story in our columns … today we salute McEnroe, the champion of Champions."

Hugh Jamieson told me how the £35,000 deal had come about: "My editor decided that it would be a very good idea to try and sign up McEnroe for Wimbledon as he was the No.1 player, plus of course the most talked about star. Negotiations started during the French Championships and he was happy to sign up a contract allowing sports interviews, as well as feature articles on his personal life plus pictures."

What conclusions had Jamieson reached?

"I found him very loyal to the paper and courteous, especially as other sections of the media still tried to muscle in on the act. He was

---

him ten dollars each year for his birthday. "I don't know if they're aware of how much money I've made. All I know is they watch me on TV. But it's that kind of thing that keeps my feet on the ground."

a little guarded at first, but I felt we built up a relationship of mutual trust and that was superb from my point of view. He wanted to get his viewpoint across and knew the pressures with so many people waiting for him to put one foot wrong. In the end he achieved what he said he would do – 'Win the title in style.'"

And what of 'The Daily Star's' counter-attack, which included claims to have talked with John's 'friends, foes, family and favourite women' and exhortations that 'others may publish yet another whitewash interview with him, ignore them!'?

Surprisingly, like McEnroe, he seemed resigned to such things:

"Yes, 'The Daily Star' were very keen to do a 'spoiler' and in fact were obsessed with the idea. They made themselves look stupid in the end by their determination to attack McEnroe on the 'Brat' lines.

"They front-paged that alleged romance with Bettina Bunge, which was wrong, and were further upset when McEnroe refused to talk to them during Queen's Club week, telling them that anything he had to say would be in 'The Sun'.

"I suppose you could say they were a section of the media that was biased against him."

'The Sun' interviews, conducted before, during and after the All England Championships included such articles as, "How I miss Stella Hall, the only girl I ever loved." The exclusives appeared on the following dates with some very interesting quotes from John.

Saturday June 23, 1984:
"I'm still learning and will continue to do so for the rest of my life…" "I'm not proud of some of the things I've done in the past and if I could change everything I'd gladly trade in a percentage of my earnings to wipe the slate clean."

Monday, June 25, 1984:
"We (Stella and I) really got on well (they split in May 1984), we liked the same things …" "I don't go for casual relationships …" "I think I'll be a good father, but I probably will want my kids to do well."

Saturday, June 30, 1984:
"I wish I could play the guitar more than anything…" "I do not dabble with drugs…" "I guess I like the right things – food, wine and women."

Monday, July 2, 1984:

"I don't accept the theories that they (my parents) pushed me into being a champion. Quite the opposite…" "She (my Mum) is a great cook and I miss her cooking. She makes great apple pies and a great chicken casserole. In fact, everything she makes is good."

Tuesday, July 10, 1984:

"If I've given pleasure to people in the last fortnight, then that has made me a happy man, especially at such a magical event as Wimbledon, which has given me problems in the past."

Monday, November 5, 1984

As John McEnroe prepared to defend his Benson & Hedges title he could have been forgiven if his thoughts lay elsewhere.

Following Stockholm's Scandinavian Open – an event he won, beating Mats Wilander – the left-hander had accrued over £6,000 in fines.

Everything occurred in his semi-final with Anders Jarryd and it was all another crazy misunderstanding. In the second set a McEnroe serve was called in by the linesman, but deemed out by the umpire. John asked why there had been no previous overrules. Instead of politely dealing with the query, the official said coldly, "Second serve."

"Answer my question. The question – jerk," screamed an indignant McEnroe.

From there things deteriorated in a chaotic spiral until John received a game penalty for smashing his racquet against the drinks' trolley.

"A powerful backhand takes the fruit juice across the court, followed by a precise forehand smash on the water bottle," ITV news sarcastically reported, carefully forgetting to say that the whole rumpus was the result of the umpire's unnecessary starchiness.

Said John, "I'm tired after years and years on the circuit of having some guy that does not know what he's doing telling me to play on when I'm asking him a completely different question. After seven years you get tired of it and that's when I get into these situations, when I'm tired."

Now he faced a 21 day suspension. Either the Wimbledon

Champion could accept the ban and miss Wembley (but be clear for the Australian Open and the Davis Cup Final), or he could appeal. If he failed to persuade the authorities his £1,650 fine in Sweden was unjust, McEnroe would be barred from those last two major events on the 1984 calendar.

It was still believed at this point that McEnroe was appearing at the Wembley Arena, opening against Peter Fleming.

* In December '84, John's father told 'The New York Post', "I'm not pleased when I watch John in some of his outbursts but I think that is over-emphasised. That may be 30 seconds out of a brilliant, three-hour tennis match, but that's all that is shown on TV.

"He has said some unpleasant things on court but mostly at himself. He is that kind of competitor. I have seen lawyers in conference say a lot more outrageous things to each other.

"Except for his tennis, John's a normal young man of his age. He likes cars, likes music I don't understand, goes out with girls I'm not aware of and enjoys spending time with his friends.

"I remember Fred Perry telling me at Wimbledon that he did worse things on the court than John ever thought of. In those days there was no television and nobody wrote about anything other than the result of the match."

Tuesday, November 6, 1984

At 1.00 a.m. on Tuesday came a fresh announcement – John McEnroe, the Wimbledon and United States Champion, had now accepted the 21 days ban that forced his withdrawal from the Benson & Hedges Championships and the following week's special event in Antwerp.

After considering all options, McEnroe had decided to miss Wembley rather than the Australian Open and Davis Cup. His eleventh hour decision prompted the deprived tournament director, Len Owen, to admit, "Faced with the same sort of decision I would probably have come to the same conclusion."

Later that day Grand Prix Supervisor Ken Farrar was to describe McEnroe's behaviour in Stockholm as "among his poorer displays."

"I think John's a very tormented young man right now. He dislikes being disliked. It upsets him. But as No.1 he feels he is carrying a burden on his shoulders." For a long time critics of McEnroe had disapproved strongly of the petty nature of the fines he received. Yet Farrar didn't agree – by his reckoning John could have made up to £200,000 in total at Antwerp and Wembley. Also, John was no longer entitled to play exhibitions prior to the Australian Open.

Many, reflecting on the whole bizarre affair, thought McEnroe was probably glad to take a rest. Considering the fatigue he was complaining about, the world Champion could not be completely unhappy about a suspension that obliged him to relax for three weeks, they said. As he himself had remarked in Stockholm, "To tell you the truth, a suspension won't be the worst thing that has happened to me."

News of McEnroe's withdrawal reached Mr. Owen by a phone call from John's father. Sadly, but quite understandably, no one would talk about Mr. McEnroe's communication.

Championship referee Colin Hess told me, "Mr. Owen regards the particular phone call as private and confidential and does not wish to indicate exactly what transpired. You will understand that it was a delicate situation and in these instances it is far better that anything said is kept entirely private."

Wednesday, November 7, 1984

Just to prove that the media could not get enough of McEnroe in this, his stellar year, the BBC Sportsnight programme broadcast an interview with him. Gerald Williams had met John at Heathrow after the Stockholm debacle.

Friday, December 14, 1984

On the eve of the Sweden v United States Davis Cup Final, Carlos Goffi, a coach at the Port Washington Tennis Academy when John was 16, spoke to Malcolm Folley in 'The Daily Mail'.

Goffi recalled, "When the Rumanian Junior Davis Cup team passed through Port Washington I'd known Mac for 15 or 20 days and knew he wasn't giving 100 per cent.

"I wondered about the guy's attitude, but still put him in against the Rumanian No.1. He hadn't shown up to practise for about three days, but he came on to court like a bull, not giving the other kid an inch.

"That was when we started to respect the abundance of his abilities and the way he put them to work. As far as he was concerned he just wanted competition. It was like he was saying, 'Give me the pressure, I'll deal with it.'"

The Brazilian added, "I don't want to come on like I'm his defence attorney. All I'm saying is, knowing the guy as I do, he is not misbehaving because he's a brat.

"People perceive the guy as a monster, who would probably come into this restaurant brandishing his racquet, breaking doors and cracking lights. He's not that sort of guy, he's extremely sensitive.

"But when the pressure is intense John asks himself to cut his mistakes to a minimum – he's excellent at doing that – and he has an expectation that no-one else should miss a call either."

At the end of 1984, it appeared that nothing was missing from John's life. He was young, talented and a world-wide superstar. He was perceived as much more than a sportsman: he was a celebrity; outspoken, witty, controversial. And he didn't just 'play' tennis: he used the game to show he was a performer, it enabled him to display his artistry and reveal his psyche. In many ways, he had turned tennis courts into the ultimate theatrical venue.

1985

Masters[19]	WON	Lendl	75 60 64
US Pro Indoors	WON	Mecir	63 76 61
WCT Houston	WON	Curren	75 61 76
Cuore Cup	WON	Jarryd	64 61
Chicago	WON	Connors	Walkover
WCT Atlanta	WON	Annacone	76 76 62
WCT Finals	Quarter-final	Nystrom	64 76 63
WCT New York	Runner-Up	Lendl	63 63
World Team Cup: beat Aguilera 67 64 64; beat Fitzgerald 61 60; beat Schwaier 75 76; lost to Lendl 67 76 63			
French Open	Semi-Final	Wilander	61 75 75
Wimbledon	Quarter-final	Curren	62 62 64
Volvo International	WON	Lendl	76 62
Canadian Open	WON	Lendl	75 63
US Open	Runner-Up	Lendl	76 63 64
Los Angeles	Semi-Final	Annacone	Withdrew
San Francisco	Quarter-final	Kriek	76 36 61
Antwerp	Runner-Up	Lendl	16 76 62 62
Stockholm Open	WON	Jarryd	61 62
Australian Open	Quarter-final	Zivojinovic	26 63 16 64 60

There is something about an athlete at the peak of his or her powers. Their invincibility instils a sense of expectation in the watching public. When McEnroe's serve was in a groove, he could shoot the ball down the centre-line or he could slice it wide with a flick of his talented wrist. Neither did he volley like the others; he always looked for the incredible angle or applied the most beautiful

---

[19] Part of the 1984 Tennis Year.

amount of backspin, which saw the ball drop dead as soon as it had cleared the net. His stroke-making was similarly idiosyncratic; with what appeared a slapdash backswing, he would hit the ball incredibly early and send it effortlessly to the most awkward parts of his opponent's side of the court. Most of all, he wanted to impress us with his flawlessness. His attention to detail was a delight to behold.

It wasn't only because of his outstanding technical ability that John's matches were anticipated with such delicious glee by the fans and the media. Another attraction was the fact that a McEnroe match was a journey into the unknown. What would irk him? Did his adversary stand any chance of success? What moments of pure skill would the New Yorker conjure up? If sport at its best is supposed to take us outside of ourselves, then John's battles in the first eight years of his career were the epitome of escapism.

Indeed, I don't think that McEnroe would deny that his breathtaking serve and volley game was at its zenith between 1977 and 1984. Between those years, despite his long-term relationships with Stacy Margolin and then Stella Hall, tennis was his life and professional success was his *raison d'être*. I cannot be certain which made him happier throughout this period; his sporting glory or his personal life, but in many ways I think it was the former. My view is that his psychological make-up dictated that, for him, it was a stipulation that he should ensure success. Only having attained his triumphs could he consider himself truly alive.

By 1985 John McEnroe had achieved; this cannot be disputed. I think he reacted by feeling that he had, at last, earned the right to ease up – if only a fraction – and he decided to concentrate on developing his social existence. Like a student liberated in the summer after weeks of exams, my belief is that he decided for the first time to divorce enjoyment from competition and winning. No doubt he embarked upon this path a little guiltily, but he sensed that he had found a soul-mate in film star Tatum O'Neal, who, like him, knew what it was like to wear the cloak of fame. It was once he had made this decision that, inevitably, his tennis career began to falter (but only if it is judged by the same excessive standards which John had habitually set himself).

So 1985 began with a scare at the '84 Masters in New York when he played Anders Jarryd. The Swede led 6-2, 3-0 and had a point for 4-0, before McEnroe asserted himself to emerge a 2-6, 6-4, 6-2 victor. After that, John made short work of Mats Wilander in the semi-final before blitzing Ivan Lendl 7-5, 6-0, 6-4.

McEnroe won eleven consecutive games during the rout of Ivan and rightly said afterwards that he had played as well as he had ever played before – "if not better."

He added, "There are still many things for me to improve – my level of concentration, my physical condition, cutting out careless shots … and there are still some technical things to work on, too."

Yet somehow John never improved upon the sparkling level of play he displayed in New York; the defeat of Lendl marked a transient pinnacle of pure excellence. In part, it was the demons within which prevented further progress.

McEnroe wasn't only troubled by the intense scrutiny of his relationship with Tatum O'Neal. He was also upset that the United States Tennis Association wanted him to sign a Davis Cup "good conduct" guarantee after Harry Merlo, chairman of team sponsor Louisiana Pacific, had threatened to withdraw financial support. Merlo had been dismayed by Jimmy Connors' obscene outbursts during the '84 Davis Cup final in Gothenburg.

Few were surprised that John refused to sign the guarantee. In March '85 he told Hugh Jamieson of 'The Sun', "I've come this far without signing a bit of paper and I'm not starting now. If that means the end of my Davis Cup career, then that's it. The bottom line is the way I feel about being told to sign – or else. No-one has been as loyal or proud to represent their country and I'm not going to be dictated to in this fashion." (Especially as team captain Arthur Ashe had said that John's behaviour in Sweden was 'fine'. In this instance, John was definitely being punished for Jimmy Connors' misdemeanours.)

In April, John was becoming world-weary, saying, "I'm beginning to appreciate the inside of my house more than the inside of an aeroplane." He was also resentful of questions about his private life, believing that his romance with Tatum was not a matter for public consumption.

Then, after failing to capitalise on a match point against Ivan Lendl in the World Team Cup, McEnroe found the going increasingly tough. He had to recover from 1-3 down in the fifth set of his French Open quarter-final against Joakim Nystrom to set up a last four clash with Mats Wilander. Mats had to save two set points at 4-5 in the third set, but otherwise he comprehensively dismantled McEnroe's game.

Before Wimbledon John's frustration was evident when he explained to Henry Fenwick in 'Radio Times' that disputing linecalls was "basically a losing proposition. It used to be when you asked [linesmen if they were sure of a call], a lot of times they'd say, 'Hey, I don't know', but now they pretty much stick with it even when they make a mistake. I suppose it's better to be consistently wrong than to mix it up – but either way you look at it it's going to be upsetting because you're always looking for a perfect match."

But the pursuit of perfection was now becoming a troublesome matter. Reports about his relationship with Tatum were the principal problem and at the All England Club John spoke out accordingly: "I don't know why people do what they do. It doesn't bother me nearly as much as it used to. I don't even read it anymore. I think it's a sad thing. I really don't know why people write things that they do and don't have the professional pride to ask anything. I get good vibes from the crowd here. I get more fan mail from here and Japan than I get from any other country. The press is making it seem a lot different than it is. I would feel a lot more anxious to come here if I didn't have to deal with that other part and that's why I'm not playing Queen's and Wembley anymore."

McEnroe's expressed intention was, in fact, not to spend "one minute longer than I have to in England." After his first round dismissal of Australian Peter McNamara, he said that since the French Open, despite missing the Stella Artois Championships, he'd practised in the normal way.

"I just thought that if Borg can win the tournament five years in a row without going to Queen's, there's no reason why I can't. That doesn't mean that I'm going to win the tournament, but it's not going to be an excuse if I lose, because I didn't have a few matches at Queen's. I just got a chance to go back and rest in the States. Paris is a tiring tournament, especially if you're in to the end. It's just not suggestable to play Queen's anymore."

Many journalists were less interested in his form ("Coming into Wimbledon I feel all right. I just hope my game gets going") than the state of his relationship with filmstar Tatum O'Neal. Was it true that they were going to wed immediately after Wimbledon, as said by freelancer Matthew Nugent?

"I didn't say to anyone that I was going to win Wimbledon, dedicate the title to Tatum and then get married afterwards. Tatum isn't over here and I don't believe she will be coming. There's a lot more things going on that are being written about that are making it a little bit difficult. It's not because of my friendship with Tatum, it's because of what the people write about it, which is a little bit different to what it is. I think it speaks for itself. The constant things that are made up and just not even asked, but what can I say? The reason she's not here is that I don't want to deal with this situation. And that's unfortunate. You're supposed to be able to come to a big thing and enjoy it.

"That's the decision I made because I want to come here and play tennis. There's a large percentage of people who have said things that are zero per cent truthful. I will be the first one to tell everyone when I get engaged."

John said he had "no idea" who Mr. Nugent was, and the latter's story embarrassed 'The Sun'. They had bought his offering and their first edition hit Fleet Street at 8.15 p.m. proclaiming that John would marry immediately after Wimbledon. At the same time, John was denying the story. Later editions carried his denial.

In the second round, John only pulled through 7-6, 6-1, 7-6 against Nduka Odizor of Nigeria. He confessed, "I feel like I just got by, just enough to win. I've been real flat a lot more this year; I was playing better last year at this point. I don't know the reason. I'm just hoping that things come together."

Incidentally, at the same press conference John was asked what he thought of American woman player Anne White's all-white body stocking. She had worn it one evening against Pam Shriver, but the match had been carried over to the following day and in the interim Alan Mills had informed her that her leotard was not acceptable tennis wear. "Different," McEnroe replied, "very different." Intriguingly, John Feinstein claimed in his 1991 book 'Hard Courts' that McEnroe and White had dated during the '84 US Open.

In truth, there was a multitude of McEnroe stories throughout every Wimbledon fortnight and the tabloids loved them all. When John was scheduled to play his fourth round game with South African qualifier Christo Steyn on Court No.2, 'The Mirror' laughed "Mac's Out In The Cold". "Banished!" screamed 'The Daily Mail' and the back page of 'The Sun' read "Angry Mac Plays In The Graveyard of Champs."

Referee Alan Mills admitted that the star "was surprised and unhappy" about the decision, but the No.1 seed emerged unscathed, 6-3, 7-5, 6-4.

And Court No.2? "The bounce was a little different, but it wasn't too bad. I don't think I should have had to play there. That's part of being the defending champion. You should have to be beaten on one of the two show courts, but what can I do about it when a decision has been made? I asked and they decided to keep me on that court.

"But I don't think they were trying to be unreasonable to me. They have been making a lot more of an effort the last three or four years. The court is not as bad as I found it five or six years ago."

When pushed further as to how The All England Cub had improved, John talked of their "tone and attitude."

"When we first came together it was two different sides of the spectrum and now both of us have made compromises. I like to make things easier now. It really is a sign of growing maturity. It sounds funny, but it's true. I'm not having more fun here, but I am in life in general and I feel a lot better about myself. I don't know if that's going to make me a better tennis player, but it's going to make me a better person which is more important."

"Do you ever look back and regret what you've done?"

"Certainly."

Yet John was again in deep water as far as the tabloids were concerned.

First, consider the following passage from Arthur Ashe's excellent 1975 autobiography-cum-diary "Portrait in Motion" (written with Frank Deford):

"About the only other place (apart from Wimbledon) you can get practice on grass is at Queen's Club, which we all hate. Queen's always holds a tournament as a warm-up before Wimbledon ... Traditionally, it offers the least prizes and hospitality – even common courtesy – of any tournament in the world ... Today, as is so often the case, it didn't suit the club to let us practise so Nikki (Pilic) and Izzy (El Shafei) and I were turned away ..."

Of the next day, June 17, 1973, Ashe had this to say, *"This afternoon, we had permission to practise at Queen's on Court 3 from 3.55 to 4.30 and then on Court 5 from 4.30 to 5.00. When no-one came to take our place on 3 at 4.30 we just did the sensible, convenient thing and completed our workout there. When we came into the locker room, a club official berated us loudly for playing 'without permission'. He just patronized us, spoke down to us with contempt."*

Little had changed at 'snooty' Queen's Club by the 1980s. 'The

Daily Mail' reported that many club members wanted the Stella Artois Championships to end and Wimbledon players to be banned from practising at the Club, since the stars' activities "interfered with their tennis playing."

Viewed in this light, it was hardly surprising that an unhappy, ill-prepared, jittery McEnroe had ended up swearing at club players before the Odizor match.

McEnroe had been granted honorary membership of the West London club in 1982 and on Friday, June 28, 1985 he was playing on a members' court for his last warm-up before travelling over to Wimbledon. Unbeknown to John, the court was booked by member Mrs. Sheila Boden, but she would not grant him 15 minutes' extra time, despite tennis being of somewhat greater importance to McEnroe's life than to hers.

After Wimbledon, high-handed Queen's Club reacted by terminating John's membership and they refused to consider him for Stella Artois wild cards.

"Let them do the thing they feel is necessary," said a weary McEnroe at the end of July '85. Distributing gifts to patients at a children's hospital in Pittsburgh, he added, "I don't think people even know what the Queen's Club membership is, much less care about it here. It kind of makes me angry when people ask me about it. It's just another story to them [reporters]. Let's put it this way, I'm glad to be in America. That's the only thing I can say about that."

But eventually, on June 26, 1989, Steve Allan of 'The Sun' announced that McEnroe and Queen's Club chairman Grant Meyrick had settled their differences. Said Meyrick, "We are delighted that old wounds have been healed." And John opined, "I'm glad the matter has been resolved and I'm looking forward to practising once again at Queen's Club."

The whole affair was manna to Fleet Street and accentuated McEnroe's low opinion of the press. As far as he was concerned, paparazzi treatment had prevented him from bringing Tatum to Wimbledon and he felt lonely without her. In a sense, he wished only for the normality of a boyfriend/girlfriend relationship and wanted to enjoy his romance away from prying eyes.

As a consequence, his mental preparation for facing fast-serving Kevin Curren in the Wimbledon quarter-finals was poor. And John Passmore of 'The Daily Mail' called it 'sensational' when after just one hour and forty-nine minutes Curren left the Centre Court a hero, having bombarded McEnroe 6-2, 6-2, 6-4. It was the worst defeat of any post-war defending Champion.

The features of a match where John never displayed any sparkle, were:

Game 5, Set 1: The decidedly shaky holder dropped serve for the first time.

Game 7, Set 1: Good reflexes gave John 40-0, but a sloppy volley, double fault and a debatable call on the sideline let Curren in at deuce. Although McEnroe earned a point for 3-4, he couldn't halt Curren from 5-2. BBC commentators sensed trouble for McEnroe like that of his 1979 downfall. "He looks as if he's asleep," said Dan Maskell.

2.05: Curren had first set 6-2 – with an easy bounce smash off a very weak McEnroe lob.

2.10: South African-born Curren broke for 1-0. "This isn't the usual John McEnroe," reiterated Maskell.

Then at 2-1, with Curren serving, McEnroe went 30-0 up. A dubious second serve winner seconds later made the score 30-30. John protested and umpire David Howie rebuked him – "Please play on, Mr. McEnroe" – a little too quickly and sharply in the player's opinion. "You tell me to play on before I've even said anything," shouted McEnroe.

McEnroe lost the next point – 40-30.

On game point Curren served a fault. "Play on, play on," said John, still troubled by Howie's words.

"Don't worry about it, John," yelled an adolescent from the crowd. "All right, you're right," replied McEnroe, with a touch of sarcasm as he acknowledged the heckler with a wave of the hand.

Curren requested two serves and umpire Howie agreed. "First serve – hindrance," he called at 2.24. McEnroe, seeing no reason why he should be penalised for spectator involvement, questioned Howie's decision. The umpire replied by meting out a code violation for 'unsportsmanlike conduct'.

"What was that for? That's 'unsportsmanlike conduct' when he yells out in the middle of the point?" argued the Champion.

"15 seconds."

"Can I have the referee please? Right now, before we play any more points," retorted McEnroe. Maskell's colleague John Barrett, realising McEnroe would question the warning, said it was the result of McEnroe's "Play on, play on." Yet Howie didn't warn McEnroe until <u>after</u> the latter had questioned the two serve decision.

Mills and the Grand Prix supervisor Ken Farrar appeared. Following a six minute conversation they upheld Howie's warning. Curren rallied for 3-1, then tightened his chokehold for 6-2, 6-2.

At 3-3 in the third set a double fault followed by three confident winners from Curren presented the 27-year old with his fifth break. More significantly, the match was effectively over.

At 3.22, the 1984 Champion, "lacking that fierce intensity" as Barrett put it, hit a forehand over the baseline on Curren's second match point. *The King is dead, long live the King!*

Given all the references to McEnroe's apparent nonchalance in the face of defeat, it seemed intriguing to ask if he was trying throughout. Hugh Jamieson, who had spoken exclusively to John McEnroe Snr. before the tournament when he had declared "MY BOY MAC WON'T LOSE TO LOVE"[20], said:

"There were a number of reasons for McEnroe's defeat by Curren. The first is that I don't think he prepared properly by missing Queen's for the first time ever. He elected to return home after the French and practise on grass in New York and Long Island with Vitas Gerulaitis and his brother Patrick. That's a lot different to getting tournament tough on grass and also getting acclimatised to the British conditions – the weather and obviously the pace of the grass. And when it came to Wimbledon he arrived on Thursday evening to find outdoor practice on grass already hit by the weather, so that his mood going into the tournament was hardly filled with confidence. He admitted within the opening week that he wouldn't retain the title playing the way he was at the time – and so it proved. He didn't have the spark, aggression and touch that should have put Curren away and he also knew it, because there were times when he looked almost disinterested. It was as if he knew he was on the way out. It left him admitting that he's got to start working harder at his game from a physical point of view, because at 26 just playing tennis – singles and doubles most of the time – is clearly not enough.

"The other factor is that his romance with Tatum O'Neal and the

---

[20] John's father said in 'The Sun' of June 24, "John knows what he's doing. Tennis is his business and the bottom line means winning. He wants that Wimbledon crown badly. He has the chance to work his way into the tournament thanks to the draw, and he can handle the pressure. He has proved it before and he'll do it again."

resultant attention in the media – especially in Britain – had also had an effect. He had already decided against playing Queen's and Wembley because of what he called 'harassment' and I think that at Wimbledon he seemed to be in no mood to dominate the place because of all his problems."

Journalist Malcolm Folley added:

"I noticed a subtle change in his attitude ever since the Volvo Masters tournament in New York in January 1985. When McEnroe lost to Joakim Nystrom in Dallas in April, many theories were offered to try to explain this surprise. Some were weird and wonderful, but after exhaustive analysis I kept returning to the fact that John was half a yard short of pace and far from disturbed by his loss. In Paris the eventual Champion Mats Wilander outclassed him on his least favourite surface – and there is no question in my mind that he had set out his stall to succeed in France that year. Coming round to Wimbledon, he complained from the very first match that he wasn't happy with his form or touch. Against Kevin Curren all his fears and self-doubts were exposed by a man playing above himself."

John said the defeat was "a combination of me being off my game and him just wanting to win."

Explaining that Curren had overpowered him, John felt it was maybe time for another switch of racquets, as "people seem to be starting to hit it harder and harder again.

"I just played a sub-par match. I certainly wasn't expecting to be broken as much as I was. I was surprised at how badly I was serving. I didn't really have any pace on my serve. When you lose, everything seems to hurt a whole lot more. It's a tough rut to get out of. I didn't feel as fresh as I'd like. I felt real old out there."

McEnroe gave the impression he had been a little light-headed on court and complained of battle fatigue. "I'm not sure if I've played yet, it's that sort of feeling. Maybe it's time to think about working a little harder. As you go on your body doesn't come back as quickly. I don't think, say, 26 is an old age. I just think that I've been on tour for eight years, I've played a lot of matches in singles and doubles and I think that at times you're not aware, it catches up with you. You have to look for ways to keep your intensity. I found it's getting to be a little overwhelming being No.1 recently. Hopefully my competitive desire will resurface on other occasions and enjoyment of the game will push me to a different level."

McEnroe cited the press as a worry. "I would look forward to coming back to Wimbledon under different circumstances and I hope the circumstances will improve in years to come. I've turned out in this country to be an easy target. I don't think that I'm that interesting a person, that I should have been harassed the way I've been. I think I'm a good person, but I've certainly never thought I warranted the kind of attention I receive here. Even people who in the papers are supposed to talk the truth and write fair things are saying things that I think are completely unjustified and it's really hard to take. I'm not going to use that as an excuse, though – he completely outplayed me."

Losing to Wilander in Paris "took something out of me also."

"It's tough to try and pull it together so quickly. I think it would be a little bit fairer if they tried to give it a little more time between tournaments. I was a little bit down after the French and I didn't mentally freshen up."

The incident in the second set still rankled. "He [Curren] asked for a let call because someone had yelled in the stand. That happens all the time, here and at other tournaments. I was having a tough enough time with his serves, so I didn't think he should get another serve. I didn't get that decision and then I received an 'unsportsmanlike conduct' for taking too long. I've been told I won't be fined for it, but I don't think I should have received anything such as that. I don't think that was even close to warranting it."

So why did Howie see fit to warn McEnroe? He explained to me that study of the videotape would show that Curren's concentration was under threat in the entire game from outside influences. McEnroe did not deliberately create these, Howie believed, but they effectively unnerved the server.

At first, when John was vexed by the "Play on, Mr. McEnroe" at 30-30, the umpire let it pass. But by the questioning of the two ball decision Howie felt it was time to step in and restore order. He also drew my attention to the following rule: *"If a player commits any act which hinders his opponent in making a stroke, then, if this is deliberate, he shall lose the point or if involuntary, the point shall be replayed."*

However, I much admire Howie's courage in admitting he should at least shoulder part of the blame. Having not umpired McEnroe for three years, it took him time to find the tone required to strike the right note with John. The touch-paper may have been lit at 30-30, he said, when he was possibly too brusque. McEnroe might have interpreted the two-ball judgement as a decision made against him. But it was not. The crowd's reaction to McEnroe's comment had disturbed Curren, Howie said.

All this I understood – except John Barrett's comment, "Frankly this must not be allowed to happen," as McEnroe spoke to Mills, inferring the player was in the wrong. The rules said otherwise: *"A player shall be entitled to require an umpire to summon the referee and the Grand Prix supervisor, but only to obtain an interpretation of these rules or to assess the competence of an official."*

Finally, was John thinking of retiring?

"That's not what I was saying at all. I think I'll be back, I just can't say when."

✄

In a later BBC TV interview with Gerald Williams, McEnroe returned to his complaints against the newspaper world. "I realise that … er … some are the prices you pay, but … er … I think it's gone way past that limit and I think people should … er … I can't rationalise talking to the press people because they're not rational people. I mean, it's very strange, it's … and I think the most important thing to realise is that I'm 26 years old and Tatum O'Neal is 21 years old and people should take that into consideration a little more when they start making up things."

Williams agreed that press treatment was affecting McEnroe's performance in England, "because John is letting it.

"The mere fact he feels such passionate alienation makes it difficult for him, surely, to play in the right frame of mind."

He went on to say: "Sometime, perhaps, in his way, John will try to make peace. He has done so before. The trouble is when he behaves bizarrely it is bound to cause adverse comment – and then the circle begins again. What will Fleet Street do? The tabloids will do much the same till their circulation falls. The heavies, I believe, are the best in the world. You can't easily stifle press comment, even if you want to. At press conferences only 'reasonable' questions should be asked, though there'll never be agreement over what is 'reasonable'.

"To sum up, sections of the press all over the world are very tough on John indeed, often unfairly, though not always."

The following day the media talked of 'McEnroe Massacre' and 'The Downfall of Superbrat'. It was as if the clock had been turned back six years.

And as for whether John gave up hope, he said no … "I was hoping maybe he'd break his ankle or something." But after he left England there were rumours that a viral infection had weakened him.

In the meantime, he and Peter Fleming still hoped to capture the doubles title. Peter, however, appreciated it would be an uphill task. He told the media: "I thought John looked bad yesterday. He wasn't so much tired as he was lost and bewildered. Physically he was not feeling that well; he wasn't moving well, nor was he hitting the ball well. He had no confidence and was not the player we are accustomed to seeing. Even if he exaggerates a little, the fact is that in his mind there are things disturbing and inhibiting him. The best performers perform the best when everything just flows and no thinking takes place. If you are tense about things, it stops – nothing flows.

"John has not had any relaxing moments with Tatum this tournament and everything snowballed. It just seems like a way of life now – this guy is as much a part of the culture here as the Royal Family in the month of June. Guys who have never been to Wimbledon will write about John in their column. Yesterday during that match John said some pretty funny things that had Connors said them, people would have laughed. But he makes a funny comment and the umpire gives him an 'unsportsmanlike conduct' warning – I don't understand that.

"John is just basically pissed off about the whole situation of why does this have to be. I've seen him this low maybe once or twice, but even then only for a very short time. Hopefully this won't last long either."

Soon the American duo were having to come to terms with a semi-finals' elimination by Pat Cash and John Fitzgerald. A few weeks later McEnroe was still struggling to eradicate his memories of Wimbledon '85. He said, "The press is why I'm not playing in England anymore. And it would not take a whole lot more for me not to play there. I am not saying right here and now that I'm not playing Wimbledon next year, but I'm definitely closer to not playing than I was."

Moreover, he revealed to Helmut Sorge and Teja Fiedler of 'Der Spiegel', "Before I won [Wimbledon], I remember saying to my father, "If I ever win this tournament, I'm never going to come back. I just went through too much in London. It's not worth it. I feel it's a total loss even to go there. I don't feel I get any enjoyment even going there. The irony of the story is I've gone back every year since."

Fortuitously, thoughts of Wimbledon were well behind John when he competed against Lendl at Stratton Mountain. He had leads of 3-0 in set one and 5-0 in set two and deservedly took the $40,000 first prize.

So why did McEnroe fall to Ivan in the final of the US Open? It should not be forgotten that it took him four hours to overcome Wilander 3-6, 6-4, 4-6, 6-3, 6-3 in an enthralling semi-final played in 118 degrees heat. In cooler temperatures, Lendl then disposed of Connors 6-2, 6-3, 7-5 after Jimmy had injured his ankle during the warm-up. The next day Ivan saved a set-point at 2-5 in the first set before John, understandably, wilted.

One could easily infer from John's post-match comments that his personal life had become more important to him than his career. He declared, "If I'm not No.1, I'll be No.2. There's a lot worse things than being No.2." But tellingly, he did add, "I think it's a major injustice to have to play two straight days in a major Championship. I'd rather take less money and screw TV. It's more important for the beauty of the game and delivering the best tennis, rather than run the risk of having two tired players out there."

A fortnight later John was hit by an intestinal infection and had to withdraw from the Los Angeles event. The following week he was still struggling with his health whilst in San Francisco, but he then went to Belgium for the European Champions' Championship hoping to inflict revenge on Lendl.

Having easily beaten the new Wimbledon Champion, Boris Becker, in the semis, John blew Ivan off the court in the first set of the final. Playing beautiful tennis, he raced to a 6-1 lead. The crunch, however, came at 4-4 in the second set tie-break when a dubious call left Lendl leading 5-4. Had the line decision gone John's way, he would have been 5-4 up with his two service points to follow. But in the end Lendl won an exciting encounter 1-6, 7-6, 6-2, 6-2 in two hours and fifty-five minutes. McEnroe reacted generously, "Lendl played a great match. Physically he's in better shape than I am right now. I need to be in tip-top condition mentally and physically and, if I am, I think I can still beat him."

It was this fighting talk which caused John to chase the Australian Open title at the end of November. But in his initial press conference in Melbourne the first question went like this, "You are going to be his new son-in-law, how do you get on with Ryan O'Neal?" Keeping his patience, John responded, "Very well."

"What about the rumours you have got married [to Tatum O'Neal]?"

"It is completely untrue," retorted John. "But it gets written so much people believe it. We're together now, we're happy. Why can't people just leave me be? It's just got so far out of control that it's affecting me at other times."

The American's exasperation was partly due to an incident earlier in the day when 'Melbourne Herald' reporter Geoff Easdown had accosted him at his hotel and had refused to leave him alone. In John's words, "If you can't go into a hotel lobby without a pressman being there, that's the lowest. I moved the guy aside and all of a sudden it's like I've physically assaulted him and he's beaten up."

John continued, "I'm not even saying leave me alone, I'm saying be reasonable."

He then discussed a newspaper story that declared he had secretly married Tatum on November 16 with President Reagan present as a guest. "I laughed at first, but I didn't laugh when there were ten reporters camped outside my hotel in Paris and I didn't laugh when I had to deny the story again in Spain and in Belgium. But no-one listened because suddenly 'The Wall Street Journal', which is probably the most conservative non-sports paper in the world, printed it as if it was fact. So by then people just assumed I was lying and that's what frustrated me. You people should be proud of what you write and take care to research it."

Quite simply, McEnroe had played out his career in the public spotlight and felt that he should protect a personal relationship which was still in its infancy. Simultaneously, he remarked, "I do love the game of tennis and I don't want to go away from it."

But even the sport itself had changed as far as John was concerned. At the back of his mind lay the thought that genuine tennis involved using his old wood Maxplys. He was bothered by the one-dimensional power shots that the new rackets had made possible. The sport's subtleties now appeared to be under threat.

It was against this emotional backdrop that McEnroe stumbled out of the last Grand Slam of '85, in effect giving up in the fifth set against Slobodan Zivojinovic. And then came the Los Angeles Herald Examiner's story that Tatum and John were planning to wed. "The truth of the matter is that she is expecting a baby," McEnroe was quoted as saying.

1986

Masters[21]	1st Round	Gilbert	57 64 61
Stratton Mountain	Semi-Final	Becker	36 75 76
Canadian Open	3rd Round	Seguso	46 63 75
US Open	1st Round	Annacone	16 61 63 63
Pacific Southwest	WON	Edberg	62 63
San Francisco	WON	Connors	76 63
Scottsdale	WON	Curren	63 36 62
Paris Open	Quarter-final	Casal	63 76
Antwerp	WON	Mecir	63 16 76 57 62
Benson & Hedges	1st Round	Cash	63 57 64

It was the Masters' defeat in early 1986 at the hands of Brad Gilbert that triggered McEnroe's decision to escape the limelight and instead bask in the warmth of his relationship with Tatum. He said, "I need to stop for a while because if I go on losing to the Gilberts of this world I'll want to stop for good. I've just got so much else on my mind right now that there's no way I can do justice to my tennis. I'm just not fit. Half the time Tatum feels sick, I feel sick, too. They say there is such a thing as a sympathetic pain, don't they?"

He duly turned his back on tennis and went on a sabbatical. Nonetheless, his business agent, Peter Lawler, stressed in April that John was practising and pushing weights (although in reality his client was actually more concerned with preparing to become a father).

Weighing eight pounds eleven ounces, Kevin John McEnroe was born in Santa Monica on Friday, May 23, 1986. His father had apparently attended all the pre-birth classes and less than two months later McEnroe married 22-year old Tatum O'Neal at St. Dominic's Roman Catholic Church on Long Island, New York. 1,000 well-wishers thronged the pavements for five hours and the couple waved to their fans. Peter Rennert acted as Best Man, whilst brothers Patrick and Mark, and Peter Fleming, were ushers.

---

[21] Part of the 1985 Tennis Year.

However, McEnroe decided not to vanish into domestic bliss. His father was quick to point out that John "will be no less intense as a performer; I suspect he will remain unhappy with himself if he is not playing well." But the player emphasised that he was willing to forego being No.1 in order to be happy.

The comeback tournament took place in Stratton Mountain, Vermont. Despite holding four match points, John crashed out in the semi-finals 3-6, 7-5, 7-6 to Wimbledon Champion Boris Becker. The American ace was so disgruntled by his opponent's celebration of victorious points that he shouted, "Someone should teach you a lesson in respect."

Afterwards, the loser claimed, "I didn't verbally abuse him or swear." He added, "I don't want to continue on the path I have been going on. I want bad press if I misbehave because I think ultimately it will help me or drive me away from the game altogether."

McEnroe's fortunes didn't improve at the US Open. He lost in the first round to 23 year old fellow New Yorker Paul Annacone; he said that he felt too 'skinny' having lost a stone during his lay-off. His absence from the Tour had also left him lacking self-belief, for he said, "I've got to look in the mirror. There's no use pretending it's there if it's not. I'm not into my matches. In fact, I'm into them less than when I stopped playing."

McEnroe's form remained erratic throughout the remainder of 1986, perhaps reflecting his shift of priorities. He won in Los Angeles and assured us, "My concentration was a lot better. I was more into the match." But at the end of October he succumbed 6-3, 7-6 to Spain's Sergio Casal in the Paris Open quarter-finals, thereby killing off any chance of qualifying for the Masters. Both players were upset with linecalls and McEnroe in fact deliberately lost one point when he believed Casal had been the victim of a bad decision. Then, at 8-7 in the second set tie-break, the New Yorker appeared to hit an ace. Relieved, he returned to his chair and sat down believing he had won the set. However, a line judge suddenly signalled the service out and British umpire Jeremy Shales upheld the decision. Enraged, McEnroe served long for his fourth double-fault and although he earned a third set-point at 9-8, he hit two shots into the net before Casal beat him with a pass into the far corner.

At the close, McEnroe informed Shales, "You're the worst umpire I ever had in my life," and he told the press that he hoped one day technology would bring an end to umpiring errors.

Typically, however, John wasn't optimistic: "Even Wimbledon's seeing eye on the service line isn't one hundred per cent." But he added that the match hadn't been decided by linecalls; Casal had played an "excellent match", while he himself had "lacked zip."

And so to England, where John had not performed for sixteen months. He started the week by smiling and posing with Tatum and Kevin outside their rented apartment in Fulham; he told photographers, "Sure, that's fine. I'll do what you want me to do."

But in the first round at the Wembley Arena, despite receiving a hero's welcome, McEnroe couldn't get the ball to dance to his tune. The trouble, as he saw it, was that he had played too much since his comeback in an attempt "to make something out of the year." Furthermore, a viral infection had left him "lacking the intensity that is a large part of my game."

Yet it was frightening that David Irvine of 'The Guardian' wrote the next day about "The man who fell to earth again". And ominously, the same experienced observer claimed that John's reactions had slowed down.

McEnroe agreed that he had "a lot to prove", but continued, "I still honestly feel that I can be a better tennis player than ever. There's something inside of me that should be coming out." All the same, he felt forced to say, "I was pathetic. That was not me out there. I apologised to Cash afterwards. He was entitled to expect more from me. At one stage I had a chance of winning, simply because I got him playing as badly as myself."

'The Daily Telegraph' believed that John had been passing around photographs of his son Kevin in the locker room and the father made his contentment obvious to the press. "That other part of my life is very fulfilling and therefore it's sometimes hard to find the motivation. That's something I need to work out for myself."

1987

Philadelphia	Runner-Up	Mayotte	36 61 63 61
Memphis	3rd Round	Kriek	75 64
Rotterdam	Runner-Up	Edberg	36 63 61
Brussels	Runner-Up	Wilander	63 64
WCT Finals	Runner-Up	Mecir	60 36 62 62
Rome	Semi-Final	Wilander	61 63
World Team Cup: beat E. Sanchez 75 36 75; beat Jaite 64 61; beat Leconte 26 75 61; lost to Mecir 75 26 21 (Mecir's scores first)			
French Open	1st Round	De la Pena	46 62 64 62
Stratton Mountain	Divided with Lendl	John led…	76 14
Montreal	Quarter-final	Connors	63 36 63
Cincinnati	1st Round	Annacone	76 64
US Open	Quarter-final	Lendl	63 63 64
Antwerp	Quarter-final	Mecir	64 64

Davis Cup:

V West Germany lost to Becker 46 15-13 8-10 62 62; beat Jelen 75 62 61

McEnroe turned 28 years old in February 1987 and the very same month his old doubles partner, Peter Fleming, disclosed that the star was having "real problems with his back." Fleming told David Irvine in 'The Guardian', "There is something inside him saying, "Don't run for that ball, because it's going to hurt," and until he loses that, he's not going to be No.1 again."

At the same time, Peter intimated that McEnroe's days of

unwavering devotion to tennis were behind him. "Back in 1980/81 no-one could touch us," recalled the right-hander. "We had that sort of arrogance when we walked on court that we just knew whatever our opponents did, it wasn't going to be good enough. Mind you, we were young then and incredibly intense. I don't think we could ever get back to that level."

But briefly, McEnroe did fight through the pain barrier to match his previous level of performance. In April, he overwhelmed Yannick Noah 7-6, 6-2, 4-6, 6-3 during the WCT Finals in Dallas and declared, "Emotion is the key to sports, especially in a one-on-one sport like tennis. At this level it all comes down to mental desire and being able to guts it out."

Nevertheless, McEnroe's back disabilities restricted his training schedule and that translated into a lack of efficacy on court.

It was sad to see him unable to live up to his early season warning that, "I'm a hell of a lot closer to my best than when I came back last year."

26year-old Tim Mayotte toppled John in the Philadelphia final and opined that the runner-up had lost some of his sharpness. In May there was talk of a hip problem and McEnroe then pulled out of Wimbledon, citing trouble with his legs.

The decision to shun London SW19 had not been taken lightly. Tatum wanted him to go there on his own and bring back the title, but McEnroe told the press, "There's no reason for me to go to Wimbledon unless I'm 100% fit. I have not been able to train adequately since I returned from Paris and I'm tired of walking onto the court worried about whether I will be able to give it my best effort."

John McEnroe Snr. could merely add, "He was looking forward to Wimbledon, but his back has been giving him trouble. What can I do? But if he is standing on two legs, this time next year, he will be back." Such was the significance of McEnroe's withdrawal from The Championships that 'The Times' carried the news on its front page.

Unfortunately John was also unable to make headlines for the right reasons in New York. He would, in time, say that it had been his nerves due to Tatum's second pregnancy which led him to behave terribly in his third round US Open encounter with Slobodan Zivojinovic.

Again he was sorry. "I made a mistake and I feel bad about it. I said something obscene and I can't justify that, even though in our open society it's tough to keep from saying those kind of words on court. I hope my children are raised not to say those words. But it happened in the heat of the moment – it just slid out."

John slid out of the US Open at the quarter-final stage and said of his conqueror, Ivan Lendl, "It's obvious why he is the No.1 player in the world. He just kept putting pressure on my serve and didn't let me into the match at all." Yet a month earlier, McEnroe had led his great rival 7-6, 1-4 in the final of Stratton Mountain's Volvo International. Unfortunately for McEnroe's confidence, torrential rain prevented an outcome and each player received runners-up prize money of $20,000.

The New Yorker was still in the hunt for a place in the end-of-season Masters, but that came to a halt when he received a two month suspension for his outbursts in the Zivojinovic match.

Unexpectedly, the 28year-old blamed 'temporary insanity' for his antics.

But John's personal life made up for the professional setbacks. Tatum gave birth to a second son, Sean Timothy, on September 23 in New York.

And it was also good to see McEnroe back where he belonged, playing Davis Cup for his country. In a relegation tie with West Germany, John battled Boris Becker every inch of the way during a marathon five-setter. The ATP Media Guide described the American's performance "as perhaps [his] finest since the destruction of Jimmy Connors in the 1984 Wimbledon final …"

৵৩

At the end of the year, Peter Fleming announced during a doubles event at the Royal Albert Hall that he was now John McEnroe's coach.

Peter said, "Maybe he can't get higher than the 1981 and 1984 levels. Some of the fire's gone. But if he got to 90% he would be practically unbeatable."

1988

Japan Open	WON	Edberg	62 62
WCT New York	1st Round	Perez	76 26 63
French Open	4th Round	Lendl	67 76 64 64
Goal Challenge	Beat Wilander 64 36 63; beat Nystrom 63 76		
Wirral Classic	Semi-Final	Van Rensburg	36 64 62
Wimbledon	2nd Round	Masur	75 76 63
US Hardcourts	Runner-Up	Becker	64 62
Canadian Open	Quarter-final	Woodforde	62 26 62
US Open	2nd Round	Woodforde	75 46 67 63 61
Los Angeles`	Semi-Final	Agassi	64 06 64
San Francisco	Semi-Final	Kriek	64 36 64
Paris Open	Quarter-final	Hlasek	76 26 76
Antwerp	WON	Chesnokov	61 75 62
Detroit	WON	Krickstein	75 62

Davis Cup:

V Argentina beat Perez Roldan 62 57 64 36 63; lost to Jaite 60 68 63

I think that John McEnroe was somewhat torn in 1988. On the one hand, as he admitted in Los Angeles in April, his place in tennis history was already assured. But he also yearned for another Grand Slam title and he told reporter Jay Axelbank of 'Inside Tennis', "I would use this analogy: I baked a great cake, but it would taste a little better if there was still icing on it."

At least his popularity was undiminished and he played some stirring tennis in '88. For instance, he thrashed Michael Chang at

Roland Garros and then, on May 31, he faced world No 1 Ivan Lendl for a place in the quarter-finals.

The match started in drizzle and John was not pleased when he slipped on the wet clay and missed a chance to break his adversary's serve. At 1-1 there was a break of 90 minutes before the New Yorker returned to grab the first set in a 7-3 tie-breaker. Lendl took the second set tie-break by the same score although the American protested fiercely that Lendl's final shot had landed beyond the baseline.

John had obviously engaged the crowd's emotions because the assistant referee had to appeal for quiet in order for the third set to begin. Suddenly McEnroe, so close to a two sets' advantage, came off the boil and Lendl sprinted to 4-1. John growled: "Will you bring on the balls that glow in the dark?" before he won the next game and play was duly suspended for the day.

On June 1 a remorseless Lendl edged through 6-7, 7-6, 6-4, 6-4. However, the Parisians roared their approval of McEnroe and he laughed, "It's like wine, you know. The older you get, the more they appreciate you."

Just nine days later Dublin's 'Evening Herald' informed its readers that tickets for the two day Goal Challenge had sold out "in double quick time" after the announcement earlier in the week that John was playing the event. All gate receipts were going to charity.

On Sunday, June 12, John practised on courts at Trinity College, which were normally croquet lawns. He told a press conference, "I wouldn't go to Wimbledon if I didn't think I could win. Losing the No.1 ranking hurt my tennis, but it helped me as a person. I was overworking and needed a rest, but I'm back now playing matches when I want to and enjoying it."

Indeed, McEnroe mastered Wilander 6-4, 3-6, 6-3 and joked, "It's nice of him to let me win the big ones. He wins the [1988] French and Australian [Opens] and gives me the Goal match."

During the contest McEnroe miscued when trying to kick a ball into the crowd and found time to quip, "I might get into the England team [which had just lost to The Republic of Ireland in The European Championships] kicking like that."

And when John contested a line decision, he instructed the crowd, "All of those in favour that the ball was out raise their hands."

But a more serious John McEnroe was on view too. He sat on the steps inside the cloisters at Trinity College and considered his past.

"It's true I want to be liked. What you are comfortable with at 20 is not what you are comfortable with at 30.

"It's a nice feeling to have the crowd behind me, as I did at the French Open. I wish it had happened earlier.

"Some of it was my problem. I wasn't brought up on the tennis court to smile. But my exterior has never been as rough as it seemed. I don't enjoy playing that way anymore."

"As you get older and see the tragedies of the world you want to do something in your own little way," John added, explaining his presence in Ireland.

"I've never felt as much electricity as I have walking onto the Centre Court to play a final," he continued. "I've had a lot of great moments there ... and some not so great. But the longer you are away the more you can appreciate it. Staying away when I was not properly fit has allowed me to get a better perspective on it and all it means."

Unfortunately, John's Wimbledon preparations did not go altogether to plan. During his stay in Dublin, he and Mats Wilander staged a charity exhibition boxing bout in front of 300 spectators at the Berkeley Court Hotel.

Though the six minute confrontation was declared a draw, referee Mike Dowling, a former Olympic boxer, admitted, "If it was a proper contest I would have had to declare McEnroe a winner by a street on points. If he had not taken up tennis he would have made a good boxer. He has an inbuilt will to win – he doesn't like to lose at anything. He has a good right jab and a long left cross."

However, the fight left John so stiff that he needed a deep massage afterwards. Indeed, a year later he confessed to 'The Sun' that he hadn't been able to lift his arms "for four days afterwards."

The next problem came when John competed on public courts in Ashton Park on the Wirral and lost a semi-final to 25year-old South African Christo van Rensburg. "I felt good in practice, but just somehow got out of synch," explained the American. "There were some calls that hurt me and his game picked up. It was just a disappointing day. I'll dig in and work out the kinks."

At Wimbledon we thought that John might play with his old passion and capture the golden trophy, just as he had in 1984. The early signs were hopeful. He destroyed his first opponent, Austrian Horst Skoff, and then talked about how much better his attitude was than it had been in 1985. "At that point, I was negative," he confirmed. "The pressure was getting to the point where I didn't want to win the match [against Curren] enough. But now it's a totally new set of circumstances."

Wally Masur should not have caused any problems in the second round; after all, hadn't the left-handed genius dispatched him on the very same Centre Court four years earlier for the loss of a mere seven games?

The early evening match began with John walking on court with a dramatic clenched fist and the crowds cheering their admiration …

He then broke Wally to thirty in the second game and we sat back in anticipation of a vintage display. But it never came. John himself dropped serve to miss the chance of a 3-0 lead, although he still managed to reach a set point at 5-4. Masur saved it with a fine shot which messed up McEnroe's volley.

Soon John was struggling. In the eleventh game he delivered three double faults to give Masur a 6-5 lead and the world's No.64 gratefully served out the set to love.

The second set was highly eventful. Again John held a set point, at 6-5, but Masur served superbly to McEnroe's backhand to thwart the American.

In the ensuing tie-break a harsh call robbed John of a vital 3-1 lead. "That ball was on the line," he shouted at umpire Rudi Berger and the TV replay indeed appeared to confirm John's opinion. Berger, however, refused to overrule his linesman and John would later downplay the incident, saying, "It's a big point you can ill afford in a tie-break. But I didn't feel I was in the match even when I was up."

In the third set John soon slumped to 0-3. At 2-4 he missed two opportunities to break back and at deuce in that game he didn't play Masur's backhand volley because he was so sure it had landed long. Berger called it in and John flung his racquet to the ground, earning a warning for racquet abuse. "Not a piece of chalk came up," he yelled. "That ball was so obviously out."

But soon it was John who was out and all he could do was express his turbulent feelings.

"I don't feel like I played well at all," he declared. "He played well though. He played a good solid match and I didn't come up with anything. Even so, I still should have won the first couple of sets. If that's the best I've got to give I'd quit tomorrow. That was a disgusting effort. I didn't get the feel of the balls. I got caught by surprise. It was just one of those days when you don't feel well. I didn't feel like competing – I didn't feel I was in the match.

"I'll probably know better in the next couple of days what went wrong, but it never felt like I was in synch with my game. You just have to learn from it. It's a real test to see how I come out of it. I expected some ups and downs. It's not that surprising that something like this happened – not surprising to me, anyhow. It's going to take more than just one match to suddenly feel comfortable again in a place where I didn't really ever feel comfortable.

"I thought the crowd was good. They were trying to pull for me. It was a good feeling and I tried to hang in there despite the fact I wasn't coming up with any good shots. I felt like I was disappointing them. Two things could happen now. I could come out of it and get a couple of good years, or just continue to stay in this mould and play inferior tennis.

"I wouldn't have won the women's tournament if I'd played [in it] today."

In 'The Sun', John explained to Hugh Jamieson "I'll Win It Next Year." The American star referred to a stomach bug which meant he "couldn't get a feel for the ball on my racquet." He added that the loss meant he "wanted to break every racquet in my bag."

Within two months, John announced his 'split' from Peter Fleming. He said, "The fact that we are such good friends meant that the coach-player relationship wasn't able to develop the way we had hoped. We were just too friendly."

At least McEnroe had the thrill of seeing his beloved US Davis Cup team return to the premier fold. In Buenos Aires he crushed experienced clay-courter Guillermo Perez-Roldan in a rousing five-setter.

And McEnroe also teamed up with Mark Woodforde to win doubles titles in Los Angeles and San Francisco. Asked why he was partnering the Australian who had twice defeated him in '88, John replied, "If you can't beat 'em, join 'em."

1989

Australian Open	Quarter-final	Lendl	76 62 76
Milan	Semi-Final	Becker	62 63
Lyon	WON	Hlasek	63 76
WCT Finals	WON	Gilbert	63 63 76
Japan Open	Semi-Final	Edberg	64 63
Beckenham	WON	Dyke	64 76
Edinburgh	WON	Connors	76 76
Wirral International	1st Round	Pugh	36 76 76
Wimbledon	Semi-Final	Edberg	75 76 76
US Hardcourts	WON	Berger	64 46 64
Canadian Open	Runner-Up	Lendl	61 63
US Open	2nd Round	Haarhuis	64 46 63 75
Toulouse	Runner-Up	Connors	63 63
Paris Open	Semi-Final	Becker	76 36 63
Silk Cut	Semi-Final	Forget	64 76
Masters	Semi-Final	Becker	64 64

Davis Cup:

V France beat Noah 63 64 61; beat Leconte 63 61

For McEnroe fans, 1989 was a year to cherish. Their idol played near his dizzy heights of 1984 and he deservedly attained a year-end ranking of No.4 in the world.

It was good to see the father of two bewitch his opponents with all his old wizardry. John brightened the entire landscape of the sport and proved that, in the age of power hitting, he could still prevail.

To be honest, we should have trusted McEnroe, who declared on his 30th birthday, "There is still a desire to do something great in tennis – even at this stage. I know I can get back to where I was, but maybe not with the total domination I once had."

True to his word, he subdued Ivan Lendl's fire in the WCT Finals. The American recovered from a set and 1-4 down to shellshock the World No 1 6-7, 7-6, 6-2, 7-5. After the four hours of drama came to a close, 16,000 people gave John a standing ovation.

The victory was no flash in the pan, for McEnroe took the £120,000 first prize the following day when he easily overcame Brad Gilbert 6-3, 6-3, 7-6. He acknowledged that the win over Lendl had been "a huge victory for me … now I'm on the way back.

"The last two years have been full of problems with injuries and suspensions," he explained. "I couldn't get into a groove. But now that has all changed. I suppose I had so much luck for eight or nine years, that something had to happen. The trouble was I let it happen instead of fighting it."

But was he really in the mood for further combat? Before Wimbledon he told Simon Kinnersley of 'Woman's Own' that he missed his family terribly when he was away for long stretches; simultaneously, "I don't believe that I've juggled between my tennis and family as well as I should have and my tennis has probably suffered as a result."

The upshot was that John decided to arrive early in England to gear up for a proper assault on the Wimbledon title. Unsurprisingly, he met with heavy rain at his first pitstop, Beckenham. He passed the time by explaining, "I really think I can win Wimbledon. It's very different to a year ago. I don't want to make excuses, but when I lost to Masur I did not feel physically right on the day. This time it could be very different because physically I'm in far better shape than I have ever been."

Inevitably, McEnroe took the Beckenham title and he laughed as he held the tiny trophy aloft, saying, "I hope to be lifting something a little heavier in a few weeks."

He still seemed in a jovial mood early the following week as he fought for further success in Edinburgh. In the first round he faced Scott Ross Matheson; the former Wimbledon Champion came through 6-3, 6-1, but he was so impressed by the 19-year old's five aces that the two later practised together. Matheson says the day remains etched in his mind for several reasons:

"1) John introduced himself to me in the locker room. Shaking my hand, he said, 'Oh, you're the guy I'm playing … Hi!'

2) The one shot that he played to break my serve for the first time. A running passing shot down the line that he turned into a topspin lob. I was sure he was going to pass me.

3) He is a "one-off" and there will be very few "one-offs" in the future of tennis.

4) He was a disciplined player. But you have to study him and his matches to realise that. Lendl played disciplined with his gift – hard work! McEnroe played disciplined with his gift, talent!

5) His serve … deceptive and tough to "pick" as his ball toss is in the same position for each serve.

6) Finally, he had a great mentality! That's why he won match after match. He was his own boss and took care of his route towards winning. He was just different."

Matheson had been delighted to help John out, but McEnroe's objectives were understandably more onerous. "I believe there's great tennis left in me," he mused. "And I'm waiting and praying the Wimbledon moment returns."

"It just so happened that I felt incredible that afternoon," he added, when asked about his awesome day of glory back in July '84. "It was one of those times when I climbed out of bed the right way. I had a few practice serves and it was all kinda clicking. The ball was that *big* and everything just slid into place.

"Now my dream is that all this returns one day in one of the majors. It would put real zip into my life. It's got to happen soon, though. I can wait a couple of years, but if things didn't start happening, well then…

"I mean, there are too many other things to do in life besides playing to about 80% of your ability. That gets on your nerves after a while."

John's comments proved beyond a shadow of doubt that he was piling more pressure upon himself. Sure enough, in the final, although he pipped Jimmy Connors 7-6, 7-6, edgy McEnroe had a significant difference of opinion with officialdom. He believed that Scottish umpire John Frame acted too harshly in warning him for tossing his racquet in the air. John swore at Frame, received a point penalty and another obscenity cost him the fifth game of the second set.

"I felt the umpire reacted inappropriately initially, then I reacted inappropriately afterwards," the winner insisted. "He was absolutely wrong to give a warning."

Yet, "I was determined to go on and play. I didn't want the story of the match to be what happened there. I wanted the focus to be on the tennis and hopefully there will be no more of that sort of thing."

The player's promise was soon compromised, however.

McEnroe again struggled when competing on Merseyside. When Jim Pugh, his first round rival, served to make it five games all in the final set, the New Yorker jumped out of the way of a serve and exploded when the ball was called in. "You have to be kidding me," he exclaimed. "That's two horrendous calls in a row – the ball was clearly out. Come on you guys, what are you trying to do?"

Happily, the Liverpool defeat didn't spell disaster for Wimbledon. Even so, John seemed to be heading for an immediate exit in his opening encounter with Australian Darren Cahill. It was the left-hander's malfunctioning serve that left him two sets to love down and he began the third set with two double faults. Thereafter, the match unfolded like an extended, compelling soap opera and the relentless veteran emerged from the quicksands after three hours, twenty-two minutes. The Centre Court applauded him wildly, mightily impressed by the courage he displayed en route to survival.

"I've certainly improved a lot in the last year," McEnroe agreed. "Since I came back a year ago my level of tennis is higher. And I feel like I've had good and bad days, but less bad and more good. But there were matches in '85, for example, where I was playing at a higher level – I mean I was one match away from being No.1 in the world that year if I had beaten Lendl in the Open."

Unfancied Richey Reneberg created an unsettling time in the second round, though John was good-humoured at the later press conference when he faced an up-front question from a pre-pubescent who was reporting for the children's newspaper, 'The Early Times'. "What do you think your chances are of winning Wimbledon after this match?" he was asked.

"Well, that's a tough question," replied the No.5 seed. "They don't get any tougher than that. I just hope to do my best. Just tell all your young friends that's all you can do."

Of course, McEnroe has always believed that 'your best' is not a finite thing; you should push yourself onwards, increasing your abilities to meet whatever challenge you have to face. When he thrashed Jim Pugh in the third round he was presumably relieved to have reversed the Wirral setback. It probably reminded him of the way that, in the past, he had sought to exact revenge for every disappointment. But now that he was older, I'm not altogether sure that he recognised the do-or-die McEnroe of the early 80s. He remembered, "I had a very intense, intimidatory way of playing, but I don't want to be the best if I have to be that way again. You have to look for the middle ground. I don't want to go over the precipice like I did between 1978 and 1986."

Besides, McEnroe had more pressing worries. He had competed against Pugh despite death threats.

A man with a London accent had phoned the All England Club to warn, "Don't let John McEnroe go on court today – or he will be assassinated." The man repeated his threat in a call to the Mirror Group offices and in a later call to Wimbledon. As a result, extra police and security guards were on duty. In the evening, security guards swarmed around John as he made his way to Court 14. Once there, he and Jakob Hlasek completed a five sets victory over Alex Antonitsch and Patrick Baur. As in his singles match, John found his serve to be more in synch and more consistent.

He then left Wimbledon with the protection of twelve security guards.

⚮

The fact that McEnroe remained the most important jewel in the crown of tennis was underlined by the publicity he generated on Monday, July 3, 1989. On court, in a match that had more twists and turns than an Agatha Christie novel, he saw off John Fitzgerald 6-3, 0-6, 6-4, 6-4 in a pulsating duel. But so many episodes involving John occurred on this day that there is no option but to look at each occurrence in isolation:

1   An argument erupted in the match when the Australian served to level at 4-4 in the first set. Fitzgerald accused McEnroe of stalling, but John yelled, "I get 30 seconds. Is this a new rule? I'd like the supervisor brought out now."

He said afterwards, "Well, I didn't know the rule, for one. I mean that's my fault, I suppose. I thought the receiver as well as the server had 30 seconds to prepare himself. And at 4-3 I was very angry at myself that I'd lost my serve twice in a row when I had started so well. And then I didn't see Fitzgerald show me the new ball. So he sort of winged a serve at me and I missed the return. And he said that he showed it to me, the umpire said that, but I didn't see it. That sort of compounded my irritation at that point because I'd been up two breaks and lost it. So I was just trying to pull myself together in what I thought was a 30 second time period. And then I got an unsportsmanlike conduct warning. So that's my mistake for not knowing it, but I was just trying to gather myself at that point so I would potentially win the set."

2   After the two hours and eleven minutes of drama on Court No.1, uncompromising Fitzgerald accused John of "gamesmanship and abuse." (Just three months later, however, the Australian was quite happy to partner Patrick McEnroe at the Seiko Classic in Tokyo. In the first round, they lost to Stefan Edberg and Jakob Hlasek 7-6, 5-7, 7-5.) John, for his part, was nonplussed by Ftizgerald's accusation. "I felt that was a sour grapes situation. He made it seem as though I was trying to pull a number on him, but as far as I was concerned he was the one trying to play that type of game."

3   'The Daily Mirror's' front page splash was headlined, "Maniac Attacks McEnroe." Nigel Clarke reported that on the first Friday of the tournament an American fan had sprayed aerosol air freshener in McEnroe's face as the star left Court 14. The incident occurred just after 8.46 p.m. when bad light had halted Antonisch/Baur –v- Hlasek/McEnroe. (The latter pair, the No.5 seeds, trailed by two sets to one, but led 3-1 in the fourth.)

Swiss journalist Renee Stauffer said, "This guy ran over to McEnroe and sprayed his face. John was alarmed. But before he could do anything, the fan fled. I chased after him, and asked him who he was and why he did it. He said his name was Tony, he came from Chicago and that he just had the can and wanted to spray McEnroe. He said he liked to follow famous people. But he had nothing against McEnroe."

John's manager, Sergio Palmieri, denied Stauffer's story. The Italian told 'The Evening Standard', "Nobody sprayed John in the eyes with an aerosol can. That's just not true."

4   There was heavy security at Wimbledon after another death threat was made against John before his game versus Fitzgerald. Chief Inspector Ray Dunn said, "The word "assassination" was used. We are treating this seriously."

John was again escorted through the crowds, this time by eight security guards and two uniformed policemen.

5   John was unnerved by the sound of a defective motor in the courtside fridge that keeps balls at the right temperature. John didn't know where the ominous whirr was coming from, so he shouted at umpire Rudi Berger, "Stop that clock. That clock is going all the time."

'The Daily Mirror' quoted McEnroe as saying, "OK, I was scared and I totally lost my concentration."

6   Finally, in the doubles, McEnroe and partner Jakob Hlasek were again banished to Court 14 where they fought Mike Depalmer and Gary Donnelly for two hours and forty-nine minutes. But they had to come off at 9.17 p.m. with the score at two sets all.

The fact that one player could initiate so many storylines in a single day explains why tennis currently lacks the vibrancy of McEnroe's heyday. Still, in early July 1989 he made news on a daily basis. He next beat Mats Wilander in a tension-filled quarter-final and stressed, "People have to realise just how on edge my nerves are at times like this. It is very difficult to contain yourself when you get into a competitive situation. Things spring up that get to you. It is heat of the moment stuff. You are on Centre Court in front of the whole world and really exposing your soul."

But the ecstasy of the big win over Wilander was clouded the following day when he suffered a torn left shoulder muscle whilst playing in the men's doubles and had to default from that event. Trainer Bill Norris utilised ultrasound and laser treatment, but warned that John would be limited on serve. He added, "When I pushed my thumb into his shoulder, John almost went through the ceiling. He was very tender indeed."

McEnroe, true to form, nonetheless took to the court for his Wimbledon semi-final versus Stefan Edberg. But the dream died; he fell 7-5, 7-6, 7-6. He said he was disappointed, but that he had tried his best and it simply hadn't been enough. He refused to blame his shoulder.

But I think McEnroe was too hard on himself. He had led by a break in the first set and had held a set-point in the third. As he himself admitted, "I really felt like some momentum was coming my way." So who knows what would have happened if he'd been truly fit?

In New York we expected McEnroe might do even better. It was his home city, there were no death threats, he was not injured. But in the second round Paul Haarhuis ambushed him in four sets. "It was one of those days you hope you'll never have in your whole career," John remarked. But he recovered by winning the US Open doubles title with Mark Woodforde – and as a result he had a short tenure back at the No.1 position on the ATP doubles computer.

McEnroe also competed well at the Masters, where he only succumbed in the semis to Boris Becker after having nine opportunities to break serve in the first set.

1990

Australian Open	4th Round	Pernfors	John disqualified when leading 61 46 75 24
Milan	Semi-Final	Mayotte	64 64
Toronto	Semi-Final	Lendl	63 62
Philadelphia	2nd Round	Reneberg	67 63 63
Stella Artois	Semi-Final	Lendl	62 64
Wimbledon	1st Round	Rostagno	75 64 64
Washington	3rd Round	Rostagno	63 16 61
Toronto	Quarter-final	Sampras	76 46 63
Cincinnati	3rd Round	S. Davis	63 57 64
Indianapolis	3rd Round	Evernden	62 64
Long Island	Semi-Final	Edberg	61 64
US Open	Semi-Final	Sampras	62 64 36 63
Basle	WON	Ivanisevic	64 46 67 63 64
Vienna	Quarter-final	Jarryd	76 62
Stockholm	3rd Round	Ivanisevic	64 64
Paris Indoor	2nd Round	Hlasek	36 63 76

Wednesday, January 17, 1990
Beat Alex Antonitsch 6-1, 6-2, 6-1 – Australian Open

John McEnroe had struck fine form in Melbourne. His win today meant he had cruised into the third round at the expense of a mere eight games.

"I have made a great start to the tournament, maybe my best at a Grand Slam event," recognised John. "If I can keep my concentration and this attitude then I have a good chance in the next round."

And he was right. He crushed Dan Goldie, who had been coached by Dick Gould at Stanford University, 6-3, 6-2, 6-2 to move into the last sixteen. The No.4 seed had refused to allow noisy spectators to distract him and he remarked, "I feel like I did a good job in keeping my cool."

But his equilibrium was shattered when he faced Mikael Pernfors, the 1986 French Open runner-up, for a quarter-final berth.

John grabbed the first set 6-1, before being broken early in the second. At the end of that game, the left-hander walked over to a lineswoman who had made a dubious call and bounced a ball on his racquet whilst staring at her. Umpire Gerry Armstrong, whose father George had handled McEnroe matches in the past, issued a warning for unsportsmanlike conduct.

McEnroe was unaware that the new ATP Tour had amended the disciplinary schedule. A warning was now followed by a one point penalty and a third offence triggered a player's default. Previously it had been the fourth indiscretion which caused a disqualification.

In the meantime, Pernfors levelled at one set all before John pulled himself together to lead 6-1, 4-6, 7-5.

In the tense fourth set, John was serving at 2-3 and deuce when he made a fateful forehand error. He threw his racquet to the ground and anyone in the stadium could hear the equipment crack. Armstrong docked John a point and suddenly Pernfors had a vital break of serve.

McEnroe was stunned by the umpire's authoritarian approach and quickly demanded the presence of referee Peter Bellenger and tournament supervisor, Ken Farrar. They upheld the point penalty and were walking from the court when John swore at Farrar. Not surprisingly, the man who had become favourite to win the tournament was immediately disqualified.

The news was broadcast around the globe; all John could say was that he had spoken in the heat of the moment. "I don't feel good about it but I can't say that I'm totally surprised by what happened," he remarked with honesty.

But should John have been disciplined for his first two 'misdemeanours'? Tellingly, in the light of the disqualification, ATP umpires were warned to be more cautious when employing the new Code.

And Boris Becker, who believes John would have captured the 1990 Australian Open crown, said at the time, "I think the rules are wrong, they are too strict. If you are out there in the heat for three or four hours it is not easy all the time to keep your cool ... Not everybody is like a computer out there. Tennis is more than that. It is excitement and it is very good we have John McEnroe."

The respective editors of the two British magazines 'Tennis' and

'Tennis World' didn't seem to think so. When I submitted to each of them my article entitled 'Debacle Down Under', neither wanted to publish it. Perhaps they just didn't like the fact I dared to mount a defence for McEnroe. In part, my story read:

"John McEnroe is now a thirty-year old father of two, strikingly different from the man in the street and torn between his new-found domesticity and lingering fires of ambition.

"The two, inevitably, clash. On the one hand, 'Daily Mirror' columnist Noreen Taylor wrote in 1982 of McEnroe's 'lashes of self-abuse'. According to her, John screamed during a match at Manchester's West Didsbury Club: 'God dammit, I'm so ashamed of myself. How can I possibly be so bad? I'm shit, man. Shit. For Chrissakes, I'm so out of it.'

"On the other hand, we have the doting family man whose charity work has been described as 'immense' and who says he knows tennis is insignificant whenever he ponders atrocities like the Tiananmen Square massacres.

"It has always been John's paternalistic, socially aware side that has had to explain the aggressive excesses that co-exist with his ardent desire for perfection. In Australia, following his disqualification, he said, 'I guess it was bound to happen and I have no-one to blame but myself.' "

I also posed that crucial question: *"...if one considers the 'crimes' Armstrong deemed worthy of punishment, are not the initial two somewhat petty?*

"The first offence was 'eyeballing' a lineswoman – no words were spoken. Yet to the umpire this was 'unsportsmanlike conduct'. 'Should I have got a warning for going up to that lady and just looking at her because she had made a horrible call?' demanded an incredulous McEnroe.

"The second offence was bouncing the racquet on the ground. True, it reared up sharply, the frame was slightly cracked, but McEnroe was quite happy to carry on playing with the instrument. Yet to the umpire this was definitely a most serious case of 'racquet abuse' ..."

"McEnroe surely had good reason to be suspicious about those two penalties.

"Hadn't Yannick Noah once got away scot-free with a tasteless 'Heil Hitler' salute to umpire Richard Kaufman?

"And when, in 1988, Robert Seguso bounced his racquet into the

turf of Queen's Club so hard that it struck a courtside photographer, Stephen Winyard announced no warning, no admonition, did not even give a steely glare. Seguso had to turn on Winyard, and swear, before he merited a code violation.

"To the umpiring fraternity John McEnroe has long been the arch-enemy. Flicking through some tabloid cuttings, I see that in 1979 one anonymous umpire declared he would like to see McEnroe banned from Wimbledon. In 1982, another uncompromisingly suggested John was 'a nutter'. A third confided, 'My main ambition in life is to disqualify McEnroe. I mean, if I were in a pub, I'd take him outside and thump him.'

"Tennis in the eighties was marked by this wall of silence between the press and officials on one side and McEnroe on the other. Maybe it was the natural result of John's separation from Everyman, but neither side gave an inch ... Gerald Williams mused aloud at Wimbledon '85 that McEnroe should throw a cocktail party for the press, but he added, 'Maybe I am being naïve. But I don't see what the alternative is.'

"The British Tennis Umpires Association failed to try and negotiate a truce with McEnroe, although in 1984 the then Wimbledon Chairman Buzzer Hadingham dropped him a personal note and explained there would be no witch hunt against the No.1 seed. John was impressed – it was a 'nice gesture' and he behaved impeccably that fortnight.

Major David Mills, however, for sixteen years Secretary of the All England Club, told the 'Sunday People' he had a poor rapport with McEnroe. Seeing John sitting in the prize money office, Mills admitted he said sarcastically, 'Oh, I wasn't aware that we have a new paymaster, Mr. McEnroe?' In the 1986 article Mills later referred to McEnroe as 'The Brat', to whom he wished, 'good riddance...'

"Now we all know the outcome of that lack of dialogue, that dearth of respect, between McEnroe and the Establishment – a messy, depressing disqualification that only debases the game's image."

And the disqualification lived with McEnroe for many months. He knew he had been playing near-flawless tennis and that perhaps his last chance of a Grand Slam title had disappeared. Now he would have to start all over again. He missed the French Open and was nearly knocked out by Ramesh Krishnan in the first round of the

Stella Artois tournament at Queen's Club.

Having eked past the Indian, he commented, "My style is like one of the last things of the past. Talent can still win out, but not as often as it did because there's more emphasis on the physical aspect of the game."

His lack of confidence was affirmed in the Queen's Club semis when Ivan Lendl outplayed him 6-2, 6-4. The former World No.1 asked a ball girl, "Is it possible I could have another ball?" Then, answering his own question, he retorted, "No, I don't deserve one."

Simultaneously, John knew that he was a competitor and therefore enjoyment, competition and success would always be inextricably linked in his life. At times it seems that the star felt a trifle ashamed about this correlation which was part of his psyche. In 1990 he told 'Woman's Own' reporter Steve Riches that tennis was "meaningless compared to other things" such as the situation in Eastern Europe and Africa. However, despite such protestations, a tennis loss still hurt McEnroe.

It was, accordingly, sad to see him bundled out of The Championships by ten past six in the evening on Day Two. Derrick Rostagno had outwitted him and at first the humid afternoon's events were too painful to consider. Asked what happened, he replied, "I got defeated." When the question was repeated, John could only forget his depression enough to answer, "I don't think there's a whole lot to say in that respect, other than I lost."

At last his determination surfaced as he explored his feelings. He was upset with "the whole picture" of his career, but, "I feel pretty strongly that this is just the beginning. But if I take a couple of steps in the wrong direction, in my opinion I'll be out of the game in six months. But I don't expect that to happen."

To recapture "the desire", as he put it, required a decoupling of family and career. "But I'm not convinced that I can't separate the two and do a helluva lot better job at this. I think that, you know, in ten years' time if I didn't, I'd feel bad about it. I don't think thirty-one is real old. It's not too late for me, as far as I'm concerned, and so it's a matter of doing it. It's that simple."

If the desire could be rekindled, was the ability still there? Or had that evaporated, maybe forever? "It's something that you have to wait and find out. I mean, it's hard to say how it is. You can't just not go hard for three, four years and then say, point blank, is the ability there? You've got to give yourself a significant amount of time. I mean, it may take three months, it may take six months, it may take a year. Look at guys that work and work and work. How many professions are there where you have to just stick with it and you have to wait for your chance to come and you have to believe that that chance is going to come? I believe it will come if I give my best."

Later, John told BBC TV: "It's not really that shocking – that's one of the disappointing things about it. Knowing that you're not really prepared …

"I just feel I need to get my mind back into the business of doing the best I can on the tennis court. I mean, tennis is my profession and you have to treat it with respect. If you don't treat your job with respect, you're going to get paid back for it. That's basically what's been happening the last few years. And so when you go out on the court you're not as confident within yourself as you would be – and that shows. People don't feel your presence.

"But the beauty of tennis is it's not like being a boxer – you may be considered a quote-unquote 'shot fighter', and so people say, 'Hey, you shouldn't go out in the ring because you may kill yourself.' In tennis we're hitting a ball over the net. So there's a lot less at stake in that regard. And I'm still young in a sense. I don't feel shot, I feel wounded."

McEnroe had recuperated by the time of the US Open. Twenty thousand fans roared him to victory against Spain's Emilio Sanchez, who would finish the year ranked eighth in the world. The four hour and twenty minute marathon was widely perceived to be one of the American's finest ever triumphs. Boris Becker told the media that no one in the entire sport could excite a crowd like John McEnroe could.

Driven John then thrashed David Wheaton 6-1, 6-4, 6-4 to set up a semi-final clash with Pete Sampras.

The nineteen-year old rookie had stunned Ivan Lendl in five sets, to leave John commenting, "I have played Lendl many times and it's nice to be able to play someone who might be one of the next great players and to be able to play him when I'm playing well. It should be a great match."

John had dismissed Wheaton with such ease that the crowd was awed into silence. Explaining his resurgence, McEnroe praised coach Tony Palafox. "He's helped me to go back to what I do well (dominating the net; combining service power with placement) and to believe that my game is good enough to beat these guys."

Wheaton had felt the full force of John's comeback. "No-one thought he was playing that well this summer, but then he played almost perfect tennis against me. I was surprised he returned so well and it kept me back a bit. Who knows what he can do now?"

Well, the supporters at Flushing Meadow backed John all the way, but Sampras subdued him 6-2, 6-4, 3-6, 6-3.

McEnroe explained, "His power really put me off. He served well when he had to. I think he's really in a groove right now." (Andre Agassi, beaten in the final the following day, would probably have agreed.)

Smiling, McEnroe continued, "I can still play better. Next year, I want to be ready for all the Grand Slams. After all, Connors won here at thirty-two and Rosewall reached the final of Wimbledon at thirty-nine. So hope springs eternal."

1991

San Francisco	Quarter-final	Cahill	76 36 63
Philadelphia	Semi-Final	Sampras	62 64
Chicago	WON	P. McEnroe	36 62 64
Indian Wells	2nd Round	Grabb	76 75
Hong Kong	1st Round	Witsken	63 57 76
Japan Open	Quarter-Final	Courier	62 62
Munich	1st Round	Pescariu	62 62
French Open	1st Round	Cherkasov	26 64 75 76
Manchester	1st Round	Caratti	76 76
Wimbledon	4th Round	Edberg	76 61 64
Washington	3rd Round	Herrera	36 62 62
Montreal	3rd Round	Rostagno	62 16 76
New Haven	Quarter-final	Ivanisevic	64 62
Long Island	Semi-Final	Lendl	63 75
US Open	3rd Round	Chang	64 46 76 26 63
Basle	Runner-Up	Hlasek	76 60 63
Paris Open	2nd Round	Ivanisevic	64 64
Birmingham	1st Round	Mronz	63 46 63

Davis Cup:

V Spain Beat Carbonell 63 62 61; beat E. Sanchez 64 36 63

Apart from an emotional Davis Cup appearance in June, the 1991 season will not linger long in the memory of John Patrick McEnroe.

I had high hopes for him when he announced in February that he had "an entirely new enthusiasm" for the game. Just two days before his 32nd birthday, John announced that he had re-hired Californian fitness coach Rob Parr to help his 1991 campaign. (The former minor league baseball player had helped John prior to the '88 US Open and he had previously assisted both Tatum and Madonna.) John also unburdened his conscience, revealing that he had "tried to cut corners so far as training is concerned" for years.

In a particularly frank disclosure, he confided the whole truth. "I knew as much as five years ago that I needed to do something different to keep my body in the best shape, but it took me until two months ago before I was ready to accept it.

"The last thing we all want to do when we wake up in the morning is sit-ups. I need someone to gee me up and say, 'Hey, come on, let's do it.' I know that if it was up to me I would talk myself out of it.

"It doesn't mean I'm going to win Wimbledon, but because I'm in better shape physically as well as mentally I'll have a better chance."

John added that in 1984 he felt his mental strength had led him to put too great a faith in his physical abilities. Yet now he had to "regain some of that speed" through training.

"I'm doing so much more than ever before, such as working with weights, going through proper stretching exercises etc., that I feel I'm already past the point I'd reached at the US Open last year."

But results didn't go John's way and it became apparent that his allies would soon be faced with the emotional end of his career. To Hugh Jamieson of the 'Daily Mirror', a journalist friend from way back, he admitted, "I want another crack at the French. The fans really like me but I still can't get that defeat (to Lendl in '84) out of my system."

Before John reached Paris he lost 6-2, 6-2 to 17-year old Dinu Pescariu in Munich. "I would have lost against my mother," he lamented. Nine days later, maintaining the family theme, Tatum gave birth to a daughter, Emily Katherine, in California.

The good news didn't improve John's fortunes on court. In the French capital, seeded 15, he played a superb opening set against Andrei Cherkasov, though in the end he was eliminated 2-6, 6-4, 7-5, 7-6. He remarked sadly, "My mind said not to come but my heart said I might get some positive things, even if I did poorly."

Soon it was time for McEnroe to enliven England once again. He joined Pat Cash on the 'Wogan' show to publicise the fact that they had assisted Roger Daltrey and two Iron Maiden stars in recording a cover version of Led Zeppelin's "Rock 'n' Roll" for the Armenian Earthquake Fund.

Said John, "We're available to do more charity work. We'd like to get up and do it as often as we could."

The studio audience cheered the genial American when he said he'd play Wimbledon "a couple more times." But he laughed, "It's the last few times so have some compassion for me – no more booing!"

McEnroe's self-deprecating charm had rarely been more evident. But he did face a couple of difficult questions. Asked by Wogan whether his sabbatical in the first half of '86 had been a mistake, John replied, "It wasn't a mistake as far as me as a person [is concerned]. I think I've developed quite a bit and matured as a person. People don't see that who just watch your tennis results. In retrospect, I should have done things a little differently as far as my career, but I think it's made me a lot better person; I have three wonderful children now and a wonderful wife and I feel I've gone a long way in that regard. At 26 years old I was all tennis and nothing else."

And, asked Wogan, should a player bring his "loved ones" over for Wimbledon?

John said feelingly, "It's not a good idea not to bring 'em, because you miss them so much and then there's the complication of bringing them because people are all over us; when we want to go for a walk in the park, there's paparazzi following us and you don't get to enjoy London the way other people do when they come on a visit. So that's hard. I wish we could come here and have that type of ability to really see London. It's a great city … So ultimately I've decided I'd rather have them with me and go through that than not have them at all and just feel alone."

∾∾

To the casual observer, the American's 7-6 (7-4), 6-1, 6-4 fourth round loss to Stefan Edberg on Wimbledon's Centre Court only proved beyond doubt that John was over the hill. It was that simple.

But inevitably, for McEnroe himself, the picture was much more confused and complicated. True, he couldn't argue against those who declared he was no longer at the peak of his powers.

Indeed, just days before The Championships commenced he had conceded a huge psychological own goal. Whilst appearing on the Wogan show, he had admitted that he needed fan support because, "I'm not playing as well as I used to."

The video of the Edberg game merely confirmed his self-analysis:

Set One, Game Two: John had a break point on Edberg's serve, but "he hit an ace on it, he put a little extra mustard on it."

Set One, Tie-break, 0-0: On the fifth shot of the rally, John, reacting slowly, prodded a backhand volley just beyond the baseline.

Set One, Tie-break, 3-1 Edberg: McEnroe's second serve was yards long. Double fault. The fallen star dropped his racquet in dismay and walked around in circles, hands on hips.

Set One, Tie-break, 6-4 Edberg: John's speed was again questionable; though his forehand return meant the Swede could only lunge to produce a volley, McEnroe failed with his favourite backhand, the one he took almost on the half volley. Unlike yesteryear, on this day his attempted pass found the top of the net. He emitted a strangled cry – game and first set, Edberg.

Set Two, 1-2, 0-30 McEnroe: John served deep to Edberg's forehand, but failed to get into position for his first volley. He took the ball close to his body, allowing Stefan to then rifle a crosscourt forehand pass. In seconds, Edberg had his break.

Set Three, 3-1 McEnroe: A disastrous game for the three times champion, who had broken the No.1 seed in the second game. A short second serve was punished. 0-15. A tentative, late half volley was netted (0-30) and so was a shoulder high volley (0-40). John pulled back a point, but another double fault proved fatal. At the changeover, he first yells, then buries his head in a towel.

Set Three, 3-3: The American went a break down. Two short serves were given short shrift by Stefan (0-30). An excellent defensive Edberg return off a great delivery left John facing three points for 3-4. He saved two, but uncharacteristic poor judgement meant he left a perfectly good topspun forehand. Had McEnroe willed the ball out? The fight was effectively over.

And yet McEnroe said afterwards he would definitely try again. In a particularly poignant moment, he told BBC's Barry Davies, "You feel so close, you want to give it another shot." To my mind, John was trying to salvage some confidence despite the comprehensive nature of the defeat. He knew his passion for the game had diminished, he didn't feel "that all consuming feeling", but he nonetheless hoped to balance that out "in other ways", whatever they were. Perhaps he could catch Becker and Edberg when those two were on an off day, he mused. Finally, he told Davies he might get "a couple of better breaks" next year.

Cornered in the pressroom, John had to exude similar optimism. "I think I can still win Wimbledon, but it's a long shot. Hope springs eternal and stranger things have happened. I'm certainly not going to pledge my life savings on it, or even a portion of it. I'm not expecting it to happen."

Rather than discuss himself, McEnroe seemed concerned to consider others during his talk with the media. "Ten percent of all [tennis] pay cheques could be donated to charity," he said. "Millions of dollars could be used to benefit people who are homeless. That would take the pressure off."

Stefan Edberg, who would eventually lose in the semi-finals to Michael Stich, said, "It's too late for John to rediscover his form. He played unbelievable tennis in 1983, '84 and '85. He has lost a little speed and consistency. But you can still see glimpses of his great touch."

⨕⨕

When Edberg had served at 4-3, 15 all in the third set, McEnroe became furious when the Swede was awarded an ace. The serve had looked wide and John yelled at umpire David Littlefield, "Come on now! That ball bounced here. You've got to be kidding me."

Over four hours after the Centre Court clash, ITN News at 5.40 p.m. transmitted a recording of the incident, with beeps replacing six expletives John had hurled at the relevant linesjudge. The umpire hadn't heard the swear words, neither BBC nor Sky TV equipment had picked up McEnroe's comments and furthermore nobody had made an official complaint to referee Alan Mills, stewards or police. But Mills requested ITN's recording of the incident.

Many journalists agreed McEnroe had suffered a bad call and John told them, "When people make mistakes, it throws you, because you hope they're into the match as much as you are. Every little point counts on grass. You get up 0-15 and it just puts a little bit of negative thinking in a person's mind."

The American added, "If I felt I wasn't in control (of my temper) I would stop playing because I've said it before, I don't want to continue along those lines."

1992

Australian Open	Quarter-final	Ferreira	64 64 64
Brussels	2nd Round	Forget	63 62
Stuttgart	1st Round	Novacek	36 76 62
Rotterdam	Semi-Final	Becker	62 76
Key Biscayne	3rd Round	Krajicek	76 64
Madrid	2nd Round	Clavet	62 61
Hamburg	2nd Round	Pescosolido	76 16 64
French Open	1st Round	Kulti	62 75 67 75
Rosmalen	Semi-Final	Stich	63 76
Wimbledon	Semi-Final	Agassi	64 62 63
Washington	2nd Round	Bates	62 16 64
Toronto	Quarter-final	Lendl	62 64
New Haven	3rd Round	Washington	76 63
US Open	4th Round	Courier	62 62 76
Sydney	Quarter-final	Edberg	63 63
Paris Open	2nd Round	Becker	64 64
Antwerp	2nd Round	Korda	64 64
Grand Slam Cup	Quarter-final	Ivanisevic	36 64 62

Davis Cup:

V Argentina with Rick Leach, beat Frana/Miniussi 67 62 62 61
V Czechoslovakia with Rick Leach, lost to Korda/Suk 63 64 64
V Sweden with Pete Sampras, beat Edberg/Jarryd 61 67 46 63 63
V Switzerland with Pete Sampras, beat Hlasek/Rosset 67 67 75 61 62

John's self-respect ensured that his final year on tour contained inspired tennis which was reminiscent of his most outstanding masterpieces.

The foundations for his perfect final year were, in fact, laid in December 1991 by former pro Larry Stefanki.[22] He had put together a video featuring John's best matches and he of course included clips of the '81 and '84 Wimbledon victories.

---

[22] Stefanki, a right-hander, hailed from Illinois where he was born in July 1957.

McEnroe watched the film over Christmas '91 at Stefanki's house in Palm Springs, California. "I think he was frightened to remember how good he was," Stefanki would later recall. "He didn't say anything, but I think he recognised a few things about how he used to play and how he should play.

"I told him that he was selling himself short, that his game was not the same as it used to be and I wanted to know why. There was no bravery in it. I could see what he was going through and I just wanted to know why."

John was obviously impressed by Stefanki's perceptions and they discussed the possibility of working together. "It really came down to a very simple question in the end," said Stefanki. "Did he really want to play or not? I think he had been living off his reputation for the last five years and I wanted him to get back to basics, to the aggressive way he played as a teenager.

"To me, he had started to believe that he couldn't play that way against all the power players of today. But that's hogwash. You can beat these new age guys by reacting quickly and taking their time away."

Stefanki's views were validated at the Australian Open. McEnroe scored a 6-4, 6-3, 7-5 win over defending champion Boris Becker. It was the kind of result that we thought was beyond the American, but he had always delighted in confounding his critics and he could rightfully take great pride from this coup. And as the year progressed we knew that tennis would never be the same again once he had gone.

John's quirky, arrogant court mannerisms marked him out as an individual. His strokes will never be duplicated and his on-court application to the task in hand was a text-book example of the virtues of persistence.

As Becker departed from the arena where a 15,000 crowd had witnessed his demise, he gasped, "I knew he could play well for one set, maybe a set and a half, but he played the whole match to a very high level and gave me no time to breathe. He played his old way."

McEnroe, as was his wont, was glad to win whilst keeping his temper in check. "The theatrics were made by the people screaming for me and not me screaming and it was really nice in that respect." He added that he hoped people would focus on his tennis when remembering him, rather than his tantrums.

He also told Richard Yallop of 'The Observer', "I've had to live with what I've done and I'm proud of my record. If I'd been quieter on court, I don't know whether I'd have won more or less, it's hard to say. Like anyone else, there are some things I wish I'd done differently."

One thing which McEnroe wished he had done differently was to emerge triumphant in the French Open, at least on one occasion. In 1992 he was destroyed in the first round in Paris. On Final's Day, when commentating for NBC TV on Courier v Korda, John proclaimed, "A part of my body is buried under that red clay." Referring to 1984, he added, "It was a bad experience."

Of course, it was to be expected that John would be in a pensive mood as he exhibited his talents for the last time at each illustrious venue. Still, it was surprising that he was even more contrite than usual; he told Malcolm Folley in 'The Mail on Sunday' on the eve of Wimbledon that in his 1981 semi-final against Rod Frawley he had "acted like a jerk; I take responsibility for that."

As he geared up for his final effort on the All England Club's lawns, he confided to Peter White in 'The Sun', "I expect never to win the title again. I just wish I could say I had another Grand Slam in me, but I can't see it."

Nevertheless, he saw off Brazil's Luiz Mattar in the first round and resolved to give The Championships his best shot. "I know that in the deep corners of my mind somewhere there's still a little tiny person telling me I still have a chance. So I'm going to give one hundred per cent," he declared.

His fighting attitude saw him through a stupendous five setter against the '87 Wimbledon winner Pat Cash. The loser opined, "I've always said he's the greatest player that ever walked on a tennis court." Next, the 33-year old breezed past the highly-touted David Wheaton in straight sets. "I love it when he throws his arms up after winning and takes the applause," said Stefanki afterwards. "I believe that has helped him."

Yes, the truth was that John McEnroe was now a crowd favourite. The Wimbledon crowds had finally understood what he was all about – intensity, courage and honesty.

Everyone wondered what he would do next against Russian qualifer Andrei Olhovskiy, the man who had sensationally upset World No.1 Jim Courier on Centre Court. McEnroe remembered what it had been like to be a qualifying 'invader' in 1977: "I know the players didn't want to play me in those rounds." So he took nothing for granted, put on a virtuoso display and defeated Olhovskiy on Court No.2. He then broke away from his security cordon in order to slap Larry Stefanki on the back. Then he kissed Tatum to the delight of the onlookers on the busy concourse.

But later John was challenged about the fact he had thrown his racquet seven times during the match. Olhovskiy had complained to umpire Sultan Gangji about the absence of a code violation warning, but John declared, "I guess it depends on the umpire, but I think Ken Rosewall was one of the greatest players in our game. He always threw his racquet. It's the way you throw it. You rarely ever break your racquet throwing it.

"I don't blame him [Olhovskiy] for trying to get an edge of some kind. He was very emotionless. I don't know him well enough to know if that's normal for him, but I think people know me well enough to know that at times it helps me to get pumped up. I was just firing up. I think it's if you break the racquet or you're endangering somebody [that you should be warned]. I didn't think that was happening.

"But I've had it called before and I've had it not called before. So you just have to go sort of with what happens. I mean, I wouldn't have continued to do it and risked it, but at the same time I agree with the umpire; I don't think there was anything malicious in it at all. I think it's good if the players show emotion. I mean, I'm one of the believers in showing emotion."

Guy Forget of France saw some of that emotion once John had won their tight quarter-final clash. The American left Court No.1 with arms aloft as he once again basked in the crowd's approval.

Later, he thanked Larry Stefanki for his improved serve: "I've been very neglectful on looking at tapes going back to say ten years ago, when I served really well. When we started working together like, nine months ago, he started looking at some tapes and he said, 'Look, this is what you did before and this is what you do now,' and I never really had bothered to look back at that. I kept thinking that I would get it together. I just thought that's always been a natural aspect of my game, but now the wind-up, and using leg strength which has improved through playing a lot and working harder, as well as the technique, they've all come together at this beautiful moment."

John continued, "Obviously it would be unbelievable to win Wimbledon."

Unfortunately, 22-year old Andre Agassi managed to thrash him in a three sets' semi-final. Before the beginning of the last point he ever played in a singles match on Centre Court, there was just time for one crowning, urgent, "C'mon John" from the stands.

Then McEnroe unleashed a thunderbolt to the backhand, Agassi replied and John's backhand volley flew wide. McEnroe's Wimbledon singles career was over. He took it well – smiling, hugging Andre, then shaking the umpire's hand. He bowed to the Royal Box and walked off ahead of his opponent. He didn't acknowledge the crowd.

"It's too early to say what this great run at Wimbledon will come to mean for me," said McEnroe. "I mean, I'm really happy with this tournament. I feel great about it. It's like every time we sit here and reflect on my great runs when I lose in the semis. It's hard to feel that good right now, but I know that I'll feel very proud of it soon."

And to Barry Davies of the BBC, John confided, "Agassi hit the ball as hard as I've ever seen it … I thought maybe in the third set he'd get struck by lightning, but it didn't work out. Everything I tried he did one step better. I got a bit of my own medicine."

ʘϒ

In the men's doubles final, play began on a worn Court No.1 at 4.53 p.m. the following day. McEnroe was broken twice as he and his German partner, Michael Stich, fell behind by two sets to one.

In the fourth, John was again broken as Jim Grabb and Richey Reneberg built up a 4-2 lead. But Grabb, for so long Patrick McEnroe's partner, lost his serve and the set went to a tie-break. The No.4 seeds came within two points of winning, but John and Michael won through 7-5 after two hours and fifty minutes' action.

And a tremendous fifth set struggle ensued. At 7-6, in gathering gloom, Grabb and Reneberg twice had Championship point on Stich's service. But the German kept his nerve, even when he had to deliver a second serve to keep the contest alive.

In the sixteenth game, McEnroe recovered from 0-30 to hold for 8-8.

At 12-12, John missed a forehand volley when the score was 30 all on Grabb's serve.

It was incredibly dark as Stich hit a near ace to make it 13-13 in an enthralling contest. The crowd didn't want it to end, but the players could hardly see the ball. McEnroe spoke with Grabb and Reneberg. Alan Mills, flanked by Ken Farrar, came on court.

It was 9.22 p.m. when umpire Gerry Armstrong intoned, "Ladies and gentlemen, due to failing light, play is now suspended. Thank you."

An hour later, when the BBC highlights programme showed Agassi's victory over Ivanisevic, it was announced that admission would be free the next day for those who wished to see whatever remained of the men's doubles final. It could have involved five minutes of tennis; it could have been an hour. But viewers watched – then took action...

Monday July 6, 1992
With Michael Stich, beat Grabb and Reneberg 5-7, 7-6, 3-6, 7-6, 19-17

The appeal of McEnroe resulted in a half-mile queue to watch him play.

In the end, 6,500 spectators witnessed his genius for thirty-six minutes and another 1,500 fans had to mill around the grounds of the All England Club.

In strong sunshine John hit a forehand topspin lob that broke Reneberg's serve at 17-17.

Suddenly, McEnroe was serving for a Grand Slam title. At 30 all Stich produced a winning smash and the crowd cheered wildly. Up in the commentary box, John Barrett enthused, "You know, I would think this next point means as much to McEnroe as any other point he's played in that long, illustrious, turbulent career."

The New Yorker served and Reneberg netted a backhand return. "Yes!" roared John as Stich lifted him high into the air. The thirty-three-year old punched the air in delight.

To a roar of approval, McEnroe then performed a lap of honour with his Cup. He handed it to four-year old son Sean, who had watched the amazing events with his mother, Tatum. Emotional John appeared to be weeping and he said later, "Having a child of mine there at a time like that was a very moving experience. It meant a hell of a lot to me. Mind you, when I told Sean to touch the cup I'm not sure he knew what was going on!"

But McEnroe had captured a dramatic Grand Slam crown in an

encounter clocked by the umpire at five hours and five minutes. And the crowd had loved him. He said, "It's certainly one of the best receptions I've ever had. It was incredible. The buzz really pumped us up. It would have been a big win for us if we'd played in front of a couple of hundred people, but as it was the excitement was unbelievable."

The previous evening John and Michael had offered to settle the final with a tie-break, but Grabb and Reneberg had not been keen. The thirty-three year old was now glad the match had been held over, though he confessed, "I was a little bit concerned how I'd feel (today) after two weeks' playing."

But when he heard the stadium was full it had been "a good motivation."

Fittingly, in what appeared to be his last Wimbledon match, the crowd had loved and admired him. Asked to explain why, his reply was at first jocular, "I lose a lot more! That's one reason and also, you know, maybe the fact that my days are numbered as far as playing and also I think one of the best things is when you settle down and have a family. A lot of people have their own family, and they just, you know, see you in a different light. They start to see you as a human being as opposed to a piece of meat and it's someone that they can relate to, and I think everyone can relate to having children and how great that is and also how difficult it can be. So I think that that puts me in a whole different light.

"Having been around – I mean people know what I'm about; it's not an act. I think they see – in fifteen years they see that I'm playing in the finals of the doubles and I'm still – I mean they know I get frustrated, but I think they understand that it's really me just being frustrated at myself and so – maybe the first time it's like they don't understand it, but now I mean they've seen it enough to know that if I throw my racquet down, for example, here it's not – I think they look at it in a different way than they would have, say, ten years ago."

McEnroe's final verdict on the last day of perhaps his last Wimbledon was, "To win a Grand Slam title is incredible. I'm very happy."

Jim Courier pummelled McEnroe in the fourth round of the 1992

244

US Open and said, "At his peak, I don't think there was anyone who could beat John when he was playing his best on grass. We are going to miss him when he's gone. You just don't replace talents like that."

∾∾

The year was not yet over. In December, whilst practising in Fort Worth, Texas for the Davis Cup Final, John released a very sad press statement. It read:

"Tatum and I are having problems. I intend to work hard at finding a sensible solution that's best for our entire family.

"This is a very painful time for me, and, I'm sure, for Tatum as well. However public are our professional activities, our personal problems are private and ... I will make no further public comment and would urge our friends to do the same."

He added that he had been forced to issue a statement following "wildly inaccurate stories" in the media, which had suggested that the break-up was due to his refusal to allow Tatum to resume her acting career. People seemed to have forgotten that McEnroe had once told Kim Cunningham in 'World Tennis' that he wanted Tatum to renew her film work.

It was a moot point as to whether the American was emotionally capable of partnering Pete Sampras in the clash against Switzerland. At least all three children were with him, and his two sons watched him train despite what Simon Barnes in 'The Times' would term the star's 'desperate depression.'

Yet amidst all his personal worries, he actually turned in a high-octane, vintage performance as he and Sampras overcame Jakob Hlasek and Marc Rosset 6-7, 6-7, 7-5, 6-1, 6-2 in four hours and three minutes. Their triumph gave the United States a crucial 2-1 lead against Switzerland and the following day Jim Courier ensured the Davis Cup was in American hands.

Sampras was full of admiration for John, "the best doubles player there's probably ever been. He was all over the guys, all over everybody, so everything just seemed to work out and my tennis got better and better."

Sampras added that McEnroe had been fully immersed in the match, "ranting and raving" in a morale-boosting tirade during the locker room break between the third and fourth sets. According to

Pete himself, John's motivational talk had helped him to produce "the two best doubles sets I've ever played."

At the end, only one question remained: How had John McEnroe been able to shrug aside his personal misery? After all, he had always said his marriage had enriched his life in so many ways. How had he managed to care so much about his tennis whilst engulfed in a sea of troubles?

After his efforts in Texas I have often been particularly impressed by two of McEnroe's strengths: his ability to banish anxieties and his capacity to concentrate on the task in hand.

⧞

Contrary to rumour, John McEnroe fulfilled his final commitment of '92 by appearing for the first time in the notoriously dollar-laden Grand Slam Cup.

But before the Munich event got under way, the thirty-three-year old emphasised, "The prize money here is obscene. For that reason I will donate my money to charity. I haven't decided who will get it. But one thing is certain – it won't be John McEnroe."

And he warned, "Should I play again, I don't want people saying, 'Aha, you can twist McEnroe with money.' "

⧞

In the quarter-final, John was pitted against power exponent Goran Ivanisevic, the Wimbledon runner-up who had terrorized opponents all season with his unplayable serve.

But in the first set, it looked as if the six-foot four-inch Croatian should have been the one contemplating retirement. McEnroe dropped just nine points on his own delivery as he raced to a 6-3 lead.

John still looked on top of proceedings in the seventh game of the second set. The players were tied at 3-3, but Ivanisevic trailed 0-30 after having hit two consecutive double-faults.

On the next point, the twenty-one-year old struck an ace which the New Yorker thought was a fault. Unwittingly, umpire Bruno Rebeuh had swung the psychological pendulum in favour of Goran and when he held to 4-3, McEnroe received a warning for verbal abuse.

The New Yorker stated afterwards, "It only takes a little thing like that [to turn a match]. If I'd won that game all I would have had to do was to hold serve twice to win. So it was a big point."

The incident no doubt unsettled McEnroe and painfully for him a missed volley on the Croatian's first break point ushered in a third set.

Suddenly John was buckling under the pressure. He bravely saw off two break points before succumbing in the fourth game and eventually Ivanisevic came through 3-6, 6-4, 6-2 in one hour and forty-two minutes.

As he left the court, the 10,000 crowd in the Olympiahalle rose to acknowledge John and he responded by raising a clenched fist in gratitude. His last full year on the professional tour was over. He would later tell the press, "I am walking out of here with my head held high."

He also said, "For the moment I'm taking a step back to re-evaluate and then I'll go from there. I'll continue to try and keep in shape, which I would like to do anyway, regardless of whether I'm playing tennis. But I feel like that is it, but I can't say one hundred per cent what is going to happen. When you have been doing something for twenty-five years, it is hard to decide you are not going to do it anymore. I feel comfortable with the decision and that is why I am not officially announcing my retirement right now … I no longer have that combination of mental and physical strength where you can push yourself to another level and because of that it's best for me to go out while I still feel I'm playing really well. I'm not as highly ranked as I was and I know I'm not at the level I was, though I proved what I wanted to this year – that I was capable of beating the top players. I don't think you will see me playing any more tournaments … maybe some more exhibitions. But I'm not going to fall off the face of the earth."

His complex, brilliant journey was over. He vowed that we would never see him "being plastered all over the place by someone who just whacks the daylights out of a tennis ball."

EPILOGUE

In May 1993, at the Paris Country Club, clothes giant Nike staged a press conference with the help of Andre Agassi, Jim Courier and John McEnroe.

McEnroe took the opportunity to confirm he wouldn't be playing at Wimbledon that year. He joked, "As an old American basketball player once said, the older I get, the better I used to be. The odds against me ever playing there again, certainly in singles, must be very long indeed."

True to his word, John's only performances at the All England Club came in his guise as CBS sports commentator. Yet freed from the discipline of an athlete's life, he enjoyed himself in London in 1993. He attended the opening of Shepherd Market's Iceni nightclub and also found time to relax at Browns in Covent Garden.

Yet he didn't completely shun competitive tennis. In October 1993 he played in the Hong Kong Championships, opening with a 7-6, 6-1 dismissal of Mark Woodforde. He commented, "It was a good start for me. I wanted to see how I would match up against top players. I think Mark had some problems, but I would rate my performance as seven out of ten."

John's self-analysis gained credence when dangerous Richard Krajicek eliminated him 6-4, 6-4.

In early '94 McEnroe informed tournament directors that he would be willing to play if a top player was forced to withdraw. Sure enough, in February, Krajicek had to pull out of the Rotterdam event due to knee surgery. When Boris Becker found out that John was Holland-bound, he suggested in one of their weekly telephone calls that they should partner each other there.

So as the time fast approached midnight on Tuesday, February 22, John and Boris took to the court against Jan Siemerink and Daniel Vacek. By 1.30 a.m. they had won through 7-6, 7-6.

The next day McEnroe faced rising star Magnus Gustafsson. The part-time player lost 6-2, 7-6. Nonetheless, once John had broken back in the second set, he thrilled the crowds and even led 5-4 in the breaker. John Parsons of 'The Daily Telegraph' thought McEnroe "looked in astonishingly good shape."

As for the doubles, the German-American combination saw off Henrik Holm and Anders Jarryd 7-6, 6-4 before succumbing to Jeremy Bates and Jonas Bjorkman 6-4, 6-4 in the semi-finals.

After that event, the New Yorker confined his displays to exhibition matches. But as Wimbledon '95 drew close, there was hope that McEnroe might once again grace the SW19 lawns. Martina Navratilova was keen to partner him in the mixed doubles and apparently the only potential obstacle was their respective television commitments.

I asked Pam Shriver, who was competing in Birmingham's DFS Classic, what Martina could expect of John. (Pam had played doubles with McEnroe in the 1990 Hopman Cup, when the United States fell to Spain.) Pam replied, "She'll have a lot of fun. I'd definitely queue up outside the grounds to see them play."

But it wasn't to be. Ms. Navratilova was destined to win the event with Jonathan Stark; McEnroe's obligations to NBC stymied the dream team's creation.

There had been a similar disappointment for the Irish the previous year. The New Yorker was scheduled to play Mats Wilander in Dublin on July 4, 1994. However, their exhibition was cancelled on July 1 because it would have clashed with Ireland's football game against Holland in the World Cup.

In 1995 he did participate on Wednesday, June 28 in Dublin's Goal Challenge charity event, held at the Fitzwilliam Club. Drama once again enveloped him – before he had even struck a ball! He missed his scheduled flight from New York and therefore had to buy a ticket to London on Concorde. Next, his connecting Aer Lingus flight from Heathrow was delayed, with the result that he required a Garda motorcycle escort to arrive in time to take on Ireland's No.1 Eoin Collins in an evening contest.

Collins remembers: "It was a full house on the indoor courts. The crowd wanted to see John win."

John lost the first set 6-4 and was broken in the fifth game of set two when he led 3-1. But he broke back immediately, capturing the set 6-3. He then seized a 7-3 tie-breaker to be declared the winner.

John O'Shea, Goal organiser, called John a "true champion". But the player was slightly sheepish in the locker room afterwards when he contemplated the fact that he had queried line calls in a charity match. "I knew I probably shouldn't have," he said, "but there you are. I am competitive and that's half the fun of sport. But no, I shouldn't really have done it in a charity match."

Despite his desire to win, McEnroe didn't lose sight of the fact that he was in Dublin to help developing countries. On court he told the crowd, "Look, this is easy for me. All I do is hit a few balls. But look at this guy John O'Shea – and they are dying out there."[23]

For English supporters hoping to see McEnroe, there was false promise in a June 1995 'Evening Standard' report which stated that he would play the Hurlingham Seniors event in 1996. John was quoted as saying, "I am really looking forward to returning to England to play." However, a plethora of commitments meant the American had to back down.

A plethora of commitments? How exactly was John occupying himself? Well, for starters, he had become an art dealer.

His interest had been aroused in Paris in 1977. He saw a Monet and became attracted to Impressionist works.

In the next couple of years, Vitas Gerulaitis introduced the youngster to photorealist paintings in New York's Louis Meisel Gallery. It was there that McEnroe bought his first painting, by the realist Audrey Flack. Next he acquired a Renoir, followed by a Picasso, from Sotheby's.

In the early eighties, Meisel himself recommended to John three top galleries in each of twelve European cities. On John's return to New York, he informed Meisel that he had made time to see thirty of the galleries.

Art came to John's rescue in 1993. Lawrence Salander recognised that the separation from Tatum had inflicted intense pain and he allowed McEnroe to work for him at the Salander-O'Reilly gallery on New York's East 79th Street.

Immersion in his passion eased the star's anguish and soon his father was telling the press that John "may well become deeply involved in the business side of art as a dealer and gallery owner."

In December '93 the former tennis star opened a gallery at 41

---

[23] McEnroe also competed in the July 6 1998 Goal Challenge at the Fitzwilliam. Irish Davis Cup player Owen Casey had what he described as the "absolute honour" to partner the American (see Appendix). Casey also told me, "It was an amazing experience. I grew up watching him compete at Wimbledon and I always pulled for him. He hasn't lost the skill." John was simply glad to make people happy. He said, "If I can play some tennis and maybe scare some people into not wanting to see me, but to give money to Goal instead, then that's great." All the gate receipts went to benefit Sudanese famine victims.

Greene Street in the SoHo district of New York. He began by exhibiting Bruno Fonseca paintings and he maintained a by-appointment-only policy until May '95 when he showed Emil Nolde watercolours and graphics.

In 1996 McEnroe followed up an exhibition of "Twentieth Century Nudes" with a display of contemporary British figurative artists in conjunction with Matthew Flowers, director of the Flowers East Gallery situated in Richmond Road, London E 8.

It was good to see McEnroe's links with England being strengthened by his love of art. And how pleasing it was that he had found a measure of composure, and such happiness, through his hobby.

John's stated ambition in art is to bring an aspiring artist to prominence. He finds peace when he studies paintings and he is glad he has found something which allows him to feel good without simultaneously eliciting in him a desire to be the very best. His gallery assistant Robin Zendell once said, "I'm sure he'll display his own works one day."

Journalists who have visited McEnroe at Greene Street describe him as totally at ease. This must mean that the fact that the Greene Street building was originally designed to be a bolthole for him and Tatum no longer caused any difficulty.

Yet the separation of John and Tatum had been pounced upon by the world's media. The tabloids displayed a lurid obsession with the financial details of their break-up, though Tatum told 'Arena' magazine that she had signed a pre-nuptial contract to marry for love, not money.

To 'Hello', Tatum admitted that John was "a devoted father with an old-fashioned sense of morals."

In the end, despite rumours that the couple might be able to resolve their differences, they in fact grew further apart.

John once again settled into a serious relationship, this time with rock singer Patty Smyth.

He explained to Malcolm Folley in 'The Mail on Sunday', "It's incredibly ironic but we actually were brought up about fifteen minutes away from each other in Queens. We're the same age and we went to the same clubs but we never met.

"Then, finally, a friend introduced us in Los Angeles on Christmas Day 1993. I thought she was fantastic and took her number but it was about eight months before I plucked up the courage to ring it. We went on a date and from that moment we have hardly been apart."

In August '95, Patty's pregnancy was announced and December 27 saw her give birth in New York to a baby girl, Anna, who briefly suffered from breathing problems. In fact, the red-haired baby arrived six weeks prematurely, weighing five pounds one ounce, and spent the first month of her life in hospital.

In the meantime, Tatum was reported to have spent time in a drug rehabilitation clinic and had allegedly been admitted to hospital due to a drug dependency problem.

The press stated that McEnroe was taking the lion's share of the responsibility for their three children and that he would fight for sole custody given his concerns about Tatum's faltering health.

But in early '96 McEnroe told reporter Milton Esterow that Kevin, Sean and Emily split their time between staying with him and with Tatum. The ex-player presumably also felt paternal towards ten-year old Ruby – "my girlfriend's daughter" – since he also mentioned her whilst conversing with Esterow …

But let us not pry too deeply into the dilemmas that John has had to face. Let us remember that he is, in essence, a good man. Ex-pro Andrea Jaeger, for instance, has often mentioned how McEnroe's largesse has aided her children's charity, the Kids Stuff Foundation. And let us also recall why John P. McEnroe is famous. He might say, "Music is so much more fun. I am trying to break away from tennis," but it is his uncanny ability with a racquet that made the world sit up and take notice.

And he does still show a lingering love for the game. He has bemoaned the decline of tennis, adding that it "used to be like chess and to me that was the beauty … we have to ensure it doesn't degenerate into a serving competition."

In an interview with Matthew Tolan of 'Racquet', John remembered that he first played tennis "by myself on the backboard … I always tried to play with some kids who were a little older than me and then go back to the backboard."

Tolan was also told, "I was perceived as constantly complaining about the umpires, but to me I was trying to do something about the horrendous calls. Instead of looking at me, they should have gotten equipment that works."

And as for what tennis had taught him, John replied, "In one sense, tennis has taught me that I can't count on anyone but myself.

It's a very individual sport. It's sad in a way. It's given me somewhat of a cynical feeling and I like to trust people. I feel like I lost some of that. Tennis is a great game when it is played well, but it has nothing to do with reality."

POSTSCRIPT

During Wimbledon '96 it was hoped that John McEnroe would play Bjorn Borg on men's finals day as a fitting finale to the 'old' Court No.1 before it was demolished.

But the previous month the Swede had collapsed at a Seniors event in the Netherlands and it was not possible to find a suitable replacement for him.

Asked at the All England Club if he had been yearning for a return to competitive tennis, John said, "When I saw the bottom half of the draw I fancied it, but there are some junior players out there who could beat me if they had a good day."

Conversely, McEnroe told Linda Pentz in the November 1997 issue of Ace Tennis Magazine, "I could beat some of these youngsters who are playing at the US Open ... Not in the shape I'm in though. But there's not a lot of guys that scare me."

Similarly, there weren't a lot of guys who impressed John. Just before Wimbledon '97, 'Sun' reporter Steven Howard quoted him thus, "I don't think people feel that strongly one way or the other about the players nowadays."

It seemed as if the old maestro was now glad to be a TV match analyst. In the same article, he remarked, "What I like about commentating is that it allows me to become more of a human being again. People who were critical of me for some of my antics as a player actually say, 'Hey, you did a good job with that commentary.'"

Away from tennis, John married Patty Smyth in Hawaii in March '97. Contrary to press reports, it was not Bjorn Borg who was Best Man, but rather John's children who performed the role.

A week before the wedding, the American star attracted intriguing headlines in the British press. Ron Atkin, writing from California for 'The Sunday Telegraph', told us that McEnroe had said he wanted to marry in "an exotic location – Hawaii maybe, or Centre Court." Apparently the New Yorker had been speaking whilst in Palm Springs, where he had undertaken a humorous autograph session to promote his fourman group, the Johnny Smyth band. He declared, "I named the band after Patty because I love her so much." The fans went home happy – their hero signed "photographs, tennis balls, baseballs and even golf balls."

But it appeared as if we would never again see McEnroe on an English tennis court. Then suddenly, when we least expected it, the word was that the 38-year old would be competing in London once more.

Peter Fleming must have understood what that meant to so many people. A few months earlier he had told Robert Philip of 'The Daily Telegraph' a story concerning an early Wimbledon; " … We drove through the gates at about ten past twelve – we were due on Court Three… and as we went past our court we noticed there wasn't an empty seat. It was packed to the rafters. Wow! John and I just looked at one another when it dawned on us that all those people were willing to sit in a cramped seat for two hours just to see us play doubles."

And now all that drama was about to be re-lived.

Honda Challenge

Monday, November 24, 1997

Unfortunately, the news from America was not good. John McEnroe could be forced out of the ATP Senior Tour of Champions event at the Royal Albert Hall owing to an orthopaedic worry.

He had a problem with the arch of his foot and described it as "potentially the most serious injury I have had."

John added, "The doctor told me it would not be safe to start practising until today or tomorrow at the earliest so that gives me about eight days to get fit."

Monday, December 1, 1997

What a difference a week makes!

All the signs now were that McEnroe, the star attraction of the Honda Challenge, would be on court in three days' time to face 45-year old Guillermo Vilas.

The publicity machine swung into action. Indeed, the BBC 1 sports programme "On Side" even featured John McEnroe, "live from his art gallery in downtown Manhattan."

Presenter John Inverdale asked, "All those tantrums, when you look back on them, do you regret them?"

"Certainly some of them I regret..." came the response.

And the 38-year old disclosed, "I have three great passions – my children, I have five to take care of now; my art I quite enjoy, my gallery here, I hope this becomes almost a full-time thing as my tennis career continues to wind down, and music is the other thing I really enjoy."

Inverdale then wondered whether there could be a British men's singles Champion at Wimbledon in the next five years.

"I'd like to think that would happen because I actually think that would be a great thing for tennis. Tell Henman[24] to get his ass out on the tennis court and start working!" As the studio audience laughed and applauded him, McEnroe raised a query of his own. "Can you say that word on TV?" he asked innocently.

Thursday, December 4, 1997

Beat Guillermo Vilas 6-3, 6-3

The morning papers seemed relieved and excited to be featuring John McEnroe once again.

In the "Independent", the star told John Roberts that Wimbledon's new Court No.1 was "beautiful." However, he couldn't help reminiscing about the old Court No.1 and his doubles triumph there with Michael Stich in 1992. "My last match at Wimbledon," he remarked. "I was actually undefeated on that court." For McEnroe, the splendour of SW19 had evidently not diminished.

Elsewhere in the papers, the New Yorker admitted that he still felt the same need to win: "I wish in my day someone had punched

---

[24] World No.17 Tim Henman in fact had a thirty-minute practice session with John at the Royal Albert Hall during the Honda Challenge. The pair also had a long talk. The 23-year old Briton said the following week, "I can show more emotion and McEnroe implied that if I let my inner feelings out a bit more it could help me. Anytime you get advice from someone who has achieved what he has you should listen."

me on the nose and made me realise how lucky I was. But it still feels similar when I'm out there losing. All the questioning in my head starts kicking off again.

"That's hard for me to take. One of the reasons I stopped playing in the first place was because of my inability to handle the losing side very well."

And the three-times Wimbledon Champion warned, "The Seniors Tour has picked up and is far more competitive and serious than I thought it would be. It's not a giggle."

❧ ☙

It was 16.57 in the resplendent Royal Albert Hall when McEnroe v Vilas got under way.

The American immediately warmed to the intimate theatre and the play was entertaining, featuring some long backcourt rallies. John found time to unfurl some big, but clever serves and he broke in the fifth game to lead 3-2.

But he clearly felt a terrible pressure to perform well. He had not played in England for five and a half years and besides, he has always believed he should dominate on a Supreme Court. Furthermore, at the back of his mind he was probably still troubled by his painful foot injury.

So, whilst McEnroe was making the game look incredibly easy, he was still likely to be ruffled by an officiating error. The latter unfortunately came at the end of the seventh game, when Guillermo struck a forehand beyond the baseline but was nonetheless awarded the point.

The American argued at the changeover with umpire John Parry, an adversary from way back. All the same, when the player got up to serve, the gallery cheered him.

The earring in John's left ear glistened under the lights as he created a delightful diagonal forehand dink to make it 40-15 in game eight…

At 5-3, 15-15 the 38-year old's backhand pass landed on the line – a shot of perfection. Vilas, once the world No.2, then fluffed a drop volley and served a double-fault. Game and first set to McEnroe, 6-3. It was like old times.

But the atmosphere soured in the first game of the second set. At break point down, McEnroe's forehand volley was adjudged to have floated wide and McEnroe scowled at the relevant linesjudge and threw his racquet at his chair. At the same time, umpire Parry had no option but to announce a code violation for audible obscenity.

Vilas ran away with the second game as John swore repeatedly at the centre service lineslady who had first irked him in the previous game. The New Yorker also growled at a spectator, "Have a couple more glasses of champagne. You're not drunk enough yet."

In the third game, McEnroe berated a baseline judge and was further angered when his serve was called out. A section of the crowd began a slow handclap, but McEnroe served an ace to cut the arrears to 1-2.

The fourth game saw further verbal exchanges with Parry. McEnroe snapped, "Give me a break. Give me one call out of eight." And seconds later, the player stormed, "Be my guest. Show me the mark if it's so clearly out." Meanwhile, composed Guillermo somehow saw off three break points and then slammed two aces of his own for a convincing 3-1 lead. "C'mon John," came a cry from the stalls.

McEnroe raced obligingly to a 40-0 lead in the fifth game. However, his crosscourt backhand was then called out. "Are you serious?" he yelled at Parry and another long argument ensued.

Vilas seemed to draw confidence from the rumpus, immediately pulling back to deuce, before John himself served two much-needed aces.

From there, McEnroe tightened the screw. First, he played his best game of the match to break back and level at 3-3. Admittedly, he slammed a ball into the majestic roof en route to 4-3 … Then he captured Vilas' serve again, thanks to a sweet backhand pass. Finally, he served out to love and playfully kicked a ball into the cheering crowd. It had been a rousing fightback.

At the press conference, McEnroe seemed a little upset by his behaviour. He was quick to describe the Royal Albert Hall as "incredible. Fabulous. But I played like crap. I'm a bit unsure of myself. I'm looking forward to playing Bjorn tomorrow. It'll be more exciting. I'll be in a more giving mood," he promised.

John said that he wished Italy had a venue like the Royal Albert Hall so that a similar Seniors event could be staged there. Looking at his agent, Milan-based Sergio Palmieri, the player joked, "I could question line calls in opera language!"

He also said sheepishly, referring to his match today: "They've got to give me a call, even if I'm wrong."

But no-one thought John was wrong when he explained what his ideal change in the tennis rules would be – a return to wood racquets. Not a soul dissented from his view that wood "separates (out) the guys who don't have the technique or feel." Besides, McEnroe said that wood racquets were perfect because when he first came to England and became angry, "they used to bend, it was beautiful!"

❧❧

The Vilas contest had been absorbing, but McEnroe's most sparkling interchanges were with barrister Clive Anderson in the evening.

The TV chat show host and the tennis professional played off each other perfectly:

Anderson: "You weren't born in America, you were born in Germany because your father was in the Forces, but if only he'd been posted to Norfolk – you'd have been British!"

McEnroe (laughing): "I don't believe they would have accepted me here."

Anderson: "Oh, I think so. McEnroe at least sounds close to being British, whereas Rusedski doesn't."

McEnroe (deadpan): "No, he sounds as if he's from Czechoslovakia."

Talk then turned to the subject of the Royal Albert Hall.

McEnroe: "Of places to play, that's fantastic. You can't beat that."

Anderson: "No, it's fine. We knocked it up especially for you."

And the star also re-affirmed his desire to win the Honda Challenge.

McEnroe: "I didn't come here to lose."

Anderson (expecting nothing less): "No."

McEnroe: "No. I've noticed even in semi-retirement that winning is a whole lot better than losing, which is something they need to teach people over here in England."

Anderson: "Well, we like to be good losers."

McEnroe: "Absolutely."

Anderson: "Let's face it, we have to be."

McEnroe (seriously): "The best press I ever got in England was when I lost."

John also described his anger as "a comic detail" at this point in his career. He further confided that he wished umpires had told him during arguments that he was "a jerk" rather than intoning such stiff reprimands as "Time delay – warning Mr. McEnroe." The audience erupted in laughter as McEnroe attempted an upper class British accent to prove his point.

* *According to tournament staff who saw John at the Hilton on Park Lane following his return from the TV studios, he was in fine spirits and had enjoyed the verbal swordplay with Anderson.*

Friday, December 5, 1997

Beat Bjorn Borg 2-6, 6-3, 10-7 (Champions' Tie-Break)

Half an hour before the re-match of these two great Champions, classical music from the violin of 27-year old Linda Brava filled the dimly-lit Royal Albert Hall. In this way the passage of time was somehow emphasised and one was put into a reflective mood. Where had all the years gone since Fire v Ice had illuminated Centre Court?

But at 13.49 McEnroe walked on court, ahead of Borg, and both players received a stirring welcome from the fans.

The 41-year old Swede looked lean and healthy. As the combatants warmed up, an anticipatory thrill ran down the crowd's collective spine. This encounter was eagerly awaited.

Bjorn played like a dream when the tussle started. He held to love and then startled McEnroe with some legendary returns. The New Yorker had to survive four break points before an ace at 14.08 gave him his first game.

The spectators loved the long, keenly fought rallies. They were quick to show their appreciation, especially when John foxed Bjorn with a breathtaking topspin forehand lob.

But Borg continued to return impeccably and McEnroe delivered a double-fault that left him trailing 3-1. In contrast, the sharp Swede ended his next service game with an ace.

In the sixth game, John led 40-30 when his first serve was deemed wide by a lineslady. Feeling the tension of the moment, the left-hander argued long and hard with umpire Kim Craven. He then went on to lose the point. The crowd shouted their encouragement for the 38 year-old and when he won the next point, he aimed a ball at the far end in the general direction of the lineslady. There was no danger of the official being hit, but Craven announced a code violation for unsportsmanlike conduct. There then followed a characteristic ace by McEnroe.

Still, Borg maintained his resolve and the errors were made by John. At 14.30 the American's forehand drifted into the tramlines and the set was Borg's, 6-2.

Fortunes changed in the second set. McEnroe served two aces in winning the second game. In the third, Borg hit two double-faults and was broken.

But the five-times Wimbledon Champion twice reached break-point in John's next service game. Typically, however, McEnroe's determination saw him through the tough times and it wasn't long before Bjorn faced a mountain at 3-5 down.

Quite simply, John was playing from memory, taking the ball at the top of the bounce and exhibiting vintage touch on the drop volley. It was as if he was still at the height of his powers.

At 15.00 the rejuvenated magician had two set-points. He choked the first one away with a netted backhand and Bjorn then served an ace. But McEnroe responded by winning a long point with a smash and an inspired backhand down-the-line pass sealed the set, 6-3.

Cries rang out for both players during the three minutes' time-out which preceded the 'first to ten points' Champions' tie-break.

The scenario was so dramatic that one could have been forgiven for thinking that the year was 1980.

Neither player conceded a point on service until 5-5. It was then that the super Swede was footfaulted on his first serve and he looked bewildered. McEnroe could only offer advice which he himself had never been able to follow. "Try and roll with the punches," he shouted amiably at his friend and the crowd loved it.

When play continued John won the point with a dinked backhand which forced a volley error from Borg.

But the 41-year old responded with a cross-court winner that conjured up further memories of that see-saw battle in the famous Wimbledon 1980 tie-breaker.

True to form, John's reply was an ace that gave him the lead, 7-6. He then put a forehand long (7-7), before passing Bjorn with an improved forehand.

McEnroe sensed victory, and another backhand down-the-line earned him a match point. Then the New Yorker served again, and the backhand return from Borg was long. 10-7, McEnroe. He raised his arms aloft and basked in the loud cheers which reverberated around the Royal Albert Hall.

And once again, he kicked a ball into the crowd.

"I wish we'd played a third set," McEnroe admitted after the one hour and 18 minutes of nostalgia. "It felt like, a little bit too quick. We're not that old! We can hang in there.

"The atmosphere felt electric to me. We're both playing better than we were a couple of years ago.

"You feel a pressure and responsibility to play well because you want to show you can still hit the ball. Once you've done that, it's more enjoyable."

McEnroe confirmed that he had felt genuinely "mad" when he hit the ball that resulted in a code violation. But he joked that his ATP Seniors contract demanded that he lose his notorious temper twice a match.

The tennis genius continued, "As far as I'm concerned, the players should be calling the lines." Journalists began to laugh, but John was quick to impress upon them, "I'm serious."

Putting the contest into context, McEnroe pondered upon his meetings with Borg between 1978 and 1981. "It was like a golden era," he said. "I feel I was part of the best time in tennis history. I feel lucky to have been part of that. Perhaps the people realize that that was a great time."

"Being a tennis player is a pretty great job," conceded the 38-year old. "Overall, I'm certainly happier now, but it wasn't so bad before. Looking back, I was so focused on winning Wimbledon, it was a pressure. I wish I'd been a little looser at that time. It seemed more important then than it actually was."

"Would you still like to play on Centre Court?" asked Barry Flatman of 'The Daily Express'.

"Sergio (Palmieri) and I and Alan Mills have thought of playing an event at Wimbledon," came the unexpected response. "That would be exciting – let's just hope they don't want 8-6 in the fifth set!" Later in the day it transpired that Alan Mills would be putting forward the idea to the Wimbledon authorities.

The last question put to McEnroe was about the surprising Borg footfault. "That was some call," said John. "Talk about a shot in the dark!"

Saturday, December 6, 1997

Beat John Lloyd 6-4, 6-4

Another day, and a change of pre-match music at the Royal
Albert Hall. This time a gospel choir provided the entertainment and
the upbeat tempo reminded us that the reassuring warmth of
Christmas was just around the corner.

In the meantime, John Lloyd, dressed in a blood-red outfit, was
determined to make McEnroe work for victory.

The 43-year old looked tremendously motivated as he pulled
ahead 2-1 on serve against a slightly slow opponent.

In response, McEnroe recognized the struggle and played some
miraculous tennis to level at 2-2.

But in the sixth game the American ace had to recover from 0-30
on serve. He kept his composure and rode his luck and it soon
became 3-3.

McEnroe kept quiet when his screaming forehand down-the-line,
which appeared good, was in fact called out at the start of the seventh
game. On the next point the New Yorker produced a superb angled
backhand pass. Yet he was still error-prone and the Briton held to 4-3.

The left-handed star finally pounced in the ninth game, breaking
serve by winning four points on the trot. He then remained serene as
he served out the set, 6-4, with an ace.

In the second set, McEnroe began with noticeably more
aggression. He gained an immediate break in a fight which was
beginning to boast some excellent all-court rallies.

At 3-2, the American served two consecutive aces to pull ahead at
40-15. But suddenly he had to save a break point with a flashing
backhand pass. John Lloyd may now be resident in California, but
he remains ever the Englishman, as typified by his response to
McEnroe's winner. "Good shot," he said sportingly.

Seconds later, Lloyd acknowledged a heavy serve from McEnroe
with the words, "Too good." That serve enabled John to forge ahead 4-2.

In the next game, the former Wimbledon Champion won an
absorbing rally and allowed himself a rare smile. Lloyd, however,
captured the next three points to decrease the deficit to 3-4.
McEnroe could be seen breathing deeply at the changeover.

The 38 year-old then decided to turn on the style. "Oh, don't do
that," wailed Lloyd when he was outwitted by a disguised forehand

dropshot in game eight. Still, the man from Essex had contributed to the fantastic strokemaking and as the pace quickened, both players seemed to enjoy the match even more.

Lloyd eventually prevailed on serve in the ninth game and the crowd gave him a huge hand.

But McEnroe then served perfectly and reached match-point with a forehand winner. An angled ace concluded the sixty-six minute showdown. The victor hit a ball high into the stands and acknowledged all four sides of the cheering arena.

Lloyd was full of admiration when he spoke to journalists later. "Like Jimmy and Bjorn, John McEnroe doesn't want to lose – even if he's playing for a tuppence ha'penny or £100,000."

He continued, "I remember seeing him play at South Orange in 1976. It was like, 'Oh, my God.' You could see there was something. He was hitting the ball so early and doing things people had no imagination to do. It's amazing when he serves and volleys and hits a drop volley – I've never seen anyone who could do that. He just feathers the ball."

McEnroe, for his own part, was modest about his performance. "I feel like I was hitting the ball well," he admitted. "I didn't pick up a racquet for five or six weeks before this tournament so it's good to play points."

He had clearly made a big effort to be at the Honda Challenge, even though he was not fully fit. "I wanted to play here," he insisted. "I knew people would be pumped up for that. It's exciting. There were more of you guys here yesterday than the combined total on the Seniors Tour this year. BBC even showed my match with Borg for thirty minutes! We're back, even if only momentarily."

McEnroe further explained, "On a good day I'm 85 per cent of what I was. On a bad day I'm 15 or 20 per cent below that. But I know how to play on this stuff."

Asked again about the possibility of his playing at Wimbledon in a seniors event, John said the plan would be to donate "a lot of money to charity and make it really positive. I don't see any reason why the All England Club wouldn't see the positive about the whole idea.[25] I'm very confident," he concluded.

---

[25] The All England Club have not progressed the idea. They reportedly decided that the proposed event would somehow take the spotlight away from the tournament proper.

Sunday, December 7, 1997

Beat Henri Leconte 6-2, 3-6, 10-5 (Champions' Tie-Break)

John won the £32,000 first prize with a theatrical, barnstorming performance.

The packed Royal Albert Hall crowd, together with a live BBC 2 audience, will long remember his all-action display. It was as if the glamour days of tennis were back.

The feisty star stated afterwards that he hadn't expected "to hit the ball that cleanly from the baseline." In truth, he created his best masterpiece for years against a player who at 34 was barely old enough for the Seniors Tour.

In the first set the New Yorker returned brilliantly and thoroughly deserved the two breaks of serve which he garnered in opportunistic style. It was a cross-court forehand pass which saw him grab the honours at 6-2.

But Leconte began to force the pace. Accordingly, McEnroe had to save a break point with a forehand volley winner before being able to scramble to 1-0 after exactly half an hour's play. The battle was obviously far from over.

The American played like his 1984 self in the second game, taking the ball very early. Nonetheless, at 30-30 a spectator shouted, "Get angry, John." However, it was the Frenchman who responded first, firing an ace to level matters at 1-1.

But in the third game a backhand return from Leconte came off his racquet frame. As the ball rose in the air, he declared aloud that it was "going in." McEnroe then netted a smash off the bounce. "Is he allowed to talk?" the American immediately interrogated umpire Kim Craven. When he didn't receive the reply he was looking for, John snapped, "The rules specifically say he can't talk during a point."

Craven, however, ruled in Henri's favour and McEnroe countered by seizing the next four points.

John received wild applause for his exploits in the fourth game, but Leconte served another ace at 30-40.

At 2-2, McEnroe netted a forehand chip to make the score 15-40. When, on the next point, he missed his first serve and simultaneously broke a string in the process, some fans goaded him by shouting sarcastically, "Take your time. Don't rush, John." He switched his racquet, but a backhand error gave Leconte the game.

The New Yorker retaliated instantaneously, harrying his opponent into a baseline mistake that gave him a chance to re-group at 3-3.

Yet the drama continued as Leconte battled his way to double break-point. On his first opportunity, his passing shot hit the tape. On the next chance, John served and volleyed to safety. An ace then improved the 38-year old's state of mind, but Henri immediately ran down a forehand dropshot to make it deuce.

A serve and volley foray by John. Advantage, McEnroe. Leconte then hit a return which was too hot to handle. Deuce.

John, off balance, hit a forehand into the net. Advantage, Leconte.

And the server then lost the next point, before slamming a ball into the roof. 4-3, Leconte. Soon it was 5-3 as the New Yorker disintegrated badly.

At 15-30 in the following game there were further problems for John. His serve down the centre was called out by linesman Syd Slawther. The player responded by walking over the net and leaving a ball where he believed it had bounced. A confrontation with Craven followed, a code violation for verbal abuse was the upshot.

Rattled McEnroe then netted a forehand to give Leconte two set points. The younger man won the ensuing long rally and his reward was frenzied appreciation from the stands.

One set all.

John argued with the umpire as they waited for Leconte to join them on court for the coin toss in respect of the Champions' tie-break. The Frenchman went on to win the toss and he elected to serve first.

Before that happened, however, McEnroe engaged in what he would subsequently call " a philosophical discussion" with Slawther. "It was a bad call," McEnroe reflected later, referring to Slawther's decision in the ninth game. "No way was it out. I asked him, why don't you just say you made a mistake? It would be nice if once in twenty years they could admit they made a bad call, but if that happened I'd fall over or have a heart attack."

"Let's play," Craven suddenly ordered McEnroe.

The tie-break began with a Leconte double-fault. McEnroe hit two vicious serves. The flashy Frenchman missed the easiest of smashes, before chalking up his first point with an ace. A hard first service winner meant McEnroe was up 5-1 at the change of ends.

Leconte's backhand went into the tramlines; a successful serve and smash routine by the 34-year old then followed. John forced a volley error, thus creating a 7-2 lead. The New Yorker struck a forehand pass when his opponent charged the net: 8-2. Leconte's backhand floated into the tramlines: 9-2 McEnroe, match point.

The crowd gasped as cool Henri captured the next three points. The tension was nearly unbearable, but Leconte finally netted a volley and it was all over.

❧

John took the Cup in one hand and the microphone in the other.

He told the gallery, "This is the best tennis I've played in the last few years. But that's not enough. You tell me to get mad, so I get mad, then you're mad at *me*!" But in victory he was happy. "See you next year," he promised his faithful band of supporters.

As for his skirmish with Craven, John informed the press, "It didn't seem to satisfy everyone when I let my racquet do the talking. So I slipped into contractual mode. In fact, the umpire was giving me the run-around. He asked me, "Is this part of the contract?" I said, "Let's take it outside." I'm serious about playing. The other part is iffy. You just don't know. That's the beauty of it!"

And the beauty of John McEnroe is that the following week he swung his racquet in the name of charity.

AFTERWORD

The popularity of tennis remained muted in 1998. The need for the sport to look backwards probably meant, if anything, that John McEnroe's fame and reputation were both accentuated throughout the year.

Almost every month there was another McEnroe happening to note. April, for instance, saw him win a Seniors event in Qatar with a 7-6 (7-5), 4-6, 10-8 (Champions' Tie-Break) defeat of Bjorn Borg. Then, at the French Open, the Roland Garros officials apparently refused to give his two-year old daughter, Anna, a ticket, so John suggested she join him in the commentary booth to plead for a complimentary pass.

In July he crushed Jimmy Connors in a Seniors' final in Detroit. And on the eve of the US Open he revealed to Richard Pagliaro in the New Jersey publication 'Passing Shot' that the real reason why he had missed Wimbledon in '86 and '87 was because he had been too perturbed by the criticism he had received in England over the years. Conversely, four months later he told Sue Mott in the 'Daily Telegraph' that he skipped those events in a misguided attempt to show the tennis world that it was dead without him.

On a less contentious note, in the autumn his art gallery exhibited botanical illustrations of Capetown Wild Flowers[26] and artist Eric Frischl was reportedly giving him painting lessons in return for tennis tuition. The old star was also teaching son Sean a few valuable lessons … such as how to behave on court. According to Malcolm Folley in 'The Mail on Sunday', John had banned Sean from tennis for a month due to the youngster's lack of sportsmanship.

By the time the Seniors Circuit arrived in London in December, McEnroe had won 7 of the 11 tournaments he had entered in '98. He felt that his game was coming together and once again he surmised that the gap between him and, certainly, the doubles players on the men's tour, was very slim. "I watch these guys and I am not impressed," he admitted.

---

[26] In May 1999 it was reported that John was closing down his gallery, but in fact it remains open 'by appointment'.

Honda Challenge

Thursday, December 3, 1998
Beat Guillermo Vilas 6-1, 6-4

McEnroe's longevity was underlined by the fact that the event was being held at Olympia, where he and Peter Fleming had smashed their way to victory in the Braniff Airways Doubles competition almost twenty years earlier.

After destroying his opponent in 64 minutes, John could only recollect that he had emerged triumphant back in January 1979, together with the fact that there had been "some pretty good crowds."

McEnroe also was quick to say that he would rather have been playing at the Royal Albert Hall where "the sound is so beautiful. But Sir Cliff is over there so we have to accept our fate!"

Although the match did not end until 12 minutes past ten at night, the New Yorker duly signed copious amounts of autographs at the finish since he knew what "it was like when I was a kid." All in all, this complicated celebrity was in an expansive mood, reiterating his belief that 10% of all the prize money in tennis should "go to charities and opportunities for kids to play the sport, environmental concerns and children's problems."

As for his own form, he stated, "I'm playing as well as I have in six to eight years. The only time I got in trouble (tonight) was when I started fiddling about."

Friday, December 4, 1998
Beat Mansour Bahrami 6-2, 7-6

John's sublime skills and Iranian Bahrami's barrage of trick shots created perfect chemistry for an appreciative Friday night crowd.

After a straightforward first set which John concluded with a subtle ace, the rallies embodied numerous 'cat and mouse' battles which provided fascinating entertainment.

McEnroe was in fact broken to love in the second game of the second set, but he broke back immediately. In the fifth game he sportingly gave a point to Bahrami, even though the linesjudge had ruled in the 39-year old's favour.

The American saved a break point in the next game before his fighting instincts took control in the tie-break. He lifted one finger in the air – to signify that only one point was needed – when he stood at match point. When the clash was over, we were all left with the feeling that McEnroe and Bahrami had given us more laughs in one evening than had been provided by the men's circuit all year long.

John was also good value on this day during his appearance on Chris Evans' TV show, TFI Friday. He lost a point of table tennis against Chris and, on cue, complained, "You cannot be serious!" But in a quieter moment he agreed, "I miss picking up that Wimbledon cup."

Saturday, December 5, 1998
Beat Henri Leconte 6-4, 6-2

Unsurprisingly the near-capacity crowd savoured McEnroe's unique tennis gifts. The player then rewarded them with the promise, "I hope to hang in there for another couple of years. You fans are fantastic here in London: thank you very much."

Seconds later he gave a courtside interview to BBC's Sue Barker and, during their chat, he spotted two jokers sporting wigs of curly hair. Automatically he was reminded of his youth. He was so pleased to see the pranksters that he ushered them over and exclaimed, "From Wimbledon '77! I wish I had hair like that now – can you bring some of that tomorrow when I play the final?!"

Sunday, December 6, 1998
Beat Yannick Noah 7-5, 6-3

Quite rightly, Olympia was a sell-out for McEnroe's title win over 38-year old Yannick Noah of France.

As ever, it was a joy to admire John's idiosyncratic service action. He starts sideways to the net, the racquet head almost scraping the ground and he finishes with a corkscrew body action. Amazing. I've never truly understood how these complex movements manage to interact and give the appearance of such fluidity.

As for the contest itself, it did much to improve the tarnished image of tennis and the plethora of breathtaking points were vigorously applauded. Many of McEnroe's shots revealed such natural brilliance that they truly could be characterised as belonging to the 1984 scrapbook.

The last game was the best. With Noah serving at 3-5, McEnroe unfurled all his greatest weapons, taking the ball at the earliest opportunity; he was really firing on all cylinders. When the Frenchman put a forehand into the tramlines at 3.12 p.m., it was all over. John punched the air with delight and later paid tribute on-court to tournament director John Beddington, "the only tournament director to give me a parting gift after 15 years on the ATP Tour: a hand-made guitar. It's not broken yet, so thank you very much."

The public's desire to see John compete remained undiminished. At the same time, should he play at this age unless he is enjoying it? With this in mind, I asked him at the press conference whether he was still pursuing perfection or was he capable of enjoying the magic moments which occur during a game against someone like Noah?

"I can do both now," he assured me. "There's more entertainment involved which is nice. You're more just working on your game, but still making sure you win it!"

Emboldened by that answer, I reminded him that 1999 represented the 20-year anniversary of his first Wimbledon title, the men's doubles with Peter Fleming. Would he compete in that event in '99 if he received a wild card?

At first John was bemused. Why would he want to put himself to all that effort when in 1992 he and Stich had prevailed 19-17 in the fifth set? Besides, who would he partner? "You find me the partner," he said to me, "because it's no longer true I could win with anyone." But then his mood changed as he reconsidered the excitement of another outing on Centre Court. He abruptly changed tack and admitted that only the previous week, in Geneva, Steffi Graf had suggested that they play the mixed doubles at Wimbledon '99. He ventured, "I guess we'd win. I mean, I suppose we could lose but it's not likely. Steffi is very tempting."

But then John decided to keep us in suspense, adding, "Ideally it would be nice. But the reality is maybe different. It's better to dream, perhaps."

Certainly, I thought to myself, it would be a dream come true if John McEnroe took to the Wimbledon lawns one more time.

Wimbledon 1999

Friday, June 25, 1999
With Steffi Graf, beat Jeff Coetzee and Eva Melicharova 6-2, 6-4

My prayers are answered. McEnroe's wife gave birth to Ava Charli on 28 March, but he remained admirably keen about the London SW19 opportunity.

Indeed, just before the French Open women's final he spoke with Steffi Graf and the partnership idea was finalised. Steffi promptly shocked a surly Martina Hingis in a three set title win. Could it be true that the thought of playing with John acted as a spur?

The 30 year-old definitely enjoyed her evening outing on Court No1 with John against South African Coetzee and Melicharova of the Czech Republic. It was McEnroe, dressed in pure white, who wrapped up the match just after 8pm when he served out to 15.

In a later joint press conference Steffi said to the American that it had been an unbelievable experience when "the two of us" walked on court. Witty John responded: "I will never forget it!" and proceeded to pretend to cry.

John and Steffi appeared full of mirth to the spectators. Both stars were a little taken aback early on by the bizarre service action of 29 year-old Melicharova. And then Graf almost fell off her chair after a remark by John during a changeover. Asked by the press what his quip had been, McEnroe replied: "That I was the greatest player of all time? But I think it was probably about that girl's serve. It reminds me of Francoise Durr's backhand. It's one of the oddest I've ever seen, it definitely needs some work!"

Joking aside, John opined that competing at Wimbledon again had left him "nervous and excited. I certainly wanted to hold up my end of the bargain. I always said that if I stepped out on a court in a major then I wanted to feel like I had a chance to win the tournament. We are in it to win."

Saturday, June 26, 1999
With Steffi Graf, level at 2-2 (15-0, McEnroe) against Eyal Ran and Vanessa Menga

Vanessa Menga, a 22 year-old Brazilian who had finished 1998 ranked 202 in the world, had lost a first round qualifying match two weeks earlier in Edgbaston. A handful of fans showed scant interest in her elimination by Evie Dominikovic.

She could, therefore, have been expected to suffer from nerves and consequently fail to connect with the service of the legendary John McEnroe in the opening game of this clash on Court No2. But instead Miss Menga won the opening point for her team when she returned McEnroe's delivery past Graf at the net. McEnroe was soon 0-30 down but won the next four points to make it 1-0.

Later, serving at 2-2, John advanced to 15-0 but during the next point rain began to fall and the groundstaff began to cover the court before the competitors had barely left the playing area.

Wednesday, June 30, 1999
With Steffi Graf, beat Eyal Ran and Vanessa Menga 6-3, 6-4

The ninth seeds' victory was overshadowed by the emergence of 18 year-old qualifier Alexandra Stevenson, who saved match points before securing a berth in the women's quarter-finals. But despite her tender years and obvious excitement she placed John back in the limelight, telling reporters that her success echoed the New Yorker's run from Roehampton back in 1977.

"I've known about John McEnroe qualifying my whole life and I'm excited to do what he did," she declared.

Friday, July 2, 1999
With Steffi Graf, beat Justin Gimelstob and Venus Williams 6-4, 6-3

Finally John McEnroe was granted his rightful place on Centre Court for a reunion with the crowds who had savoured his brilliance so often in the past.

The early evening excitement took place in perfect conditions – with the stadium bathed in sunshine and packed to the rafters. Admittedly, shadows gradually drew across the lush surface as play progressed, but it was, nonetheless, a beautiful tennis scene which quite simply epitomised the very best qualities of Wimbledon. The fortunate onlookers participated in a purely happy occasion which was given defining force and poignancy by the silky, evergreen skills of the 40 year-old McEnroe.

The American performed with breathtaking quality. A break of

Gimelstob's serve had been enough to clinch the opening set, but Graf was also broken in the initial game of the second and John knew that he had a battle on his hands.

He rose to the occasion with relish. His exquisite return to feet secured the break back and he then aced Venus and Justin to move within four games of another Wimbledon semi-final.

As expected, the awesome Williams, an admirer of McEnroe in her formative years, maintained the pressure and John had to rely on his excellent reactions at the net to help his partnership edge ahead 3-2. He and Steffi high-fived when that mini-feat had been accomplished.

The charged atmosphere was much to John's liking, and he clenched his fist when another of his perfect service returns set up Graf for a volley opportunity which she seized, thus meaning they had broken 22 year-old Gimelstob to love.

The crowds were also revelling in the drama, and McEnroe responded to cries of "C'mon on John!" with some vicious serving to the ad court which enabled him to hold to love and make the score 5-2 at 6.35pm.

Venus kept plugging away in the eighth game, winning an absorbing net exchange with John, although he also conjured up a sublime backhand return to her feet which completely flummoxed her. Still, she showed sufficient composure to hold her serve again.

At 5-3 Graf endured three break points, but eventually the ninth seeds came out on top in a thrilling rally and Steffi then served an ace which was much to McEnroe's delight as it gave them match point.

Venus then muffed her backhand return and John kissed Steffi on both cheeks before raising his arms in jubilation as the appreciative crowds gave their roar of approval.

The veteran loved this nostalgic, life-affirming moment and enthused: "It's still the same feeling on Centre Court. There didn't seem to be a spare seat." He was enjoying the party. "It's magical," he murmured.

Saturday, July 3, 1999

To lose any Wimbledon semi-final is intensely disappointing for a player. It is hard to overcome that feeling of "what might have been". But for poor John the scenario was made worse because he was fit and yet he didn't hit a ball against opponents Jonas Bjorkman and Anna Kournikova.

Steffi Graf withdrew from the mixed doubles event, citing a thigh muscle strain which had required strapping during her semi-finals singles defeat of Mirjana Lucic of Croatia.

In his column in the "Sunday Telegraph", McEnroe barely concealed his inability to come to terms with the situation. He had gratefully accepted the adrenalin rush associated with competing again on Centre Court and he felt he had lost the chance to say a proper goodbye as a player to the Wimbledon Championships.

It probably did not help the former Champion's equilibrium the following day when commentator John Barrett described Steffi as moving "like a gazelle" as she slithered to defeat against Lindsay Davenport. Afterwards the German revealed that the injury had occurred "days ago" and had not been much of a factor in the final.

Robbed of the appropriate All England Club farewell he deserved, John returned to the States and drew some comfort seven days later when he was inducted into the International Tennis Hall of Fame in Newport, Rhode Island.

He reflected: "I hadn't played at Wimbledon in seven years... The one thing I asked of Steffi, if you start a tournament you should finish it. She just didn't fulfil her responsibility. It was a slap in the face. Luckily I have this great occasion here in Newport, otherwise I might still be stewing about this for a few more weeks."

At the ceremony John added: "Sure, I wore my emotions on my sleeve [during my career] and I couldn't get away from the labels like the next Nastase or the next Connors. When you think about it, nobody would give a hill of beans about my behaviour if I wasn't winning championships."

"But I think I brought energy to the game," the 40 year-old ventured. "I brought a style that has not been duplicated. In that respect I tried to do what my idol Rod Laver did."

Honda Challenge

Wednesday December 1 1999
Beat Bjorn Borg 7-5, 6-4

McEnroe arrived in a sunny but bitterly cold England as the new US Davis Cup captain.

The Wimbledon mixed doubles debacle was a fading memory ("I really felt like we were going to win it. It was awfully close,") and he was generally loving life again.

His happiness was typified by his post-match analysis. Borg, he said, "has less hair and I have grey hair," but it was "always fun to play" the Swede in front of "really supportive" Royal Albert Hall crowds.

John was playing five times per week ("I basically coach myself,") and he planned to compete on the Seniors' Tour for perhaps another four years "depending on motivation". "I don't want to go out there and do poorly. I have pride. But the fact that people come and watch you do something you like to do, to me that is the best way to make a living."

Thursday, December 2, 1999
Beat John Lloyd 6-3, 6-2

Another night game for John. Watched by Boris Becker and Ilie Nastase, he exhibited decorative skills and announced afterwards, "I'm here to win the tournament."

Friday, December 3, 1999
Beat Jimmy Connors 6-1, 6-0

"It's nice to have a great day," remarked the victor after a flawless effort, broadcast live on TV.

The athletic New Yorker took Connors' serve outrageously early, producing authoritative returns. He hit with confidence (and some topspin) during absorbing baseline duels. He served impressively. In short, he was dynamite!

Despite the scoreline, the entertainment value was sky-high. Also, McEnroe was on his best behaviour and, in an innocent tone, he wittily insisted: "It's important for the tennis to stand on its own – it's not important for us to stand on our head every match." Another McEnroe aside was that the contest had represented the fourth and fifth set of the Wimbledon '84 final!

The three times SW19 Champion won 14 consecutive points and reminded us that he had the "perfect game to play a lot of people." However, "If I thought I could go out there and still win Wimbledon, I'd be out there playing it."

Saturday, December 4, 1999
Beat Jeremy Bates 6-3, 6-7 (4-7), 10-4 (Champions' Tie-break)

In a stunning encounter, John was in control when serving at 6-3, 5-4. He no longer appeared to be struggling, having recovered from 1-3 in the first set and 0-2 in the second. But Bates broke back to 5-5 and John endured two discussions with umpire Grime over line calls before winning through

"I lost a set I should have won and it became a bit of a 'roll of the dice'," he stated before signing autographs for fans from the doorway of the Royal Albert Hall's Elgar Room.

Sunday, December 5, 1999
Beat Henri Leconte 6-2, 4-1 (Leconte retired)

A third Honda Challenge title for 40 year-old John, courtesy of his distinctive yellow-framed Volkl racket. Admittedly Leconte hurt his back, but the American deserved this special moment in London, especially after that mixed doubles pain inflicted by Steffi Graf.

The German conceded that when she told John she was pulling out, "he wasn't so happy. He said 'Come on, we can win this.' I felt terrible."

Today McEnroe might have disappointed Sue Barker, who previewed the final by bemoaning his lack of bad temper throughout the event, but the crowds went home happy since he declared: "This is my favourite tournament. I want to come back at least one more time."

His other goals for 2000 were well defined. As Davis Cup captain, he hoped to demonstrate that there was "no reason why someone shouldn't be given a chance to prove they have grown up and are responsible." And he aimed to be involved in shaping the direction of tennis, acting as "some sort of commissioner".[*]

---

[*]Footnote: John McEnroe was asked to be a BBC TV commentator for Wimbledon 2000. The critics praised him for bringing intelligence and colourful insight to the role. The Centre Court crowd also cheered him the loudest during the Millennium Parade of Champions. Moreover, on Sunday July 2 he and Bjorn Borg competed on a hard court in the grounds of Buckingham Palace. The great friends played for the NSPCC charity; the honours fell to John 6-3 7-6 (7-5). The 41 year-old overcame both a 3-5 games deficit and heavy rain which triggered his skyward (and good-humoured) shout: "You cannot be serious!"
But he was earnest and true when he volunteered: "We just want to be invited back." McEnroe relished the possibility of "a little tea and scones". The televised match, seen by a billion worldwide, raised over

Honda Challenge

Tuesday, December 5, 2000

The American had stepped down as Davis Cup captain the previous month, even though his team had reached the semi-finals (before losing away on clay 5-0 to Spain).

In resigning, he cited frustration regarding the lack of availability of the top stars, and he was also upset that the USTA had not really utilised his abilities for the benefit of junior development.

A couple of weeks after the Honda Challenge, John's brother Patrick would become the new Davis Cup captain. No doubt he was aware that his elder sibling still cherished hopes of playing doubles in the competition, for John said on this day in London: "It's a realistic option on my part. I felt awkward picking myself to play [doubles] so I didn't do so. At least I can say that I won five Davis Cups – they can't take that away ... I haven't seen anyone out there that plays a better game of doubles than I do."

And John was similarly blunt about claims by the Williams' sisters that they could win matches on the regular men's tour. The 41 year-old responded by stating that competitors on the men's seniors circuit could trounce Venus or Serena, and Donald Trump dramatically entered the fray by putting up a million dollars for McEnroe to fight the ultimate "battle of the sexes" exhibition. John's view was that the sum on offer was not nearly enough, though he cautioned: "I wouldn't take the money myself, it would go to charity."

As for playing again at the Royal Albert Hall, McEnroe observed wistfully: "It's nearly over. We've been lucky to get another chance and it's a hell of a lot better than being completely forgotten."

Wednesday, December 6, 2000
beat John Lloyd 7-5, 6-3

"I always have very good feedback when I play here. I have confidence already."

---

one million pounds for the fight against cruelty to children. That fact alone made certain that 2000 was some kind of golden year for the three-times Wimbledon Champion.

Thursday, December 7, 2000
Beat Mansour Bahrami 6-3, 6-4

Boris Becker was in the newspapers amidst suggestions that he was having an affair. Asked to comment, McEnroe retorted: "The media should go out with a drink because they've contributed to it. The people who do this for a living have no shame – their karma will get them eventually. They will end up in a miserable place."

John brightened slightly to admit: "What I'm doing this week is easy for me – it's something I've done since I was a kid." But on the subject of children, his mood again darkened: "People don't take seriously the job of being a parent, they just don't spend the time with their kids."

Friday, December 8, 2000
beat Bjorn Borg 7-6 (7-4), 6-3

In an evening confrontation widely touted to be their last ever in England, John performed immaculately to make light of being 1-3 down in the tie-break. At 3-3 in points he executed a cunning drop shot and he chipped and charged at 4-4 to earn a mini-break. An ace and a deep second serve eased him a set ahead.

He broke Borg in the Swede's first service game of the second set, and that proved to be the key to victory.

McEnroe later said: "What Bjorn has done for tennis is what superstars like Pele and Maradona have done for soccer. I wish him happiness with his family and himself."

Saturday, December 9, 2000
Beat Henri Leconte 6-2, 7-5

John's grey Nike shirt matched his hair, but he demonstrated focus and youthful effort to see off his French rival.

In a close second set, the New Yorker threw his racket to the ground on at least three occasions, and he saw a break point opportunity disappear in the seventh game. John twice served aces in the following game to nullify break points in favour of Henri.

At 5-5 the former Wimbledon Champion won a brilliant 15 shot rally, which triggered a smile. A little later his sense of satisfaction was enhanced because he broke Leconte.

Serving for the match, McEnroe needed a great ace down the middle to recover to 30 all. There was an altercation on the next point when John thought he had hit another ace. "That was a beautiful looking serve," he exclaimed to umpire John Parry, but the call was not reversed and the Frenchman seized a further break point. Yet again, an ace pulled McEnroe level and he convincingly captured the ensuing two points. After 1 hour and 9 minutes, he was into his fourth consecutive Honda final. He told BBC's Sue Barker courtside: "I came out smoking today."

Sunday, December 10, 2000

Lost to Pat Cash 6-7 (3-7), 7-5, 14-12 (Champions' Tie-break)
The spectators certainly received value for money, but John was unlucky to succumb after 2 hours and 18 minutes to the Australian who is six years his junior.

John tried to compensate for the age gap by hard graft, and to this end he practised his return of serve for 45 minutes before the final.

His dedication appeared to be paying off when he quickly moved to break point in the first game. However, he uncharacteristically hit a forehand long off a Cash second serve, and it was clear that from then on it would be a long afternoon's battle.

The strokeplay was enchanting, and the level of interest heightened when John stepped up in game ten to serve to save the set. At that stage, the left-hander believed he had delivered a sweet ace, and Cash, in recognition, began to move to the other side of the court. Unfortunately, umpire Parry disagreed with the players' analysis and the 41 year-old had to rely on his second serve to win the point. Stung by the dispute, he reacted in the best possible way by in fact taking the game to love.

He even recovered from 40-0 down at 5-5 to startle his opponent by rattling off four points in a row. John then saw an ace whistle past him but he had the strength of character to carve out two more break point chances. Much to his chagrin, he mistimed backhand returns on both occasions and the right-hander from Melbourne held to 6-5.

In the tie-break, by contrast, McEnroe was decisive. His tremendous forehand return put him ahead 1-0 and soon it was 4-

0…then 7-3 in points after 33 minutes.

Pat retaliated by improving his consistency off the ground. Still, McEnroe would probably have survived the onslaught if he hadn't gifted Cash a second break-point with a bad volley error. It was another simple error – delivered from well inside the service line – which gave the Australian a 1-0 lead. McEnroe's racket went flying to the other end of the court.

The rage within was immediately accentuated when Cash served fiercely to stave off two McEnroe break points. Indeed, John then had to scrap to circumvent a 3-0 disaster.

At 2-4, John had another disagreement with Parry over a disputed ace. This time the American remarked: "See that mark right there? That's where I've just served. The ball caught the outside of the line."

McEnroe lost the argument although he successfully scrambled to 3-4. But the 1987 Wimbledon Champion served out to love for 5-3.

It was at this juncture that the awesome left-hander showed his customary superhuman qualities. He channelled his resources beautifully and showed all his skills to acquire 9 of the next 11 points. Accordingly, the score moved to 5-5.

Yet it wasn't to be John's day. He dropped the set 7-5 and the Champions' tie-break unfolded. Our hero kept the faith and at 8-8 he earned a well-deserved match point. Cash retorted with an ace. At 10-10, John produced an ace of his own. Second match point. But the Aussie again served big and John's blocked backhand return flew long.

The standard of play remained enthralling. At 12-12 there was a thrilling 14 shot rally and then we saw a similarly scorching 13 stroke duel. It was all over – it was Cash's day and John McEnroe did the right thing by hugging his nemesis at the end.

As always, McEnroe had wanted to win. In addition, he had shown the London crowds that he could, and would, play on "for as long as possible." Long may he continue…

By doing so, the star was simply obeying the oft-heard command of many a Wimbledon umpire: "Please play on Mr McEnroe."

APPENDIX

John McEnroe's results in the British Isles are as follows:

1977

Wimbledon Qualifying

Beat Roger-Vasselin 6-4, 6-3
Beat Marten 6-8, 6-4, 6-4
Beat Moretton 6-2, 6-4, 6-4

(With Gene Scott)
Beat Crawford/Lofgren 7-5, 2-6, 6-1
Lost to Carnahan/Wayman 4-6, 9-8, 6-3

Wimbledon

Beat El Shafei 6-0, 7-5, 6-4
Beat Dowdeswell 9-7, 6-3, 6-1
Beat Meiler 6-2, 6-2, 5-7, 6-3
Beat S Mayer 7-5, 4-6, 6-3, 6-1
Beat Dent 6-4, 8-9, 4-6, 6-3, 6-4
Lost to Connors 6-3, 6-3, 4-6, 6-4

(With Mary Carillo)
Beat Wilson/Fayter 5-7, 9-8, 7-5
Beat J. Lloyd/Simmen 6-4, 6-3
Beat Carmichael/Kloss 6-2, 5-7, 6-2
Lost to Ralston/Navratilova 6-8, 6-3, 10-8

1978

Rawlings International

Beat Fleming 4-6, 7-5, 6-3
Beat El Shafei 6-3, 6-4
Beat G. Mayer 7-5, 6-0
Beat Tom Gullikson 4-6, 6-2, 6-4
Beat Dibley 6-3, 8-9, 6-2
Lost to Roche 8-6, 9-7

(With Peter Fleming)
Beat Dupre/Menon 6-0 retired
Beat S. Mayer/Stewart 6-4, 9-8
Lost to Hewitt/McMillan 6-4, 6-4

Wimbledon

Lost to Erik van Dillen 7-5, 1-6, 8-9, 6-4, 6-3

(With Fleming)
Beat C. Fancutt/McNamee 6-1, 6-2, 7-5
Beat Lutz/S. Smith 4-6, 6-1, 6-3, 8-9, 13-11
Beat Alvarez/Pecci 6-2, 6-4, 6-4
Beat McNair/Ramirez 9-7, 8-6, 9-8
Beat Fibak/Okker 1-6, 6-3, 9-7, 6-4
Lost to Hewitt/McMillan 6-1, 6-4, 6-2

(With Stacy Margolin)
Beat T. Lloyd/R. Lewis 6-2, 6-2
Lost to Kachel/Kloss 8-9, 7-5, 9-7

Benson & Hedges

Beat D. Lloyd 6-4, 6-2
Beat Okker 6-2, 6-3
Beat Barazzutti 6-0, 7-6
Beat Stockton 6-4, 6-3
Beat Tim Gullikson 6-7, 6-4, 7-6, 6-2

(With Fleming)
Beat Gunthardt/Teltscher 6-4, 6-2
Beat Smid/Taroczy 6-3, 6-3
Beat Fibak/Okker 6-1, 6-3
Beat Hewitt/McMillan 7-6, 4-6, 6-4

1979

Braniff Airways Doubles

(With Fleming)
Beat Panatta/Bertolucci 6-1, 6-1
Beat Nastase/Stewart 7-6, 4-6, 6-3
Beat Hewitt/McMillan 6-3, 6-3
Beat M. Cox/D. Lloyd 6-3, 6-7, 6-3
Beat Nastase/Stewart 3-6, 6-2, 6-3, 6-1

Stella Artois

Beat Pasarell 6-4, 6-4
Beat James 3-6, 6-3, 6-2
Beat V Amritraj 7-6, 6-1
Beat S. Mayer 3-6, 6-2, 6-4
Beat Tanner 6-4, 7-5
Beat Pecci 6-7, 6-1, 6-1

(With Fleming)
Lost to Manson/Pattison 6-2, 7-6

Wimbledon

Beat Moor 7-5, 6-1, 6-4
Beat Mottram 6-7, 6-2, 7-6, 6-2
Beat Tom Gullikson 6-4, 6-4, 7-6
Lost to Tim Gullikson 6-4, 6-2, 6-4

(With Fleming)
Beat Fitzgerald/Pascoe 4-6, 7-5, 6-2, 6-1
Beat Moore/Tanner 7-5, 7-6, 6-3
Beat Winitsky/Ycaza 6-3, 6-2, 6-4
Beat Case/Masters 6-3, 6-2, 6-3
Beat Hewitt/McMillan 6-3, 7-6, 6-1
Beat Gottfried/Ramirez 4-6, 6-4, 6-2, 6-2

Benson & Hedges

Beat J. Lloyd 6-4, 6-1
Beat R. Drysdale 6-2, 6-2
Beat Fibak 6-2, 6-1
Beat Ocleppo 6-3, 6-0
Beat Solomon 6-3, 6-4, 7-5

(With Fleming)
Beat Ocleppo/Roger-Vasselin 6-4, 6-2
Beat Taygan/Docherty 6-4, 6-4
Beat Fibak/Okker 6-3, 7-6
Beat Smid/S. Smith 6-2, 6-3

1980

Stella Artois

Beat Leonard 6-3, 6-4
Beat McNamee 6-4, 7-5
Beat Gottfried 7-6, 7-6
Beat V. Amritraj 6-2, 6-2
Beat Pecci 6-4, 6-0
Beat Warwick 6-3, 6-1

(With Peter Fleming)
Beat Taygan/Tanner 6-7, 7-5, 7-5
Beat Gerulaitis/F. Stolle 6-2, 6-3
Lost to Tim/Tom Gullikson 6-4, 6-1

Wimbledon

Beat Walts 6-3, 6-3, 6-0
Beat Rocavert 4-6, 7-5, 6-7, 7-6, 6-3
Beat Okker 6-0, 7-6, 6-1
Beat Curren 7-5, 7-6, 7-6
Beat Fleming 6-3, 6-2, 6-2
Beat Connors 6-3, 3-6, 6-3, 6-4
Lost to Borg 1-6, 7-5, 6-3, 6-7, 8-6

(With Fleming)
Beat Collings/Hampson 7-6, 6-4, 7-5
Beat van Dillen /van Patten 7-6, 6-1, 7-5
Beat Gonzalez/Prajoux 7-5, 7-5, 6-2
Beat Gunthardt/McMillan 6-3, 6-4, 5-7, 6-4
Lost to McNamara/McNamee 6-3, 6-2, 6-3

Benson & Hedges

Beat Waltke 6-1, 6-1
Beat Lutz 6-2, 6-1
Beat Meyer 6-3, 6-3
Beat Solomon 6-3, 6-2
Beat G. Mayer 6-4, 6-3, 6-3

(With Fleming)
Beat Fibak/Smid 4-6, 6-4, 6-1
Beat Curren/Denton 6-4, 7-6
Beat Dibley/Kronk 6-1, 6-0
Beat Scanlon/Teltscher 7-5, 6-3

1981

Stella Artois

Beat Feaver 6-1, 6-2
Beat Edmondson 6-3, 6-3
Beat Scanlon 6-3, 6-2
Beat Pfister 6-2, 7-5
Beat Teacher 6-3, 6-4
Beat Gottfried 7-6, 7-5

(With Fleming)
Beat Gonzalez/Moretton 7-6, 6-3
Beat Frawley/C. Lewis 6-3, 6-4
Lost to Austin/Buehning 6-4, 6-7, 6-3

Wimbledon

Beat Tom Gullikson 7-6, 7-5, 6-3
Beat Ramirez 6-3, 6-7, 6-3, 7-6
Beat Lutz 6-4, 6-2, 6-0
Beat S. Smith 7-5, 3-6, 6-1, 6-2
Beat Kriek 6-1, 7-5, 6-1
Beat Frawley 7-6, 6-4, 7-5
Beat Borg 4-6, 7-6, 7-6, 6-4

(With Fleming)
Beat Aguilar/J.Edwards 6-1, 6-2, 3-6, 6-3
Beat Moore/van Dillen 7-6, 4-6, 6-3, 6-4
Beat Fitzgerald/Pascoe 6-4, 6-2, 6-2
Beat A/V Amritraj 4-6, 6-2, 6-1, 6-4
Beat Okker/Stockton 6-3, 6-2, 6-4
Beat Lutz/S. Smith 6-4, 6-4, 6-4

Benson & Hedges

Beat Feaver 6-1, 6-1
Beat Birner 6-2, 6-2
Beat Gottfried 6-1, 6-2
Beat S. Mayer 6-3, 6-3
Lost to Connors 3-6, 2-6, 6-3, 6-4, 6-2

(With Fleming)
Beat S. Mayer/McMillan 6-3, 6-4
Beat Delatte/Waltke 6-3, 7-6
Beat Mayotte/Wilkison 6-4, 6-4
Lost to Stewart/Taygan 7-5, 6-7, 6-4

1982

Manchester

Beat Campbell 6-2, 6-1
Beat Fulwood 6-2, 6-0
Beat Lapidus 6-3, 6-4
Beat Alexander 6-3, 7-6
Beat Simpson 6-3, 6-7, 10-8

(With Peter Rennert)
Lost to Levine/Steyn 6-4, 4-6, 8-6

Stella Artois

Beat Andrews 6-4, 6-2
Beat C. Fancutt 6-3, 6-2
Beat Sadri 6-3, 6-2
Beat Hooper 6-3, 6-4
Beat C. Lewis 6-0, 6-2
Lost to Connors 7-5, 6-3

(With Rennert)
Beat Gitlin/Nichols 7-5, 6-4
Beat Estep/Kronk 6-3, 6-4
Beat Gerulaitis/Leconte 6-4, 6-2
Beat Andrews/Sadri 6-4, 7-6
Beat Amaya/Pfister 7-6, 7-5

Wimbledon

Beat Winitsky 6-2, 6-2, 6-1
Beat E. Edwards 6-3, 6-3, 7-5
Beat Bourne 6-2, 6-2, 6-0
Beat Pfister 6-4, 6-4, 6-4
Beat Kriek 4-6, 6-2, 7-5, 6-3
Beat Mayotte 6-3, 6-1, 6-2
Lost to Connors 3-6, 6-3, 6-7, 7-6, 6-4

(With Fleming)
Beat Dyke/P. Johnston 6-2, 6-4, 6-4
Beat Frawley/C. Lewis 7-6, 3-6, 8-6
Beat Dowlen/Odizor 6-4, 7-6
Beat Hocevar/Soares 3-6, 7-5, 6-2
Beat Curren/Denton 6-2, 6-4, 2-6, 6-3
Lost to McNamara/McNamee 6-3, 6-2

Benson & Hedges

Beat C. Panatta 7-5, 6-2
Beat Dickson 6-3, 6-4
Beat Leconte 6-3, 7-5
Beat Denton 6-1, 6-4
Beat Gottfried 6-3, 6-2, 6-4

(With Fleming)
Beat R. Lewis/McMillan 6-3, 6-4
Beat Amaya/Teacher walkover
Beat Fromm/Glickstein 6-3, 7-6
Beat Gunthardt/Smid 7-6, 6-4

1983

Stella Artois

Beat Borowiak 6-3, 6-3
Beat Sauer 6-1, 7-6
Beat Motta 7-5, 6-2
Beat Gottfried 6-0, 6-1
Beat Curren 7-5, 7-6
Lost to Connors 6-3, 6-3

(With Fleming)
Beat Hooper/Rennert 6-3, 6-3
Beat Andrews/Sadri 6-2, 6-3
Beat Dowlen/Odizor 7-6, 6-7, 6-4
Lost to Gottfried/McNamee 7-5, 6-4

Wimbledon

Beat Testerman 6-4, 7-6, 6-2
Beat Segarceanu 4-6, 6-2, 6-3, 6-3
Beat Gilbert 6-2, 6-2, 6-2
Beat Scanlon 7-5, 7-6, 7-6
Beat S. Mayer 6-3, 7-5, 6-0
Beat Lendl 7-6, 6-4, 6-4
Beat C. Lewis 6-2, 6-2, 6-2

(With Fleming)
Beat Bradnam/Lloyd 6-4, 6-4, 6-3
Beat B. Cox/Hlasek 7-6, 7-5, 6-3
Beat Mitton/Moore 6-4, 6-2, 6-4
Beat Alexander/Fitzgerald 4-6, 6-1, 6-4, 6-3
Beat Jarryd/Simonsson 6-2, 6-2, 6-4
Beat Tim/Tom Gullikson 6-4, 6-3, 6-4

Davis Cup (v. Ireland)

Beat Sorensen 6-3, 6-2, 6-2
With Fleming; beat Doyle/Sorensen 6-2, 6-3, 6-4
Beat Doyle 9-7, 6-3, 6-3

Benson & Hedges

Beat J. Lloyd 6-2, 6-4
Beat van Patten 7-5, 6-2
Beat Denton 6-3, 6-3
Beat Jarryd 6-3, 6-1
Beat Connors 7-5, 6-1, 6-4

(With Fleming)
Beat S. Simonsson/Sundstrom 7-5, 6-0
Beat Giammalva/J.Lloyd 6-3, 6-4
Beat Slozil/Smid 7-6, 7-5
Beat Denton/Stewart 6-3, 6-4

1984

Stella Artois

Beat M. Davis 7-6, 6-2
Beat Winitsky 7-5, 6-0
Beat Meister 6-4, 6-3
Beat Visser 6-3, 6-4
Beat Connors 6-2, 6-2
Beat Shiras 6-1, 3-6, 6-2

(With Rennert)
Lost to Cash/McNamee 6-3, 3-6, 17-15

Wimbledon

Beat McNamee 6-4, 6-4, 6-7, 6-1
Beat Harmon 6-1, 6-3, 7-5
Beat Masur 6-0, 6-4, 6-3
Beat Scanlon 6-3, 6-3, 6-1
Beat Sadri 6-3, 6-3, 6-1
Beat Cash 6-3, 7-6, 6-4
Beat Connors 6-1, 6-1, 6-2

(With Fleming)
Beat Menon/Michibata 6-3, 6-3, 4-6, 6-3
Beat Gitlin/Hooper 6-4, 6-4, 7-6
Beat Purcell/van Patten 7-6, 6-1, 7-5
Beat Alexander/Fitzgerald 6-4, 6-4, 4-6, 6-4
Beat S. Mayer/Taygan 7-6, 7-6, 6-4
Beat Cash/McNamee 6-2, 5-7, 6-2, 3-6, 6-3

1985

Wimbledon

Beat McNamara 6-4, 6-3, 6-4
Beat Odizor 7-6, 6-1, 7-6
Beat Steyn 6-3, 7-5, 6-4
Beat Maurer 6-0, 6-4, 6-2
Lost to Curren 6-2, 6-2, 6-4

(With Fleming)
Beat Purcell/van Patten 6-3, 6-4, 3-6, 6-4
Beat C. Fancutt/Lendl 7-6, 3-6, 6-3, 6-2
Beat B. Cox/Kohlberg 6-3, 6-4, 6-4
Beat Tim/Tom Gullikson 6-3, 6-4, 7-6
Lost to Cash/Fitzgerald 7-6, 2-6, 6-1, 6-4

1986

Benson & Hedges

Lost to Cash 6-3, 5-7, 6-4

(With Fleming)
Beat Acioly/Bahrami 6-4, 6-4
Beat Steyn/Visser 6-4, 7-6
Beat Cash/McNamee 7-6, 6-3
Beat Stewart/Warwick 3-6, 7-6, 6-2

1987

Did not play in The British Isles

1988

Goal Challenge

Beat Wilander 6-4, 3-6, 6-3
Beat Nystrom 6-3, 7-6

(With Fleming)
Lost to Nystrom/Wilander 6-3, 6-3

Wirral Classic

Beat Volkov 7-5, 6-4
Beat Lundgren 4-6, 6-4, 6-2
Lost to van Rensburg 3-6, 6-4, 6-2

Wimbledon

Beat Skoff 6-1, 7-5, 6-1
Lost to Masur 7-5, 7-6, 6-3

1989

Beckenham

Beat Baur 6-2, 6-3
Beat Michibata 6-2, 6-2
Beat Goldie 7-5, 6-4
Beat Annacone 6-3, 6-2
Beat Dyke 6-4, 7-6

(With Gary Muller)
Bye
Beat Baur/Warder 6-3, 6-4
Beat Broad/Kruger 7-6, 7-6

Edinburgh

Beat Matheson 6-3, 6-1
Beat de le Pena 6-3, 6-3
Beat Krickstein 6-4, 6-4
Beat Connors 7-6, 7-6

Wirral International

Lost to Pugh 3-6, 7-6, 7-6

Wimbledon

Beat Cahill 4-6, 4-6, 6-2, 6-3, 8-6
Beat Reneberg 6-3, 3-6, 6-3, 7-5
Beat Pugh 6-3, 6-4, 6-2
Beat Fitzgerald 6-3, 0-6, 6-4, 6-4
Beat Wilander 7-6, 3-6, 6-3, 6-4
Lost to Edberg 7-5, 7-6, 7-6

(With Jakob Hlasek)
Beat Antonisch/Baur 6-3, 3-6, 4-6, 6-3, 6-3
Beat Depalmer/Donnelly 6-7, 6-4, 3-6, 7-5, 10-8
Retired when Doohan/Warder trailed 3-6, 6-4, 4-6, 4-2

Privilege Challenge

Beat Edberg 2-6, 6-4, 6-4

Silk Cut Championships

Beat S. Davis 6-3, 6-3
Beat Jelen 6-4, 6-1
Beat Mecir 2-6, 6-4, 6-3
Lost to Forget 6-4, 7-6

(With Hlasek)
Beat Mansdorf/Vajda 6-3, 4-6, 6-3
Beat Forget/Ison 7-5, 6-1
Beat Aldrich/Visser 7-6, 7-6
Beat Bates/Curren 6-1, 7-6

1990

Stella Artois

Beat Krishnan 4-6, 6-4, 6-2
Beat Paloheimo 6-0, 6-7, 7-5
Beat Fromberg 6-7, 6-3, 7-5
Lost to Lendl 6-2, 6-4

Wentworth Classic

Lost to J. Svensson 9-6
Lost to Forget 9-7

Wimbledon

Lost to Rostagno 7-5, 6-4, 6-4

1991

Manchester

Lost to Caratti 7-6, 7-6

Wimbledon

Beat Oncins 6-1, 6-2, 6-4
Beat S. Stolle 7-6, 5-7, 6-0, 7-6
Beat Fleurian 6-2, 7-6, 6-1
Lost to Edberg 7-6, 6-1, 6-4

(With Goran Ivanisevic)
Beat Leach/Pugh 6-3, 6-4
Lost to Courier/D.Flach 3-6, 7-6, 6-4

Birmingham

Lost to Mronz 6-3, 4-6, 6-3

1992

Wimbledon

Beat Mattar 5-7, 6-1, 6-3, 6-3
Beat Cash 6-7, 6-4, 6-7, 6-3, 6-2
Beat Wheaton 6-3, 6-4, 6-4
Beat Olhovskiy 7-5, 6-3, 7-6
Beat Forget 6-2, 7-6, 6-3
Lost to Agassi 6-4, 6-2, 6-3

(With Michael Stich)
Beat Carbonell/Rikl 6-2, 6-2, 6-3
Beat Fitzgerald/Jarryd 6-3, 7-6, 6-3
Beat Kinnear/Salumaa 6-3, 6-2, 6-4
Beat Haarhuis/Koevermans 6-3, 6-4, 6-4
Beat Forget/Hlasek 7-6, 6-3, 7-6
Beat Grabb/Reneberg 5-7, 7-6, 3-6, 7-6, 19-17

1993-1994

Did not play in The British Isles

1995

Goal Challenge

Beat Collins 4-6, 6-3, 7-3 (tie-break)
(With Peter Fleming)
Lost to Casey/Collins 9-8 (7-4)

1996

Did not play in The British Isles

1997

Honda Challenge

Beat Vilas 6-3, 6-3
Beat Borg 2-6, 6-3, 10-7 (tie-break)
Beat J. Lloyd 6-4, 6-4
Beat Leconte 6-2, 3-6, 10-5 (tie-break)

1998

Goal Challenge

Beat Wilander 6-1, 3-6, 6-2*

(With Owen Casey)
Beat Cash/Wilander 8-7 (7-4)*

Honda Challenge

Beat Vilas 6-1, 6-4
Beat Bahrami 6-2, 7-6
Beat Leconte 6-4, 6-2
Beat Noah 7-5, 6-3

1999

Wimbledon

(With Steffi Graf)
Beat Coetzee/Melicharova 6-2 6-4
Beat Ran/Menga 6-3 6-4

Beat Woodbridge/Davenport walkover
Beat Gimelstob/V Williams 6-4 6-3
Scratched to Bjorkman/Kournikova
Honda Challenge

Beat Borg 7-5 6-4
Beat J Lloyd 6-3 6-2
Beat Connors 6-1 6-0
Beat Bates 6-3 6-7 (4-7) 10-4 (tie-break)
Beat Leconte 6-2 4-1 (Leconte retired)

2000

ATP Seniors, Dublin

Beat Pernfors 6-1 6-3
Beat C Panatta 6-2 6-3
Beat Forget 6-3 6-7 10-6 (tie-break)
Beat Leconte 6-4 6-3

NSPCC Exhibition Match

Beat Borg 6-3 7-6 (7-5)

Honda Challenge

Beat J Lloyd 7-5 6-3
Beat Bahrami 6-3 6-4
Beat Borg 7-6 (7-4) 6-3
Beat Leconte 6-2 7-5
Lost to Cash 6-7 (3-7) 7-5 14-12 (Champions tie-break)

2001

KPMG Challenge

Beat Borg 7-6 (7-3), 6-7 (3-7), 10-4 (tie-break)
Beat Pernfors 6-1, 6-2
Beat J. Lloyd 7-5, 6-3
Beat Forget 7-6 (9-7), 7-6 (8-6)

*These results were kindly provided by Owen Casey